Specialties of the House

A Cookbook to Benefit
the Endowment Fund of
The Ronald McDonald House

Library of Congress Catalog Number: 95-74920

ISBN: 0-9647955-0-7

First Printing October 1995 10,000 copies
Second Printing November 1996 10,000 copies

About the Book

The book you are now holding represents the culmination of thousands of hours of effort by the extended family of the Ronald McDonald House of Rochester.

The project began with a call for recipes, and the many friends of *The House That Love Built*® responded enthusiastically. More than 2,000 recipes – tried-and-true family favorites as well as good-enough-for-company fare – arrived from all over New York state as well as many other states and Canada. Chefs from some of the area's favorite restaurants, well-known cooking teachers and other food professionals were among the contributors.

Volunteer members of the Cookbook Committee prepared each recipe at least twice, testing recipe methods and judging results for flavor and culinary merit with family and friends. More than 350 were selected to fill these pages.

The recipes are organized with ten tabbed sections. *Cook's Notes* are added to facilitate food preparation. Symbols indicate recipes that can be made ahead or require advanced preparation, making entertaining and meal planning simpler. The *Cook's Pantry* section is intended to be a resource providing basic recipes and techniques. Our professionally prepared index will allow every recipe to be referenced with ease. All this is packed into an easel-style binder that stands by itself.

And it stands tall because of the effort of the many people who gave it life. We hope *Specialties of the House* will find a happy home in your kitchen.

Kathy Lindsley, Food Editor
Democrat & Chronicle/Times-Union
Rochester, New York

Symbol indicates recipes that require preparation in advance.

✓ Symbol indicates the point to which the recipe can be prepared ahead.

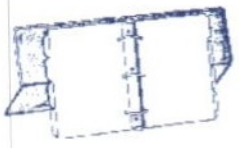

The stand-up binder is ideal for counter reference. Lay the book flat and fold at the crease.

About the House

After 5 years of planning, fund raising, construction and furnishing, the Ronald McDonald House of Rochester was dedicated on February 18, 1990. Its 20 bedrooms and communal living areas provide shelter and comfort to families of critically ill children who travel to Rochester for treatment at The Children's Hospital at Strong and other excellent area health care facilities.

Before that time, distraught families slept on cots or in chairs in a child's hospital room, in hospital lounges or even in their vehicles. Children receiving outpatient treatment frequently had to make arduous daily trips to the hospital from outlying counties. For a modest fee, families can live comfortably in home-like surroundings, where they can share their concerns with others who understand and care. No one is ever turned away for inability to pay.

The first Ronald McDonald House opened in Philadelphia in 1974. The idea soon caught fire and by 1995 there were almost 170 Houses around the world. Although McDonald's Corporation provides a start-up fund and local McDonald's operators contribute generously, each House must raise its own operating funds.

A charitable community has built and furnished *The House That Love Built®* and hundreds of volunteers put the heart in the House. Your purchase of this book will help us to continue to assist families in need at a most stressful time. All proceeds which the Rochester Ronald McDonald House receives from the sale of the book will go directly to the Endowment Fund for the support of the House.

We wish you good health and bon appétit.

Nancy Robbins
First President of the Board
Ronald McDonald House of Rochester

Additional copies of *Specialties of the House*
can be obtained from:

Ronald McDonald House
333 Westmoreland Drive
Rochester, New York 14620

or by mailing an order blank from the back of the book.

Underwriters

The Ronald McDonald House and the Cookbook Committee would like to express their sincere appreciation to the individuals, businesses and organizations who generously supported *Specialties of the House* through monetary donations and gifts-in-kind.

Founders
$1,000 and up

Allens Creek Office Park
Alling & Cory
Canfield & Tack
Glenda Nothnagle, GN Design Studio
Refrigeration Service Engineers Society
Rochester's McDonald's Operators Association

Benefactors
$500-999

Automatic Rolls of New York
Leonard & Mary DeWolf
Golden State Foods of Rochester
Daniel & Nancy Robbins
Richard & Margaret Schenkel
Ronald & Jacquie Sonkin
Daniel & Martha Tack
Van Den Bergh Foods Company
Wegmans Food Markets, Inc.

Patrons
$250-499

Brighton Dental Group
Harold S. Feinbloom Charitable Lead Trust
Hessler, Keogh & Millard Associates, Inc.
IMPCO Direct Response Marketing
James & Lauretta Kmet
Andrew & Sharon Lonthair
Walter & Sue Millard
Ernest S. & Ann L. Olson
Quaker Oats Company
RIT School of Food, Hotel & Travel Management
Rochester Colonial Manufacturing Company
Sharel Enterprises
Woods, Oviatt, Gilman, Sturman & Clarke LLP

Donors
up to $249

Andre's Unisex
Beaumont & Stork, Inc.
Barbara Blake
Bucket Brigade
John U. & Mary Jo Coniglio
H. Thomas Erbland
Forward Design, Inc.
Melanie Ferniz, MF Designs
Melissa Frontuto
David P. & Susanne Harris
Henderson's Drug Store, Inc.
Italian-American Civic Organization
Kate's Salon, Inc.
Raymond & Glenda Nothnagle
Rush Lions Club
Joseph & Margaret Shero
Vincent J. Stanley
Donald Stork
Margaret Thirtle
Van Dyke Agency
Ellen Wagner
Dr. & Mrs. Robert Weis
Dr. Jeffrey A. Welch

Cookbook Committee

Chairpersons

1994-1995	Sharon Lonthair, Jacquie Sonkin
1996	Nancy Robbins
1997	Judie Griffin

Paula Ayers	Special Events
Jackie Colicchio	Promotions
Mary DeWolf	Direct Sales
Carl Dumbauld	Publicity
Glenda Nothnagle	Art Director
Bill & Betty Oswald	Finance
Julie Paternico	Marketing
Nancy Robbins	Editor
Jean Sobraske	Marketing
Martha Tack	Recipes & Testing
Margaret Schenkel	Secretary
Lorrie Weis	Recipes & Testing

Advisory Committee

Jane Andrews	Nutritionist, Wegmans Food Markets
Jackie Cannizzaro	Cooking Teacher and Demonstrator
Dick & Ginger Howell	Seasonal Kitchen Cooking School
Kathy Lindsley	Food Editor, *Democrat & Chronicle/Times-Union*
Sue Millard	President, Ronald McDonald House Board
Daniel Tack	Fundraising, Ronald McDonald House Board

Our Special Thanks To

Artist: Carl Zollo, creator of the design element "Carl's Kids" derived from his sculpture *Friendship*.

Illustrator: Richard Lubey, who beautifully captured the essence of the Ronald McDonald House in the sketches for the tab dividers.

Cover Design: Bill Buckett, Adjunct Professor, RIT.

Art Director: Glenda Nothnagle, GN Design Studio, book typography.

Index: Members of the Western New York Chapter of the American Society of Indexers.

The garden and Zollo sculpture, "Friendship"

Dips & Spreads

Cold Appetizers

Hot Appetizers

First Courses

Sauces

Beverages

HERBED CHEESE with SUN-DRIED TOMATO PESTO

Yield: 6 cups

1½ cups fresh basil leaves
6 ounces oil-packed sun-dried tomatoes, drained
2 tablespoons olive oil
1 garlic clove
¼ cup freshly grated Parmesan *or* Romano cheese
3 tablespoons walnuts
1 pound mascarpone *or* soft farmer's cheese
1 pound cream cheese, softened
1 teaspoon freshly ground black pepper
1 teaspoon minced fresh garlic
1 teaspoon dried *or* 1 tablespoon minced fresh basil
½ teaspoon dried *or* 1½ teaspoons fresh thyme
½ teaspoon salt, optional
½ cup chopped walnuts for garnish

- To prepare pesto, in food processor fitted with metal blade, purée basil leaves, tomatoes, oil, garlic, Parmesan cheese and nuts until smooth. Set aside.
- In clean processor bowl, blend mascarpone and cream cheese, along with pepper, garlic, basil, thyme and salt.
- Spread half the cheese mixture in a quiche dish or other serving plate. Place in freezer for about 15 minutes, or until firm.
- To create second layer, spread with pesto. Return to freezer briefly until firm.
- Top with final layer of cheese and sprinkle with chopped walnuts. Cover with plastic wrap and refrigerate for 6 hours.
- Decorate with basil leaves and serve with crackers.

Cook's Notes

Sun-dried tomatoes can be purchased dry-packed or packed in oil. If using dry-packed, rehydrate by covering with hot water and letting stand 30 minutes.

SUN-DRIED TOMATOES and GOAT CHEESE

Yield: 24 to 30 servings

- **1** **8-ounce jar sun-dried tomatoes, oil-packed**
- **2** **large garlic cloves, *or* more to taste**
- **⅔** **cup chopped pitted Kalamata olives**
- **12** **ounces soft goat cheese**
- **milk**
- **French bread baguette**

- In a food processor with metal blade, combine sun-dried tomatoes with their oil and garlic. Blend until as smooth as possible. Add olives and blend until olives are minced.
- Mash goat cheese with a fork and add a little milk, if necessary, to make a smooth paste.
- Spread cheese on a 10-inch round serving plate and cover completely with tomato mixture.
- Serve with thinly sliced baguette.

ROASTED RED PEPPER and GARLIC SPREAD

Preheat broiler

Yield: 8 to 10 servings

- **6** **sweet red peppers**
- **2** **garlic cloves**
- **4** **tablespoons olive oil**
- **½** **cup freshly grated Parmesan cheese**
- **salt and pepper to taste**
- **2** **large loaves ciabatta bread *or* 1 large loaf French bread**

- Halve red peppers, remove core and seeds and place on a cookie sheet, cut side down. Squash with palm of your hand. Broil until charred.
- Put peppers in paper bag, tied securely, and let steam 10 to 15 minutes, until cool enough to handle. Remove skins.
- **Preheat oven to 375°F.**
- With motor running, drop garlic down feed tube of food processor. Add peppers, olive oil, Parmesan cheese, salt and pepper; purée.
- Heat bread 5 to 10 minutes. Slice bread and serve with spread.

Dick and Ginger Howell
–The Seasonal Kitchen

SPINACH and ARTICHOKE DIP

Preheat oven to 350°F   Yield: 2 cups

1 14-ounce can artichoke hearts, drained and chopped
1 cup sour cream
1 cup freshly grated Parmesan cheese
1 garlic clove, minced
1 10-ounce package chopped spinach, thawed and well drained
sliced green onions and chopped tomatoes for garnish

- Mix artichoke hearts, sour cream, cheese, garlic and spinach.
- Spoon into a 9-inch pie plate.
- Bake, uncovered, in preheated oven 20 to 25 minutes or until lightly browned.
- Sprinkle with onions and tomatoes. Serve with tortilla chips or crackers.

HOT and SPICY SPINACH DIP

Preheat oven to 350°F   Yield: 4 cups

2 10-ounce packages frozen chopped spinach
2 tablespoons butter *or* margarine
½ cup finely minced onion
½ cup finely minced celery
2 tablespoons flour
½ cup milk
½ teaspoon freshly ground white pepper
1 teaspoon Worcestershire sauce
6 ounces jalapeño Muenster cheese, shredded

- Cook spinach in microwave according to package directions, using no extra water. Drain, pressing spinach dry, and reserve liquid.
- Melt butter over moderate heat in a saucepan. Add onion and celery; cook until soft but not brown, about 2 to 3 minutes. Add flour, stirring until bubbly and smooth.
- Remove from heat; add milk and ½ cup spinach liquid slowly, stirring constantly to avoid lumps.
- Return to heat and bring to a boil; simmer until smooth and thick, stirring constantly. Add seasonings and cheese; blend in spinach.
- Put into a buttered 1-quart casserole and bake in preheated oven until bubbly, approximately 15 to 20 minutes.

✓ *Can be made ahead and refrigerated. If so, bake for 30 minutes.*

CURRY PÂTÉ

Yield: 2 cups

6 ounces cream cheese, softened
4 ounces sharp Cheddar cheese, grated
¼ teaspoon salt
½ teaspoon curry powder *or* to taste
2 tablespoons dry sherry
chutney

- Mix by hand all ingredients except chutney. Spread onto a serving plate to about ½-inch thickness. Refrigerate until firm.
- At serving time, spread with chutney and serve with crackers.

FROSTED ORIENTAL PÂTÉ

Preheat oven to 325°F

Yield: One 9-inch loaf

2 tablespoons pared and chopped fresh ginger
1 garlic clove, peeled
4 large green onions
1½ pounds skinless, boneless chicken breasts
3 eggs
2 tablespoons peanut oil
2 tablespoons dry sherry
2 teaspoons oriental sesame oil
2 tablespoons soy sauce
½ teaspoon freshly ground black pepper
1 bottle oriental hoisin sauce
fresh vegetables for garnish: red *or* green sweet peppers, carrots, etc.
assorted cocktail breads

- In a food processor fitted with a metal blade, process ginger and garlic until minced. Add green onions and process, on and off, until chopped. Add chicken and process, on and off, for 1 to 2 minutes. Add eggs, peanut oil, sherry, sesame oil, soy sauce and black pepper. Process until mixture is smooth.
- Oil a 5x9-inch loaf pan, pour mixture into pan and cover with foil. Bake for 1 hour in preheated oven. Let cool 20 minutes, turn out onto a flat plate and cool completely.
- Cover with hoisin sauce and refrigerate at least 6 hours.
- Garnish with fresh vegetables and serve with cocktail breads.

SMOKED WHITEFISH PÂTÉ

Yield: 2 cups

½ pound smoked whitefish
4 ounces softened cream cheese, regular *or* low fat
4 ounces unsalted butter, softened
1 tablespoon minced onion
1 teaspoon Cognac
½ teaspoon Worcestershire sauce
2 tablespoons fresh lemon juice

- In a food processor, purée all ingredients, scraping down side of bowl several times.
- Transfer pâté to a small bowl and serve with crackers.

✓ *Pâté keeps for 3 days, covered with plastic wrap and chilled.*

Dick and Ginger Howell
–The Seasonal Kitchen

SHRIMP MOUSSE

Yield: 6 cups

1 10½-ounce can tomato soup, undiluted
6 ounces cream cheese, broken into chunks
1½ tablespoons unflavored gelatin, softened in 2 tablespoons cold water
1 cup mayonnaise
½ cup finely chopped celery
½ cup finely chopped onion
2 cups cooked shrimp, shredded
cucumber slices for garnish

- In a medium saucepan, bring soup to a boil. Remove from heat and add cream cheese. Stir until well blended.
- Add remaining ingredients and mix well..
- Pour into an oiled 6-cup mold; refrigerate until firm.
- Unmold onto a plate, decorate with cucumber slices and serve with crackers.

CLAMS CASINO SPREAD

Preheat oven to 450°F — Yield: 3 cups

- 2 small onions, diced
- ½ sweet green pepper, diced
- 3 tablespoons butter
- 3 6-ounce cans minced clams, drained, reserving half the liquid
- 1 2-ounce jar chopped pimientos
- 6 tablespoons dry Italian bread crumbs
- ¼ teaspoon hot pepper sauce
- 3 tablespoons mayonnaise
- 8 slices bacon, cut into bits, fried crisp and drained

- Sauté onions and green pepper in butter. Add remaining ingredients, mix well and add reserved clam juice.
- Place in a 3-cup baking/serving dish and bake uncovered in preheated oven for 30 minutes.
- ✓ *This dish can also be frozen, thawed and baked later.*
- Serve with crackers.

CRAB MEAT DIP DELUXE

Yield: 3½ cups

- 1 cup crab meat
- 8 ounces cream cheese, softened
- ½ cup chopped green onion
- ½ cup chopped celery
- ½ cup chopped water chestnuts
- dash of hot pepper sauce, optional

- Mix all ingredients in a small bowl.
- Chill and serve with crackers.

Dick and Ginger Howell
–The Seasonal Kitchen

Cook's Notes

To speed softening of *cream cheese*, remove foil and place on microwave-safe plate, uncovered. Cook an 8-ounce block for 1 minute on medium, 3 ounces for about 30 seconds. Let stand 1 minute.

PEPPERONI PIZZA DIP

Preheat oven to 350°F Yield: 3½ to 4 cups

8 ounces cream cheese, softened
½ cup sour cream
1 teaspoon dried oregano
⅛ teaspoon garlic powder
⅛ teaspoon crushed red pepper, optional
½ cup pizza sauce
½ cup chopped pepperoni
½ cup sliced green onion
¼ cup chopped sweet green pepper
½ cup freshly shredded mozzarella cheese

- In a small mixing bowl, beat cream cheese, sour cream, oregano, garlic powder and red pepper. Spread evenly in a 9 to 10-inch quiche dish or pie plate.
- Spread pizza sauce over the top and sprinkle with pepperoni, green onion and green pepper.
- Bake 12 minutes in preheated oven. Remove from oven; top with mozzarella cheese. Bake 5 minutes more, or until cheese is melted and mixture is heated through. Let sit 5 minutes before serving.
- Suggested accompaniments: sweet pepper strips, broccoli florets or crackers.

LOBSTER SPREAD

Yield: About 4 cups

12 ounces lobster meat, thawed if frozen
8 ounces cream cheese, regular *or* low fat, softened
¾ cup mayonnaise
½ sweet green pepper, chopped
1 medium onion, chopped
Worcestershire sauce, fresh lemon juice and hot pepper sauce to taste

- Blend all ingredients and store, refrigerated.
- Remove from refrigerator about ½ hour before using and serve with crackers.

CURRY DIP for VEGETABLES

Yield: 2 cups

- ½ small carrot
- ½ small onion
- ¼ small sweet green pepper
- 2 sprigs parsley
- 2 tablespoons vinegar
- 1 cup mayonnaise
- ½ cup cottage cheese
- ¼ teaspoon salt
- ½ teaspoon curry powder
- raw vegetables

- In a blender jar, purée first five ingredients. Add remaining ingredients except vegetables and mix until smooth.
- Serve with assorted raw vegetables, such as carrots, cucumbers, cauliflower, broccoli, etc.

LIME DILL DIP for MELON BALLS

Yield: 1½ cups

- 3 ounces cream cheese, softened
- ½ teaspoon grated fresh lime rind
- 1½ tablespoons fresh lime juice
- ¼ teaspoon dried dill weed *or* ¾ teaspoon fresh
- dash of salt
- 1 cup sour cream
- 2 melons: honeydew *or* cantaloupe

- Combine cream cheese, lime rind, lime juice, dill weed and salt until smooth. Blend in sour cream and chill.
- Cut melons into balls and chill. Serve with dip.

Dick and Ginger Howell
–The Seasonal Kitchen

Cook's Notes

A fruit's flavor is concentrated in the *zest*, or the outer rind, of a citrus fruit. Remove only the thinnest layer of rind with a fine grater, or peel it with a sharp paring knife. Be careful not to cut into the pith or bitter white layer beneath the color.

TZATZIKI

Yield: 3 to 4 cups

1½ cups plain yogurt
1½ pounds cucumbers, pared, seeded and coarsely chopped
½ teaspoon salt *or* to taste
1 teaspoon minced garlic
2 tablespoons chopped fresh mint leaves
½ tablespoon fresh lemon juice *or* more to taste
dash of hot pepper sauce, optional
½ tablespoon olive oil

- Let yogurt drain for 2 hours in a fine sieve lined with rinsed and squeezed cheesecloth or a coffee filter.
- Toss cucumber with salt and let drain 1 hour in a colander.
- In a bowl, combine the yogurt, garlic, mint, lemon juice, red pepper sauce and oil. Add cucumber and mix well.
- Serve with pita bread, cut into bite-sized chunks, for dipping.

HUMMUS

Yield: About 3 cups

4 garlic cloves *or* to taste
2 15-ounce cans chick peas, drained, reserving ¼ cup of liquid
½ cup tahini *(sesame seed paste)*
¼ cup freshly squeezed lemon juice
paprika
olive oil
pita bread *or* fresh vegetables

- Using food processor with metal blade, mince garlic. Add chick peas, reserved liquid, tahini and lemon juice. Process until smooth.
- Place mixture in a serving bowl, sprinkle with paprika and drizzle a small amount of olive oil over top. Serve as a dip with wedges of pita bread or fresh vegetables.

Cook's Notes

Hollow out bell peppers and purple cabbage to use as *dip containers* or holders for other cut-up vegetables.

EGGPLANT DIP

Preheat oven to 400°F — Yield: 2 cups

1 **large eggplant, about 1 pound**
¼ **cup chopped fresh parsley**
1 **garlic clove, peeled**
1 **small onion, quartered**
½ **teaspoon salt *or* to taste**
¼ **teaspoon freshly ground black pepper**
2 **tablespoons olive oil**
2 **teaspoons fresh lemon juice**
Sesame Pita Triangles–*recipe follows*

- Prick whole eggplant several times with a fork.
- Place on a baking sheet and bake for 1 hour in preheated oven. Remove from oven and let cool.
- **Alternate microwave method**: place eggplant on a double thickness of paper toweling. Microwave at 100% power for 12 minutes, which helps retain the eggplant's color. Let cool.
- In food processor with metal blade, mince parsley and garlic. Add onion and chop.
- Cut eggplant in half lengthwise and scoop out flesh. Add to processor, along with salt and pepper. Process until mixture is coarsely chopped.
- Transfer to a serving bowl. Stir in oil and lemon juice until well blended.
- Serve at room temperature with Sesame Pita Triangles.

SESAME PITA TRIANGLES

Preheat oven to 350°F — Yield: 64 triangles

4 **6-inch pita pockets, white *or* whole wheat**
3 **tablespoons butter *or* margarine, melted**
2 **teaspoons sesame seeds**

- Split pitas horizontally and cut each half into eighths. Place on cookie sheet, smooth side down.
- Brush with melted butter and sprinkle with sesame seeds.
- Bake in preheated oven for 10 to 15 minutes until crisp and lightly browned.
- Use with your favorite dip or salsa, or use as a bread or cracker with soup.

REUBEN DIP

Preheat oven to 375°F Yield: About 4 cups

8 ounces cream cheese, softened
½ cup sour cream
1 cup drained, chopped sauerkraut
½ pound cooked lean corned beef, chopped
2 teaspoons chopped onion
1 tablespoon catsup
2 teaspoons spicy brown mustard
1 cup grated Swiss cheese
rye crackers *or* rye Melba toast

- Cut cream cheese into bits and combine with sour cream, sauerkraut, corned beef, onion, catsup, mustard and Swiss cheese.
- Place in 1-quart ovenproof casserole and bake, covered, in preheated oven for 30 minutes, or until bubbles form around edges.
- Remove cover and bake an additional 5 minutes until golden.
- Serve warm with rye crackers or Melba toast.

BRIE with SUN-DRIED TOMATOES

Yield: 6 servings

8 ounces very ripe brie cheese, top rind removed
6 sun-dried tomatoes in oil
4 small garlic cloves
2 tablespoons minced fresh parsley
2 tablespoons freshly grated Parmesan cheese
1 teaspoon dried basil
bland crackers

- Remove brie from refrigerator early in the day to bring to room temperature.
- Remove tomatoes from oil and chop, reserving oil. Mince garlic cloves and mash to a paste.
- Combine parsley, Parmesan cheese, tomatoes, garlic and basil. Add reserved oil until mixture is of spreading consistency. Let stand 1 hour.
- Spread tomato mixture over brie and let stand 1 hour more before serving with crackers

ONION DIP

Preheat oven to 375°F Yield: 3 cups

1 **cup chopped Vidalia onion**
4 **ounces Swiss cheese, grated**
1 **cup mayonnaise**
chopped fresh parsley
crackers for dipping

- Mix onion, cheese and mayonnaise; pour into 3-cup ovenproof serving dish.
- Bake 25 minutes in preheated oven.
- Garnish with a sprinkling of parsley and serve with crackers.

SMOKED SALMON APPETIZER

Yield: 1½ cups

4 **ounces smoked salmon**
8 **ounces nonfat cream cheese, softened**
¼ **cup nonfat mayonnaise**
1-2 **green onions with tops, chopped**
1 **tablespoon freshly squeezed lemon juice**
2 **tablespoons chopped fresh parsley**
French bread baguette

- Cut salmon into small pieces; set aside.
- Combine cream cheese, mayonnaise, onions, lemon juice and parsley. Mix well. Gently stir in salmon.
- Cut a French bread baguette in half lengthwise, remove most of the center and fill with spread. Put top back on, wrap and chill several hours. Cut bread into thin slices.
- Spread can also be served with crackers.

GOUGÈRE

Preheat oven to 400°F — Yield: 6 to 8 servings

1 cup flour
pinch of freshly grated nutmeg
⅛ teaspoon cayenne pepper
1 cup water
½ cup butter
¼ teaspoon salt
4 eggs
4 ounces Swiss cheese, shredded
1 egg, lightly beaten

- Butter, and then flour, a large baking sheet. Mark a 9-inch circle in middle.
- In a bowl, combine flour, nutmeg and cayenne pepper.
- In a pan over medium heat, combine water, butter and salt until water boils and butter melts.
- Reduce heat and add flour mixture all at once, stirring briskly with a wooden spoon, until mixture leaves sides of pan and forms a ball. Leave over low heat about 1 minute more to dry.
- Remove from heat. Add eggs, one at a time, beating well after each addition. Stir in cheese.
- Drop by ¼-cup mounds inside the marked 9-inch circle on baking sheet. Brush top lightly with beaten egg.
- Bake 30 minutes in preheated oven. **Turn oven off** and leave gougère in oven another 30 minutes.
- This can be made in 2 smaller rings using heaping tablespoons of pastry. These puffy pastries are also good eaten as bread with salad.

Cook's Notes

Firm *cheeses*, such as Swiss, are easier to shred if they are cold. If using the food processor, coat the disk first with cooking spray for easier cleanup.

DEVILED EGGS in the WILD

Yield: 16 appetizers

- 8 eggs, room temperature
- ½ cup cooked wild rice
- ¼ cup chopped pimiento-stuffed olives, reserving olive juice
- ¼ cup mayonnaise, more if needed
- 8 pimiento-stuffed olives, halved, for garnish

- Put eggs in a large saucepan and add cold water to cover. Bring to a boil and cook for 10 to 12 minutes. Plunge eggs into cold water to cool. Crack and peel eggs; then split in half lengthwise.
- Place yolks in a small bowl and mash. Stir in cooked rice, chopped olives and enough mayonnaise to moisten the mixture. Stir in olive juice a little at a time to suit your taste.
- Fill egg white halves with a rounded teaspoonful of rice mixture. Top each half with a slice of pimiento-stuffed olive.
- Cover and refrigerate several hours before serving.

BEEF STICK

Yield: 2 sticks

- 2 pounds ground sirloin
- 2 teaspoons salt
- 1 teaspoon freshly ground pepper
- ½ teaspoon liquid smoke
- 3 teaspoons mustard seed
- ½ teaspoon garlic powder
- ½ teaspoon onion powder

- Prepare this recipe at least 2 days before using.
- Mix all ingredients in a large bowl and shape into 2 rolls 10 to 12 inches long. Wrap separately in plastic wrap and refrigerate 24 to 36 hours.
- **Preheat oven to 200°F.**
- Unwrap rolls, place on baking sheet and bake 4 hours.
- Cool and refrigerate in aluminum foil.
- Cut into thin slices and serve with thinly sliced bread and a good mustard.

✓ *This can be stored up to 3 days in refrigerator or up to 6 months in freezer.*

ZESTY SHRIMP

Yield: 12 servings

- dash of garlic powder
- 3 pounds raw shrimp, peeled and deveined
- 1 large red onion, thinly sliced
- 1 lemon, thinly sliced
- 1 sweet red pepper, thinly sliced
- ¾ cup fresh lemon juice
- 6 tablespoons olive oil
- 3 teaspoons white wine vinegar
- 2 garlic cloves, finely chopped
- 1 bay leaf
- 1½ tablespoons dry mustard
- coarsely ground black pepper
- ½ teaspoon salt
- dash of cayenne pepper *or* hot sauce, optional

- Add dash of garlic powder to a large pot of boiling water. Add shrimp and boil 3 to 5 minutes. Shrimp should be pink but not overcooked. Drain, cool and place in a large serving bowl.
- Add onion, lemon and pepper slices to shrimp.
- Mix remaining ingredients thoroughly and pour over shrimp; mix well.
- Cover and refrigerate several hours or overnight, tossing occasionally.
- Drain if desired, or serve as is, with toothpicks.

Cook's Notes

Because most *marinades* contain acidic ingredients, always marinate in a non-metallic container. To save cleanup, use a large zip-closure bag. Place it on a plate and refrigerate. Turn the bag occasionally to distribute marinade.

MARINATED ROASTED RED PEPPERS

Preheat broiler

Yield: About 1 pint

2 large sweet red peppers
3 tablespoons olive oil
2 tablespoons balsamic vinegar
1 large garlic clove, cut into 8 pieces
½ teaspoon salt
½ teaspoon freshly ground black pepper
1 teaspoon chopped fresh basil
or ¼ teaspoon dried
1 teaspoon chopped fresh mint
or ¼ teaspoon dried
½ teaspoon fresh oregano
or ⅛ teaspoon dried

- Cut peppers in half lengthwise and remove seeds, stem and ribs. Lay skin side up on broiler pan and broil 3 to 4 inches from heat until skins are charred.
- Place peppers in paper bag. Fold over top and let peppers steam for 15 minutes, or until cool enough to handle.
- Remove from bag and peel the charred skins. Cut each pepper into 4 pieces and place in a container with a cover.
- Mix remaining ingredients and pour over peppers. Mix well and cover. Refrigerate at least 3 hours.
- Bring to room temperature at least 30 minutes before serving. Drain before using, removing garlic pieces.
- Serve as a vegetable, for a salad or as a topping for sandwiches. The peppers are also a nice antipasto item.

Cook's Notes

Mash a *garlic clove* with the flat side of a knife and the husk will slip off easily.

When using fresh garlic, split the clove in half and remove the green sprout, which is bitter.

TORTILLA PINWHEELS

Yield: 32 appetizers

8 ounces low-fat cream cheese, softened
4 ounces Cheddar cheese, grated
½ cup salsa: mild, medium *or* hot
4 10-inch flour tortillas
½ cup finely chopped green onions
2 cups washed and stemmed spinach leaves, coarsely chopped

- With an electric mixer, combine cream cheese, Cheddar cheese and salsa until spreadable. Cover each tortilla with this mixture.
- Sprinkle tortillas evenly with green onions and then with spinach.
- Roll tortillas as tightly as possible and wrap each in plastic wrap. Chill at least 8 hours. Make the day before using if possible.
- To serve, unwrap tortillas, trim ends and cut each into 8 slices.

CHEESE-STUFFED BREAD

Preheat oven to 375°F

Yield: 6 to 8 appetizers

1 pound frozen bread dough, defrosted and brought to room temperature
1 pound Monterey Jack cheese, shredded
2 eggs
½ cup sour cream
1 egg, lightly beaten with 1 tablespoon water

- Butter a 9-inch deep-dish pie plate.
- Roll bread dough into an 18-inch circle; place on top of pie plate, dropping excess dough over sides.
- In a large bowl, mix cheese, eggs and sour cream. Spoon filling into center of dough so it is evenly distributed. Gather the excess dough to the center, twisting ends into a topknot.
- Brush dough with the egg wash and bake 35 minutes in preheated oven.
- Cool about 2 hours; cut into wedges. Refrigerate to store.

COCKTAIL MEATBALLS with TWO SAUCES

Preheat oven to 350°F — Yield: 60 meatballs

- 2 slices white bread, broken up
- ¾ cup milk
- 2 pounds ground beef
- 1 medium onion, chopped
- 2 teaspoons salt
- ¼ teaspoon garlic powder
- ¼ teaspoon freshly grated nutmeg
- ⅛ teaspoon ground allspice
- 1 egg

- In a large bowl, soak bread in milk; mix in remaining ingredients. Shape into 1-inch balls and place on a jelly roll pan.
- Bake 20 minutes in preheated oven. Pour off accumulated fat and drain on paper towels.
- Place meatballs in a large saucepan with one of the following sauces and simmer for 1½ hours. Serve hot in a chafing dish.

SAVORY SAUCE for MEATBALLS

Yield: About 4 cups

- ⅓ cup chopped onion
- 2 tablespoons butter *or* margarine
- 2½ tablespoons sugar
- ½ cup + 3 tablespoons water
- 1 cup catsup
- ¼ cup white vinegar
- 2 teaspoons prepared mustard
- 2 tablespoons Worcestershire sauce
- ½ teaspoon salt

- Brown onion in butter and add remaining ingredients. Add to meatballs and proceed as above.

CRANBERRY SAUCE for MEATBALLS

Yield: About 4 cups

- 2 cans whole cranberry sauce
- 3 tablespoons orange marmalade
- 14 ounces tomato juice
- ⅓ cup raisins

- Mix cranberry sauce, marmalade and tomato juice in a large saucepan. Add meatballs and proceed as above for 1¼ hours. Add raisins and simmer 15 minutes.

BEEF on a STICK

Yield: 20 appetizers

- ½ cup red wine vinegar
- ½ cup olive oil
- 1 large shallot, minced
- 1 teaspoon Worcestershire sauce
- salt and pepper to taste
- 2 pounds beef, sirloin *or* top round, sliced into thin strips
- 20 bamboo cocktail skewers
- Mustard Sauce for Dipping–*recipe follows*

- Combine all but beef and skewers in a glass dish. Stir in beef strips and marinate for several hours or overnight.
- Soak cocktail skewers for 1 hour.
- Thread meat onto skewers. Broil lightly to rare stage and serve with Mustard Sauce for Dipping.

MUSTARD SAUCE for DIPPING

Yield: About 3 cups

- 4 tablespoons butter *or* margarine
- 4 tablespoons flour
- 3 tablespoons grainy stone-ground mustard
- 2 cups water, divided
- 1 teaspoon green peppercorns, crushed
- ¼ cup heavy cream
- 1 tablespoon fresh lemon juice
- salt to taste

- In a small saucepan, melt butter. Add flour and whisk until butter is absorbed.
- Mix mustard with 1 cup water. Add to flour/butter mixture slowly, stirring constantly. Heat until thick.
- Add peppercorns and remaining water. Heat and stir until thick and smooth. Keep warm.
- Whip heavy cream to sour cream consistency. Stir into sauce, add lemon juice and season to taste. Serve warm.

Cook's Notes

Slicing raw *beef* into thin strips is done most easily if the beef is partially frozen.

CHICKEN DIJON TIDBITS

Yield: About 50 servings

½ cup unsalted butter
3 heaping tablespoons Dijon mustard *or* to taste
2 garlic cloves, crushed
2 tablespoons minced parsley
2 tablespoons fresh lemon juice
2 whole boneless chicken breasts, skinned and cut into bite-sized pieces

- In a large skillet, melt butter; stir in mustard, garlic, parsley and lemon juice.
- Add chicken and sauté over medium high heat approximately 10 minutes, turning chicken until lightly browned on all sides.
- Serve warm as an appetizer. These tidbits make an equally good entrée.

Marcia Canale-Bracken
–Caterer

CHINESE CHICKEN WINGS

Yield: 8 to 10 servings

⅔ cup dark brown sugar, firmly packed
5 ounces soy sauce
1 tablespoon hot Chinese mustard *or* to taste
½ teaspoon ground ginger
2 teaspoons garlic powder *or* to taste
3 pounds chicken wings, cut in sections, tips discarded

- In a large bowl, mix sugar, soy sauce, mustard, ginger and garlic powder. Stir in chicken wings, cover and refrigerate overnight.
- Preheat oven to 325°F.
- Place wings in single layer on cookie sheet and bake for 1 hour and 15 minutes, turning halfway through the baking.

SOUTHWESTERN SHRIMP

Preheat oven to 375°F

Yield: 8 appetizers

8 extra large shrimp
peeled and deveined, tails left on
8 ounces cream cheese, softened
¾ teaspoon ground cumin
¼ teaspoon chili powder
2 tablespoons milk
3 green onions, minced
8 sheets phyllo dough, thawed
½ cup butter, melted
red and green salsas for garnish

- Rinse shrimp, pat dry and set aside.
- Mix cream cheese, cumin, chili powder, milk and green onions; set aside.
- Refer to page 261 for suggestions regarding handling of phyllo dough.
- Working with one sheet at a time, brush half of a sheet of phyllo with butter. Fold other half over it and repeat the process, folding over 2 more times.
- Place a generous tablespoon of cream cheese in the center of phyllo strip. Place shrimp on top of cheese crosswise with tail extending beyond dough. Moisten edges of dough and fold down over shrimp, sealing around tail. Fold each side over and over to make a little packet, Completely sealing shrimp and filling inside. Pinch tightly around tail.
- Repeat the process with the remaining 7 shrimp and place all on a baking sheet. Sprinkle packets with a little water and bake in preheated oven for 15 minutes.

✓ *Packets can also be prepared 1 to 2 hours ahead and baked at serving time.*

- Serve hot shrimp surrounded by red and green salsas.

Cook's Notes

P*hyllo pastry* is paper-thin sheets prepared from flour, water, cornstarch and vegetable oil. Phyllo is lower in calories and fat than a traditional butter or oil pastry.

SAUSAGE in a CRUST

Preheat oven to 375°F | Yield: 24 appetizers

- 2 6-inch sausages, such as mild *or* hot Italian, kielbasa, andouille *or* chorizo
- 1 sheet frozen puff pastry
- 1 egg, beaten with 1 teaspoon water
- Dijon-style mustard

- Prick sausages in 5 or 6 places and place in pan with water to cover. If using kielbasa, andouille or chorizo, boil gently for 5 minutes. Set aside to cool. If using uncooked Italian sausage, simmer uncovered for 45 minutes; drain, cool and remove casing.
- While sausage is cooling, thaw puff pastry about 20 minutes.
- On a floured board, roll out pastry to about 11 by 12 inches. Cut in half. Center a cooled sausage on one of the pastry rectangles. Wrap sausage, leaving a 1-inch overlap. Brush seam with egg wash and press down. Cut excess pastry from ends, brush ends with egg and tuck in firmly.
- Cut small pieces of pastry into decorative shapes and place on pastry roll. Brush whole roll with egg wash.
- Repeat with second sausage; place rolls on ungreased baking sheet, seam side down. Bake in preheated oven 30 to 40 minutes, or until brown and puffed. Let cool slightly and cut into ¼-inch slices. Serve with mustard.

PISTACHIO-STUFFED MUSHROOMS

Preheat oven to 350°F | Yield: 20 appetizers

- 20 medium mushrooms
- 3 tablespoons minced onion
- 4 tablespoons butter *or* margarine
- ⅓ cup dry bread crumbs
- ¼ cup pistachios, shelled and chopped
- 2 tablespoons chopped fresh parsley
- ¼ teaspoon dried marjoram
- ¼ teaspoon salt
- 3 tablespoons butter, melted

- Remove stems from mushroom caps and chop finely. Sauté stems and onion in 4 tablespoons of butter until tender.
- Add bread crumbs, pistachios, parsley, marjoram and salt. Mix well.
- Spoon stuffing into mushroom caps. Place on baking sheet and drizzle with melted butter.
- In preheated oven, bake for 10 minutes, or until hot.

APPLE CHEDDAR QUESADILLAS

Yield: 8 large
or 24 small appetizers

- ⅓ cup sugar
- ½ teaspoon ground cinnamon
- 2 cups thinly sliced pared apples
- ½ teaspoon rum flavoring
- ⅓ cup raisins
- 1½ cups shredded low-fat Cheddar cheese
- 8 6-inch flour tortillas

- Mix sugar with cinnamon. Reserve 1 tablespoon of mixture.
- Spray large skillet with butter-flavored vegetable spray. Cook apples over medium heat until tender. Remove from heat and stir in remaining sugar-cinnamon mixture, rum flavoring and raisins.
- Using all the cheese, top each tortilla to within ½-inch of the edge. Spread apple mixture over cheese.
- Coat a clean skillet with vegetable spray, heat to medium, place tortillas in skillet, filling side up, and heat 1 minute. Remove and quickly fold in half. Cover and keep warm while cooking remaining quesadillas.
- To serve, leave whole or cut quesadillas into thirds and sprinkle with reserved sugar-cinnamon mixture.
- **Alternate microwave method**: Place 1 to 2 filled tortillas on wax paper in microwave and heat on High for ½ to 1 minute, or until very warm. Remove from microwave and quickly fold in half. Cover and keep warm while cooking remaining quesadillas.

–New York Apple Association, Inc.

Cook's Notes

The best way to store *apples* is in a plastic bag in the refrigerator. This helps retain moisture so they stay crisp longer.

To keep cut apples from turning brown, toss with a citrus juice, or dip them in 1 quart of cold water mixed with 3 tablespoons of lemon juice.

PESTO CROSTINI

Yield: 10 servings

¼ cup shelled pistachio nuts, chopped
¼ cup toasted almonds, chopped
8 ounces sun-dried tomatoes, oil-packed, drained, reserving tomato oil
¼ cup freshly grated Parmesan cheese
¼ cup freshly grated Romano cheese
1 garlic clove
¼ cup packed parsley sprigs
¼ cup packed basil leaves
¼ teaspoon salt
1 teaspoon fresh lemon juice
Italian *or* French bread

- In food processor with metal blade, chop nuts and add sun-dried tomatoes. Process until smooth. Add remaining ingredients except bread.
- With machine running, add enough reserved oil to make a smooth, moist paste.
- To serve as an appetizer, spread mixture on thin slices of Italian or French bread. Heat under broiler until warm.

ROASTED RED PEPPER CROSTINI

Preheat oven to 375°F

Yield: 12 servings

12 slices French bread, cut ½ to ¾ inch thick
3 garlic cloves, halved
2 Marinated Roasted Red Peppers, sliced-*see page 16*
¼ pound mozzarella cheese, grated

- Toast French bread until golden brown. Rub both sides of slices with a cut half of garlic.
- Place bread in a single layer on a baking sheet. Top each slice with red peppers. Place in preheated oven and bake 4 minutes.
- Remove from oven; sprinkle each piece with mozzarella cheese. Return to oven; bake 1 to 2 minutes or until cheese is bubbly.

WHOLE ROASTED GARLIC with GOAT CHEESE

Preheat oven to 350°F — Yield: 6 to 12 servings

6 heads fresh garlic, unskinned
½ cup extra virgin olive oil
salt and pepper
6 sprigs fresh thyme, leaves only
6 ounces fresh goat cheese
crostini *or* crackers

- Cut each head of garlic in half horizontally. Brush each cut surface with olive oil and sprinkle with salt, pepper and thyme leaves. Put the garlic heads back together and wrap each in aluminum foil.
- Bake in preheated oven until garlic is completely soft, about 1 hour.
- Spread goat cheese on crostini and top with soft garlic squeezed from the skin. Accompany with good green olives and a great Chardonnay.

Mark Cupolo
–Victor Grilling Co.

RAVIOLI with WALNUT CREAM SAUCE

Yield: 8 servings as a first course

9 ounces refrigerated cheese ravioli
1 cup walnut pieces
1¼ cups heavy cream
½ cup freshly grated Parmesan cheese
salt and pepper
2 tablespoons finely chopped parsley
chopped chives *or* green onions, optional

- Cook ravioli according to package directions.
- In bowl of a food processor fitted with a metal blade, process walnuts until finely ground.
- In a small saucepan, heat cream, stir in nuts and cheese; season to taste. Heat through but do not boil.
- When ravioli are cooked, drain and transfer to a heated serving bowl or platter. Pour nut sauce over ravioli and sprinkle with parsley. If desired, sprinkle with chopped chives or green onions and serve hot.

MUSSELS DAISY

Yield: 6 servings as a first course

- 1 teaspoon dried basil
- 1 teaspoon dried oregano
- 1 teaspoon dried thyme
- 1 teaspoon dried marjoram
- 1 teaspoon minced fresh garlic
- pinch of salt and pepper
- 1 cup olive oil
- ½ cup red wine vinegar
- ½ cup chopped parsley
- ½ cup water
- juice of 2 lemons
- 4 pounds fresh, tightly closed mussels, scrubbed and debearded

- In a 5-quart kettle, combine all ingredients except mussels; bring to boil. Add mussels and poach, covered, about 4 minutes or until mussels open. Do not overcook. Discard any that do not open.
- Serve as a first course or pour cooked mussels into a large pasta bowl. Let guests help themselves to mussels and hunks of crusty bread.

Cook's Notes

Store *clams and mussels* in the refrigerator, covered only with a damp cloth, for up to 2 days.

Select only those clams and mussels which have tightly closed shells or those that shut when tapped on the sink or counter. Discard any with broken shells.

Scrub well with a stiff brush, under cold, running water. Pull out the dark threads — the beards — which protrude from mussel shells.

MUSSELS MARINARA

Yield: 4 servings as a first course

- Fresh Marinara Sauce–*recipe follows*
- 3 garlic cloves, chopped
- 2 tablespoons olive oil
- 2 pounds fresh, tightly closed mussels, scrubbed and debearded
- salt and pepper to taste
- ½ cup dry white wine
- 2 tablespoons chopped fresh parsley

- Prepare Fresh Marinara Sauce and keep warm.
- In a sauté pan over low heat, cook garlic in oil for 1 minute.
- Add mussels, salt and pepper and let simmer, covered, for 2 minutes.
- Pour in wine and cook, uncovered, for about 2 minutes more, until mussels have opened. Discard any mussels that do not open.
- Add parsley and sauce and cook 3 to 4 minutes more, until done.

FRESH MARINARA SAUCE

Yield: About 4 cups

- 2 tablespoons olive oil
- 2 garlic cloves, chopped
- 1 28-ounce can Italian plum tomatoes in juice
- salt and pepper

- Heat olive oil in a sauté pan over low heat. Add garlic and cook until golden, stirring constantly.
- Add entire can of tomatoes with juice and crush with a fork. Cook over low heat about 20 minutes. Season to taste.

–Portobello Ristorante

LITTLENECK CLAMS in CASINO BUTTER

Yield: 4 servings as a first course

1 cup unsalted butter, softened
½ cup chopped green onions
½ cup chopped parsley
½ cup chopped sweet red and green peppers
2 tablespoons fresh lemon juice
½ teaspoon Worcestershire sauce
½ teaspoon freshly ground black pepper
2 slices slab bacon, each ¼ inch thick
24 littleneck clams, scrubbed and tightly closed
½ cup water

- To make Casino Butter, mix butter, chopped vegetables, lemon juice, Worcestershire sauce and black pepper until well blended. Reserve.
- Dice bacon and fry over medium heat until browned and crisp. Drain.
- Place clams in a shallow pot with ½ cup water; cover and cook over high heat until clams pop open. Discard any which do not open. Reduce heat to low and add casino butter and bacon.
- Remove clams to 4 warm soup plates; continue to heat broth and butter until butter is thoroughly melted. Pour broth and bacon over clams. Serve with regular or oyster crackers.

Mark Cupolo
–Victor Grilling Co.

Cook's Notes

To get the most juice out of *lemons and limes,* bring them to room temperature, or pop them into the microwave oven on High for 20 to 30 seconds. Roll them on the counter with the flat of your hand while pressing down on the fruit.

Look for lemons with the smoothest skin and the smallest points on each end. They have more juice and better flavor.

BALSAMIC EGGPLANT

Preheat broiler — Yield: 4 servings as first course

Balsamic Dressing-*see page 87*
1 large eggplant, unpared
olive oil
8 medium radicchio leaves
2 tablespoons balsamic vinegar
4 thin slices prosciutto
4 thin slices mozzarella cheese, smoked or plain

- Prepare Balsamic Dressing and keep warm.
- Cut 8 thin slices from eggplant. Brush both sides lightly with olive oil and place in a single layer on a baking sheet. Broil until just tender, turning once.
- Wash radicchio leaves and place in a small saucepan with only the water clinging to the leaves. Add balsamic vinegar, cover and simmer until leaves are just wilted.
- On baking sheet, make a sandwich: layer 1 slice of eggplant; top with 1 slice of prosciutto, cut or folded to fit; add another slice of eggplant, offset slightly, and 1 slice of mozzarella cheese. Repeat to make 3 more servings.
- Place under broiler until cheese is just melted.
- To serve, place 2 radicchio leaves on each of 4 plates. Top each with an eggplant sandwich and spoon a little warm dressing on top.

Cook's Notes

Baking a whole *eggplant* in the microwave will help to maintain its nice green color.

Choose eggplants that are firm and heavy for their size. Male eggplants have fewer bitter seeds than the females. The males have smooth blossom ends, while the females are usually indented.

FROZEN DAIQUIRIS

Yield: 8 to 12 servings

1 6-ounce can frozen lemonade
1 6-ounce can frozen limeade
5 cups water
2 cups light rum
sugar to taste

- Combine all ingredients and pour into a freezer container. Freeze until hard, 1 to 2 days.
- To use, scoop out desired amount and place in a blender container. Whip in blender for a second or two. Pour into cocktail glasses.

CRANBERRY CITRUS PUNCH

Yield: 6 to 8 servings

2 cups low-calorie cranberry juice
½ cup grapefruit juice
½ cup orange juice
16 ounces sugar-free club soda
sherbet, optional

- Mix all liquid ingredients. Add ice *and/or* sherbet.

HOT SPICED WINE

Yield: About 36 servings

2 cinnamon sticks
6 whole cloves
3 cups water
2 cups superfine sugar
½ cup slivered almonds
1 cup raisins
juice of 1 lemon
1 gallon red wine

- Place cinnamon sticks and cloves in a cheesecloth bag.
- In a large stock pot, bring water, sugar, cinnamon, cloves and almonds to a boil. Cook 2 minutes. Remove cinnamon and cloves.
- Add raisins and lemon juice; simmer ½ hour. Add wine and heat until warm.

✓ *This can be made ahead and stored for several weeks. Reheat only what you plan to use.*

The portico shelters families and friends

Bread & Breakfast

Bread & Breakfast

Yeast Breads

Quick Breads

Muffins, Scones & Coffee Cakes

Pancakes & Cereals

Eggs

Accompaniments

HERBED CASSEROLE BREAD

Yield: 1 loaf

1 package active dry yeast
2 teaspoons sugar
¼ cup warm water–105° to 115°F
2 cups flour, divided, more if needed
1 cup cottage cheese
1 egg
1 teaspoon dried basil
1 teaspoon dried thyme
1 teaspoon garlic powder
1 teaspoon salt

- Dissolve yeast and sugar in warm water; let stand 10 minutes.
- In large mixer bowl, combine 1 cup flour, cottage cheese, egg, basil, thyme, garlic powder, salt and dissolved yeast. Beat at low speed until moistened. Beat an additional 3 minutes at medium speed.
- Stir in enough remaining flour to form stiff batter. Cover and let rise in a warm place until light and doubled in size.
- Stir dough down. Place in buttered 1½-quart baking dish or 9-inch loaf pan. Cover; let rise in warm place until doubled in size.
- **Preheat oven to 350°F.**
- Uncover dough and bake 40 minutes or until golden brown and loaf sounds hollow when lightly tapped. Remove immediately from baking dish; cool on wire rack.

–American Dairy Association and Dairy Council, Inc.

Cook's Notes

To put a sheen on the crust of *homemade bread*, take it out of the oven when it is almost baked, brush the top with white or cider vinegar, then return it to the oven until done.

RAISIN BREAD

Yield: 2 loaves

1 cup milk
¼ cup butter *or* margarine
½ cup sugar
1 teaspoon salt
½ cup warm water–105° to 115°F
2 packages active dry yeast
1 egg
4½ cups unsifted flour, divided
1 cup seedless raisins

- Heat milk, butter, sugar and salt until butter is melted. Cool to lukewarm.
- Pour warm water into a large warmed bowl. Sprinkle yeast over water, stirring until yeast is dissolved. Let stand a few minutes until mixture bubbles slightly.
- Stir in lukewarm milk mixture, egg and 3 cups of flour. Beat by hand until smooth. Stir in remaining flour to make a stiff batter. Beat until batter leaves sides of bowl. Cover and let rise in a warm, draft-free place until doubled in bulk, about 1 hour.
- Stir batter down with a spoon until it is reduced to almost its original size. Beat in raisins. Turn into 2 greased 9-inch loaf pans. Press raisins below top surface to prevent burning.
- **Preheat oven to 350°F** and bake 40 to 50 minutes. If bread browns too quickly, cover pans with a piece of heavy brown paper for last 10 minutes of baking.
- As soon as breads are done, remove them from pans to cool on wire racks, right side up.

Cook's Notes

Do not bake with "lite" *butter or margarine*. The water content can be detrimental to results.

To grease a baking pan, heat the pan briefly and grease will apply more easily.

WHEAT GERM BREAD

Yield: 4 loaves

- 2 packages dry yeast
- ½ cup warm water–105° to 115°F
- 4 cups hot milk + 1 cup dry milk
- 6 tablespoons sugar
- 4 teaspoons salt
- 6 tablespoons vegetable oil
- 2 eggs, beaten
- 1 cup wheat germ
- 10 cups flour, divided

- Dissolve yeast in lukewarm water in a large bowl.
- In another bowl, combine milk mixture, sugar, salt and oil; cool to lukewarm. Stir in beaten eggs.
- Add wheat germ and 2 cups of flour. Add to yeast mixture and beat until smooth. Gradually add remaining flour until you have a stiff dough. Knead 5 minutes until smooth and elastic. Add more flour if dough is too sticky.
- Place in a large greased bowl; turn to coat evenly. Cover with a towel and let rise in a warm draft-free place for 1½ hours.
- Punch down and let rise again 45 minutes.
- Cut dough into 4 pieces. Shape into loaves and place in well-greased 9-inch metal loaf pans. Let rise 1 more hour.
- **Preheat oven to 350°F.**
- Bake 30 minutes. Cover with foil if crust starts to get too brown.
- Remove from pans at once and cool on a rack. This bread can be frozen.

Cook's Notes

Wheat germ has high oil content and is very perishable. Store in the refrigerator for up to 3 months.

CHERRY NUT BREAD

Preheat oven to 350°F | Yield: 4 small loaves

- 2 cups flour
- 1 cup + 2 tablespoons sugar
- 1½ teaspoons baking powder
- ¼ cup solid vegetable shortening
- 1 egg
- 1 tablespoon grated peel from navel orange
- ½ cup orange juice
- 2 tablespoons cherry juice *or* warm water
- 1 cup canned pitted tart cherries, well drained and coarsely chopped
- ½ cup chopped nuts

- Grease four 5-inch loaf pans.
- Sift together flour, sugar and baking powder. Cut in shortening until mixture resembles coarse crumbs.
- Stir in egg, orange peel, orange juice and cherry juice. Fold in cherries and nuts. Pour into prepared loaf pans and bake 25 to 30 minutes in preheated oven.

–New York Cherry Growers Association

NO-EGG DATE NUT LOAF

Preheat oven to 350°F | Yield: One 9-inch loaf

- 1 cup pitted dates
- 1 cup boiling water
- 1 teaspoon baking soda
- 1 cup sugar
- ½ cup canola oil
- 1 cup chopped walnuts
- 1¾ cups flour

- Grease and flour a 9-inch loaf pan.
- Soak dates in boiling water with baking soda for 10 to 15 minutes.
- Blend sugar and oil. Mix nuts with flour. Combine all mixtures alternately.
- Place in prepared loaf pan and bake in preheated oven 1 hour, or until loaf tests done. If not eating soon, wrap and freeze.

SWEDISH BANANA BREAD

Preheat oven to 350°F Yield: One 9-inch loaf

1 cup brown sugar
½ cup solid vegetable shortening
3 very ripe bananas, mashed
1 teaspoon vanilla extract
1 whole egg + 1 egg white
2 cups flour
½ teaspoon salt
2 teaspoons baking powder
2 teaspoons ground cinnamon
¼ teaspoon freshly grated nutmeg
½ teaspoon ground cardamom
1 cup raisins
½ cup chopped nuts, optional

- Coat a 9-inch loaf pan with vegetable spray.
- Beat sugar with shortening until light and creamy. Add bananas, vanilla, egg and egg white.
- In a separate bowl, mix flour, salt, baking powder and spices. Add flour mixture to banana mix, stirring well. Add raisins and nuts. Pour into prepared pan and bake in preheated oven 1 hour, or until done.

APPLE and ORANGE BREAD

Preheat oven to 325°F Yield: 1 loaf

1 cup sugar
⅓ cup solid vegetable shortening
1 egg
⅓ cup orange juice *or* more if needed
1 cup grated pared apple
¾ cup raisins
2 cups + 3 tablespoons flour
¾ teaspoon salt
1 teaspoon baking powder
½ teaspoon baking soda

- Grease and flour a 9-inch loaf pan.
- In the bowl of an electric mixer, cream sugar and shortening until light and fluffy. Mix in egg. Add orange juice, grated apple and raisins; mix well.
- Sift together flour, salt, baking powder and baking soda. Add to other mixture and blend well. Pour into prepared loaf pan; bake in preheated oven 40 to 45 minutes, or until done.

RHUBARB STRAWBERRY BREAD

Preheat oven to 325°F | Yield: Two 8-inch loaves

1½ cups firmly packed brown sugar
⅔ cup vegetable oil
2 egg whites
1 cup buttermilk
1 teaspoon salt
1 teaspoon baking soda
1 teaspoon vanilla extract
2½ cups flour
1 cup diced fresh rhubarb
½ cup diced fresh strawberries
½ cup sugar
½ teaspoon ground cinnamon
1 tablespoon softened butter *or* margarine

- Coat two 8-inch glass loaf pans with vegetable spray and then with flour.
- In a large mixing bowl, combine brown sugar, oil, egg whites, buttermilk, salt, baking soda, vanilla and flour. Add diced rhubarb and strawberries or, if preferred, 1½ cups rhubarb and no strawberries. Pour into prepared loaf pans.
- Blend sugar, cinnamon and butter until crumbly. Sprinkle evenly over batter.
- Bake 1 hour in preheated oven; cool well. Can be frozen.

PUMPKIN BREAD

Preheat oven to 325°F | Yield: Two 8-inch loaves

4 eggs
3 cups sugar
1 cup vegetable oil
⅔ cup water
1 teaspoon ground cinnamon
1 teaspoon ground cloves
1 teaspoon freshly grated nutmeg
3½ cups flour
½ teaspoon baking powder
2 teaspoons baking soda
1½ teaspoons salt
2 cups canned pumpkin

- Grease two 8-inch loaf pans.
- Beat eggs and sugar until fluffy, add remaining ingredients and mix well. Pour into prepared pans and bake in preheated oven 1¼ hours, or until done.

PEAR BREAD

Preheat oven to 350°F Yield: One 9-inch loaf

½ **cup butter *or* margarine, softened**
1 **cup sugar**
2 **eggs**
2 **cups flour**
½ **teaspoon salt**
½ **teaspoon baking soda**
1 **teaspoon baking powder**
⅛ **teaspoon freshly grated nutmeg**
¼ **cup plain yogurt *or* buttermilk**
1 **cup coarsely chopped fresh pears**
1 **teaspoon vanilla extract**

- Grease a 9-inch loaf pan.
- Cream butter and sugar. Beat in eggs, one at a time.
- Sift together flour, salt, baking soda, baking powder and nutmeg. Add to creamed mixture alternately with yogurt or buttermilk.
- Stir in pears and vanilla. Pour into prepared loaf pan and bake in preheated oven 1 hour, or until done.

IRISH SODA BREAD

Preheat oven to 350°F Yield: 1 loaf

3 **cups flour**
¼ **cup brown sugar**
1 **teaspoon salt**
1 **tablespoon baking powder**
1 **teaspoon baking soda**
4 **tablespoons butter**
¾ **cup white raisins**
2 **eggs, slightly beaten**
1 **cup buttermilk, more if needed**

- Grease a 10-inch round pan.
- Combine flour, sugar, salt, baking powder and baking soda in a large bowl. Cut in butter. When mixture resembles coarse crumbs, add raisins.
- Mix eggs with buttermilk. Add to flour mixture and mix until a soft, loose dough is formed. Add more buttermilk if needed.
- Turn onto a floured board and knead 10 times. Shape dough into round loaf and place in prepared pan. With a sharp knife, make a cross on top about ½ inch deep. Bake in preheated oven about 1 hour, until cake tester comes out clean.

SCOTTISH BREAKFAST SCONES

Preheat oven to 400°F | Yield: 12 to 14 scones

- **⅔ cup currants**
- **1½ tablespoons Scotch whisky *or* water**
- **2 cups flour**
- **1 tablespoon baking powder**
- **½ teaspoon salt**
- **⅓ cup sugar**
- **5 tablespoons cold unsalted butter**
- **2 tablespoons grated fresh orange rind**
- **½ cup buttermilk**
- **2 large eggs**

- Dust cookie sheet with flour.
- Soak currants in Scotch or water, stirring occasionally.
- In a large bowl, mix flour, baking powder, salt and sugar. With fork or pastry blender, cut in butter, adding it in small pieces.
- When flour mixture resembles crumbs, stir in currants with Scotch and orange rind.
- In a medium bowl, beat together buttermilk, 1 egg and 1 egg yolk, reserving the extra white.
- Add buttermilk mixture to flour mixture and stir until dough lumps together. Place dough on a floured board or counter; knead and turn dough about 6 times.
- Reflour counter and press dough with your hands into a circle ½ to ¾ inch thick. With a 2 to 3-inch biscuit cutter or round cookie cutter, cut scones and place on cookie sheet. Gather scraps, make a new ball of dough, press and cut. Continue until all dough is used.
- Beat reserved egg white until foamy and brush tops of scones. Sprinkle lightly with sugar.
- Bake 15 to 20 minutes in preheated oven. Tops of scones should be fairly well-browned. Serve warm with butter and good-quality Scottish marmalade or jelly.

CRANBERRY ORANGE SCONES

Preheat oven to 375°F Yield: 8 large scones

- 1 large egg
- ⅔ cup buttermilk
- 3 cups flour
- 4 teaspoons baking powder
- ½ teaspoon baking soda
- ½ teaspoon salt
- 8 tablespoons cold, unsalted butter
- 1 cup fresh *or* frozen cranberries, chopped
- ½ cup sugar
- 1 teaspoon freshly grated orange peel

- Beat egg into buttermilk and set aside.
- Combine flour, baking powder, baking soda and salt in a bowl and mix well with a spoon.
- Cut butter into flour mixture, using 2 knives or a pastry blender, to form fine granules.
- To flour mixture, add cranberries, sugar and orange peel; toss lightly. Add buttermilk mixture to flour mixture and stir briefly to form a soft dough.
- Turn out onto a lightly floured board and knead just until mixed. Handle dough as little as possible as it tends to toughen. Form dough into a ball and cut into 8 wedges. Shape each wedge into a ball; place on an ungreased cookie sheet, not touching.
- In preheated oven bake 20 to 25 minutes or until medium brown. Remove to a rack and let cool at least 1 hour before serving.

Ellie Klein, Owner
–*Dartmouth House Bed and Breakfast*

Cook's Notes

If a recipe calls for *buttermilk* or *sour milk*, you can make your own. For 1 cup of buttermilk, add 1 tablespoon lemon juice or white vinegar to enough sweet milk to make 1 cup. Let stand a few minutes to thicken.

APPLE MUFFINS

Yield: 12 muffins

- ½ cup brown sugar
- ½ cup white sugar
- 1¾ cups pared and diced apples
- 1½ cups flour
- ½ teaspoon baking soda
- ½ teaspoon salt
- 1 teaspoon ground cinnamon
- 1 egg
- ½ cup butter *or* margarine, melted and cooled
- ½ cup chopped walnuts, optional

- In a large bowl, combine sugars. Add apples and stir. Let stand 15 minutes.
- **Preheat oven to 325°F.**
- Mix flour with baking soda, salt and cinnamon. Set aside.
- Beat egg into butter and add to apple mixture. Stir in flour mixture and then walnuts.
- Spoon into greased or paper-lined muffin tins and bake 40 to 45 minutes.

PEACH ALMOND MUFFINS

Preheat oven to 350°F

Yield: 12 muffins

- 4 fresh ripe peaches *or* canned equivalent
- 1 cup white flour
- ¾ cup whole wheat *or* white flour
- ½ teaspoon salt
- ½ teaspoon baking soda
- ⅔ cup sugar
- 2 eggs, lightly beaten
- ½ cup vegetable oil
- ½ teaspoon vanilla extract
- ¼ teaspoon almond extract
- ½ cup sliced almonds, toasted

- Peel peaches, chop and set aside.
- Combine dry ingredients in large mixing bowl; make a well in center. Add eggs and oil. Stir just until all ingredients are combined. Add peaches, extracts and almonds; stir until blended.
- Spoon into greased or paper-lined muffin tins. Bake 20 to 25 minutes in preheated oven.

FRUIT and NUT GRANOLA

Preheat oven to 250°F — Yield: 24 to 30 servings

½ **cup canola oil**
½ **cup honey**
6 **cups oatmeal, not quick-cooking**
1 **cup raw wheat germ**
1 **cup raw sunflower seeds**
1 **cup chopped *or* sliced nuts**
chopped dried fruits, optional

- In a very large pot, heat oil and honey just until blended. Stir in remainder of ingredients except for dried fruits.
- Spread out on 2 cookie sheets and bake in preheated oven until golden brown, about 50 to 60 minutes.
- Remove from oven and separate grains by pressing with back of a wooden spoon. Cool. Dried fruits can be added at this point.
- Place in jars with tight-fitting lids and keep refrigerated. Can be frozen.

YORKSHIRE PUDDING

Preheat oven to 450°F — Yield: 12 servings

¼ **cup beef drippings from roasting pan**
1 **cup unbleached flour**
¼ **teaspoon salt**
2 **eggs**
1 **cup milk**
1 **tablespoon chopped fresh chives**
1 **teaspoon fresh thyme leaves**
or **¼ teaspoon dried**

- Place 1 teaspoon of drippings into each cup of a 12-cup muffin tin. Place tin in preheated oven to heat while batter is being prepared.
- Combine flour and salt in a large bowl. In a smaller bowl, beat eggs and milk together. Make well in flour mixture, add egg mixture and combine with a few swift strokes.
- Fill cups half full; sprinkle tops with chives and thyme.
- Bake until puffed and golden, 15 to 20 minutes. Serve immediately with roast beef.

LEMON PANCAKES with RASPBERRY BUTTER

Preheat griddle — Yield: 6 servings

1½ cups whole milk ricotta cheese
8 tablespoons unsalted butter, melted
½ cup flour, measured by dip-and-sweep
6 large eggs, separated
¼ cup sugar
2 tablespoons lemon zest
2 generous pinches salt
¾ teaspoon cream of tartar
⅔ cup Raspberry Butter–*recipe follows*

- In food processor, process ricotta, butter, flour, egg yolks, sugar, lemon zest and salt until well blended. Remove to a large bowl.
- In another large bowl, beat egg whites on medium speed until foamy. Add cream of tartar and continue beating, gradually raising speed to high, until stiff peaks form when beater is raised slowly. Using a large whisk or rubber spatula, fold whites into cheese mixture.
- The griddle or frying pan should be just hot enough to sizzle a drop of water. Lightly butter it and pour batter in 3-inch rounds, about 2 tablespoons of batter.
- This delicate pancake batter tends to brown quickly. Test for doneness by lifting an edge of each pancake with a metal spatula.When golden brown, turn it over and cook about 1 minute on other side.
- Remove pancakes to warm plates and keep warm in a low oven while cooking remaining batter.
- Serve with Raspberry Butter.

Rose Levy Beranbaum, Author
–The Cake Bible

Cook's Notes

When *separating eggs*, make sure not a speck of yolk is left with the white if whites are to be beaten.

Egg whites will beat up better if they are allowed to come to room temperature before beating.

RASPBERRY BUTTER

Yield: 1⅓ cups

- 2 cups fresh raspberries
- ¼ cup water
- 2 tablespoons granulated sugar
- 8 tablespoons unsalted butter, softened
- ¼ cup confectioners' sugar
- 2 teaspoons Chambord *(black raspberry liqueur)*

- In a medium saucepan, stir together raspberries, water and granulated sugar. Over medium heat, bring to a boil and cook, stirring often, until thickly bubbling and reduced to a scant cup, about 5 minutes. Strain to remove seeds and cool to room temperature. You will have about ¾ cup.
- Process raspberry purée with butter, confectioners' sugar and Chambord until smooth. Store tightly covered.
- Any leftover butter keeps 2 weeks, refrigerated, or 3 months, frozen.

Rose Levy Beranbaum, Author
–The Cake Bible

SOURDOUGH PANCAKES

Yield: 18 to 20 four-inch cakes.

- 3 eggs
- 1 cup flour
- 6 ounces plain yogurt
- 1 cup milk
- 2 tablespoons sugar
- 2 teaspoons baking powder
- 4 tablespoons butter, melted
- 1 teaspoon salt
- 1 teaspoon baking soda

- In a large bowl, beat eggs until frothy. Add flour, yogurt and milk. Beat until smooth. Still beating, add remaining ingredients.
- Let mixture stand 10 minutes.
- **Heat a griddle** until drops of water dance across surface. Pour ¼ cup of batter onto hot griddle and make one test pancake, turning when bubbles have formed on top. Adjust heat if pancake gets too brown; grease griddle if pancake sticks.
- Continue making pancakes.

SOUR CREAM PUMPKIN COFFEE CAKE

Preheat oven to 325°F Yield: 12 to 16 servings

½ cup butter *or* margarine, softened
¾ cup sugar
1 teaspoon vanilla extract
3 eggs
2 cups flour
1 teaspoon baking powder
1 teaspoon baking soda
1 cup sour cream
1 16-ounce can solid-pack pumpkin
1 egg, lightly beaten
⅓ cup sugar
1 teaspoon pumpkin pie spice
1 cup firmly packed brown sugar
⅓ cup butter
2 teaspoons ground cinnamon
1 cup chopped walnuts *or* pecans

- Cream ½ cup butter, ¾ cup sugar and vanilla in mixer bowl. Add eggs, one at a time, beating well after each addition.
- Combine flour, baking powder and baking soda. Add dry ingredients to butter mixture alternately with sour cream; set aside.
- Combine pumpkin, beaten egg, ⅓ cup sugar and pie spice; set aside.
- Spoon half of batter into greased 9x13-inch baking dish, spreading to corners.
- Cut brown sugar, ⅓ cup butter and cinnamon together until blended. Stir in nuts. Sprinkle half of this streusel mixture over batter. Spread pumpkin mixture over streusel. Carefully spread remaining batter over pumpkin mixture. Sprinkle remaining streusel over top.
- In preheated oven bake 50 to 60 minutes, or until toothpick inserted in center comes out clean.

–Cornell Cooperative Extension Service

CRANBERRY ALMOND KUCHEN

Preheat oven to 350°F	Yield: 10 to 12 servings

8 tablespoons butter
or margarine, softened
1 cup sugar
2 eggs *or* ½ cup egg substitute
1 teaspoon baking powder
1 teaspoon baking soda
½ teaspoon salt
2 cups flour
½ cup sour cream
1½ teaspoons almond extract, divided
1 16-ounce can whole cranberry sauce
½ cup chopped walnuts, optional
¾ cup confectioners' sugar
1-2 tablespoons warm water

- Grease and flour a 10-inch tube pan.
- With mixer, cream butter and sugar in a large bowl. Add eggs, one at a time, beating after each addition.
- Mix dry ingredients; add to egg mixture alternately with sour cream. Mix well. Add 1 teaspoon almond extract and mix.
- Put layer of batter in bottom of pan. Spread half of cranberry sauce over batter; sprinkle with half of chopped nuts. Top with remaining batter, cranberry and nuts.
- In preheated oven bake 55 minutes, or until done. Cool and remove from pan.
- Mix remaining ½ teaspoon almond extract, confectioners' sugar and water in a small bowl. Drizzle over top.

Cook's Notes

Keep *sour cream* tightly covered in the refrigerator for up to four weeks. Freezing is not recommended because the sour cream will separate as it thaws.

In cartons of soft dairy foods, such as sour cream, yogurt and cottage cheese, spots of mold on the top usually mean there is mold present throughout the food. Throw them away.

BREAKFAST OVEN SOUFFLÉ

Preheat oven to 325°F

Yield: 10 to 12 servings

4 cups herbed croutons
2 cups shredded Cheddar cheese
8 eggs, lightly beaten
4 cups milk
1 teaspoon prepared mustard
1 teaspoon onion powder
¼ teaspoon freshly ground black pepper
12 slices of bacon, partially cooked, fat reserved
paprika, optional

- Grease a 9x13-inch baking dish.
- Layer croutons and cheese in baking dish.
- Combine eggs, milk, mustard, onion powder and black pepper. Pour mixture over croutons and cheese.
- Top casserole with slices of bacon. Drizzle some bacon fat over top. Sprinkle with paprika.
- Bake in preheated oven for 55 to 60 minutes, covered. Let rest 15 minutes before serving.

✓ *Recipe can be assembled the night before for a fast breakfast.*

Ellie Klein, Owner
–Dartmouth House Bed and Breakfast

BREAKFAST EGGS

Yield: 10 servings

1 pound bulk pork *or* turkey sausage
6 eggs
2 cups milk
½ teaspoon salt
1 teaspoon dry mustard
3 slices of bread, cubed
12 ounces Cheddar cheese, shredded

- The night before, cook and drain sausage.
- Beat eggs, milk, salt and mustard in medium bowl.
- Put layers of bread, sausage and cheese in 9x13-inch baking dish. Pour egg mixture over all. Cover and refrigerate overnight.
- **Preheat oven to 350°F.**
- Bake 40 to 45 minutes.

SAUSAGE and CHEESE in PHYLLO ROLLS

Preheat oven to 375°F Yield: 5 servings

Filling:

2 tablespoons butter *or* margarine
2 tablespoons flour
1 cup milk
⅓ cup shredded Swiss cheese
2 tablespoons freshly grated Parmesan cheese
dash of salt
⅛ teaspoon cayenne pepper
⅛ teaspoon freshly grated nutmeg
¼ pound bulk breakfast sausage
5 eggs, beaten
½ teaspoon dried thyme
3 tablespoons chopped fresh parsley

Pastry:

5 sheets frozen phyllo, thawed
½ cup butter *or* margarine, melted
¼ cup dry bread crumbs

Topping:

2 tablespoons freshly grated Parmesan cheese
6 tablespoons chopped fresh parsley

- Melt 2 tablespoons butter in a small saucepan. Blend in flour and cook over medium heat until smooth and bubbly, about 1 minute. Gradually add milk and cook, stirring constantly, until mixture boils and thickens, about 1 minute.
- Add Swiss cheese, 2 tablespoons Parmesan cheese, salt, cayenne pepper and nutmeg. Stir until cheese is melted; set aside.
- In medium skillet, brown sausage; drain. Stir in eggs and thyme. Cook over medium heat until eggs are set. Stir in cheese sauce and 3 tablespoons of parsley. Cool completely.
- Refer to page 261 for suggestions regarding handling of phyllo.
- Brush 1 phyllo sheet with melted butter; sprinkle with crumbs. Fold in half lengthwise; brush with melted butter. Place ½ cup filling on bottom of short side of phyllo, leaving a 1-inch edge on bottom and sides. Turn up edge, fold in sides and roll up. Place seam side down on ungreased cookie sheet.
- In a small bowl, mix topping. Brush rolls with melted butter; sprinkle with topping. Repeat with remaining phyllo sheets, filling and topping.
- Bake in preheated oven 15 minutes, or until crisp and light brown.

APPLE CARAMEL FRENCH TOAST

Yield: 8 servings

- 1 cup brown sugar
- ½ cup butter
- 2 tablespoons light corn syrup
- 2 apples, pared and sliced
- 1 loaf French bread
- 5 eggs
- 1½ cups milk
- 1 teaspoon vanilla extract
- Apple Syrup-*recipe follows*

- Cook brown sugar, butter and syrup in a small saucepan until thickened. Pour into greased 10x14-inch baking pan. Place apples over syrup.
- Slice bread into ¾-inch slices and lay on top of apples.
- Whisk together eggs, milk and vanilla and pour slowly over bread. Cover and refrigerate overnight.
- Preheat oven to 350°F.
- Bake, uncovered, 40 minutes. Flip slices upside down to serve. Can be served alone or with Apple Syrup.

APPLE SYRUP

Yield: About 2 cups

- 1 cup applesauce
- 1 10-ounce jar apple jelly
- ½ teaspoon ground cinnamon
- ⅛ teaspoon ground cloves

- While French toast is baking, prepare syrup. Combine all ingredients in a medium saucepan over moderate heat. Stir until jelly melts and syrup is hot.

Cook's Notes

Apple yields: 1 pound fresh = 2 large, 3 medium or 4 small; 2 to 2½ cups chopped or sliced.

Apples that are past their prime lose moisture and flavor. Revive them by chopping coarsely, then covering with cold apple juice and refrigerating for 30 minutes.

PHILADELPHIA FRENCH TOAST

Yield: 4 servings

8 **slices Italian bread, thickly cut on the diagonal**
4 **tablespoons cream cheese, softened**
4 **tablespoons strawberry preserves**
3 **eggs**
1 **cup milk**
2 **tablespoons sugar**
¼ **teaspoon freshly grated nutmeg**
1 **tablespoon butter *or* margarine**
Strawberry Sauce–*recipe follows*

- The night before, spread each of 4 slices of bread with 1 tablespoon of cream cheese and the other 4 each with 1 tablespoon of preserves. Make 4 sandwiches from the bread and put in a 9x13-inch baking dish.
- Mix eggs, milk, sugar and nutmeg in a bowl. Slowly pour half of this mixture on one side of each sandwich. Turn sandwiches over and repeat process, making sure that all bread surfaces have some egg mixture on them. Cover with wax paper and refrigerate overnight.
- In the morning, **preheat oven to 200°F.**
- Heat a large skillet over medium heat; add 1 tablespoon of butter. Fry sandwiches about 4 minutes on each side. Keep warm in preheated oven. Serve with Strawberry Sauce.

STRAWBERRY SAUCE

Yield: About 2½ cups

2 **cups chopped strawberries**
½ **cup sugar**
½ **teaspoon cornstarch**
¼ **cup water**

- Combine all ingredients in a small saucepan. Bring to a boil and watch carefully so that it doesn't boil over. Boil several minutes until mixture cooks down and thickens.

✓ *This can be done the night before, refrigerated and then reheated.*

Ellie Klein, Owner
–Dartmouth House Bed and Breakfast

OMELETTE MILANESE

Yield: 8 to 10 servings

4 eggs
½ cup chopped green onion
2 sheets puff pastry, thawed
2 10-ounce packages frozen chopped spinach, thawed and squeezed dry
16 ounces mozzarella cheese, cut into 12 to 15 slices
2 12-ounce jars Italian roasted peppers, drained
4 slices smoked ham, cut ⅛ inch thick
1 egg beaten with 3 tablespoons water
sliced tomatoes for garnish

- Coat an 8-inch omelette pan with vegetable spray and heat.
- Mix eggs with onions. Place half the mixture in the pan and cook until firm. Turn the omelette carefully in one piece. Continue cooking until done. Remove to a plate to cool. Repeat with remaining eggs.
- **Preheat oven to 400°F.**
- Roll 1 sheet of puff pastry large enough to line a 9-inch springform pan bottom and sides with a 1 inch overhang.
- Spread 1 package of the spinach evenly over the pastry. Cover with overlapping slices of cheese. Place 1 omelette over cheese. Layer jar of peppers and then 2 slices of ham.
- Continue layering, changing the order: omelette, peppers, ham, spinach, ending with mozzarella cheese. Roll another sheet of pastry to cover top. Seal edges.
- Decorate top with scraps of pastry moistened with water. Brush top with beaten egg mixture.

✓ This can be prepared several hours ahead, covered and refrigerated. Increase baking time by 10 minutes.

- Bake in preheated oven 30 minutes, or until pastry is brown and crisp.
- Let cool 20 minutes. Remove ring from pan, slice omelette and place on plate decorated with sliced tomatoes.

Families are welcomed at the front door

Soups & Salads

Hot Soups

Cold Soups

Vegetable & Fruit Salads

Main Dish Salads

Salad Dressings

SHERRIED CRAB SOUP

Yield: 4 servings

½ pound crab meat
2 tablespoons dry sherry
¼ cup chopped onion
¼ cup chopped sweet green pepper
2 tablespoons butter
¼ teaspoon sugar
1 teaspoon chili powder
1 tablespoon flour
2 cups half-and-half
salt and pepper to taste

- Heat crab meat and sherry in top of double boiler.
- Sauté onion and green pepper in butter over medium heat until just softened.
- Mix sugar, chili powder and flour. Add ½ cup half-and-half and stir well until smooth.
- Add to onion and pepper in sauté pan; stir until well blended. Add balance of cream; cook gently until bubbly and a little thickened.
- Pour mixture over crab and stir. Thin with more milk or cream if needed.

ROASTED GARLIC and ONION SOUP

Preheat oven to 350°F

Yield: 6 to 8 servings

½ pound peeled garlic cloves
1 pound sliced onions
½ teaspoon dried thyme
1 bay leaf
¾ teaspoon cracked pepper
6 cups chicken broth–*see page 262*
3 tablespoons butter
2 cups heavy cream

- Roast garlic and onions in a large roasting pan with herbs, pepper, chicken broth and butter for 2 hours in preheated oven.
- Let cool briefly; purée in a blender or food processor.

✓ *Purée can be refrigerated at this point for several days or can be stored in freezer.*

- To serve, add cream to purée, stir well and heat soup.

Daniel Lombardo, Chef
–Mendon House Restaurant

CUBAN BLACK BEAN SOUP

Yield: 6 to 8 servings

1 pound dry black beans
1 sweet green pepper, left whole
10 cups water
½ cup olive oil
1 large onion, chopped
1 large sweet green pepper, chopped
4 garlic cloves, crushed
¼ teaspoon dried oregano
4 ounces pimientos, chopped
4 teaspoons salt
½ teaspoon freshly ground black pepper
1 bay leaf
2 tablespoons white vinegar
2 tablespoons dry sherry
lemon wedges
finely chopped onions for garnish

- Wash beans in 2 or 3 changes of cold water. Soak beans and whole green pepper in 10 cups of water. Beans are ready when they swell up, about 4 to 6 hours.
- Bring beans to boil in same water and reduce heat to slow boil for 1 hour, or until beans are almost cooked. Stir occasionally, being careful not to break green pepper.
- Heat oil in skillet and sauté onion until soft; add chopped green pepper. When onion starts to brown, add crushed garlic and oregano. Stir for a few seconds and add pimientos; sauté for 1 minute more.
- Take out about 1 cup of beans, mash with a fork and add to onions. Return mixture to soup pot, adding salt, pepper and bay leaf. Return to slow boil, partially covered, for 1½ hours.
- Remove and discard whole green pepper, being careful not to break it. Add vinegar and sherry; simmer for another hour. Taste for seasoning; soup may need more salt or vinegar. Serve with lemon wedges and chopped onion.

Cook's Notes

To hasten soaking of *beans,* place them in a large pot, cover with water and bring to a boil. Remove from heat, cover and let stand 1 to 2 hours.

PORTOBELLO MUSHROOM SOUP

Yield: 2 quarts

- 2 tablespoons butter *or* margarine
- ¾ cup chopped onion
- 1 pound fresh portobello mushrooms, coarsely chopped
- ½ cup chopped celery
- 1 medium garlic clove, minced
- 2 bay leaves
- 10 peppercorns
- few sprigs of fresh parsley
- 2 quarts beef broth
- ¾ teaspoon Worcestershire sauce
- 3 tablespoons cornstarch mixed with ½ cup cold water
- ¾ cup sauterne wine

- Heat butter in a large saucepan or medium stock pot. Add onion, mushrooms, celery, garlic, bay leaves, peppercorns and parsley. Cook 10 minutes over moderate heat, stirring occasionally, or until vegetables become almost black.
- Remove from heat and slowly pour in beef broth while stirring. Add Worcestershire sauce and return to heat.
- Bring to boiling, reduce heat and simmer, partially covered, for about 45 minutes.
- Stir up cornstarch and water and add gradually to soup mixture. Bring to boiling and cook about 5 minutes longer, stirring.
- Remove bay leaf and purée soup in a processor or blender. Return to pot. Mix sauterne into soup. Serve hot but do not boil.

Cook's Notes

To clean *mushrooms* ahead and keep them fresh, moisten a clean cloth with lemon juice. Wipe away dirt, leaving mushroom clean and protected from discoloration.

PARSNIP VELVET SOUP

Yield: 8 to 10 servings

4 tablespoons butter
2 small onions, minced
2 teaspoons ground coriander
1 ripe pear, pared, cored and cut into chunks
2 potatoes, pared and cut up
2 pounds parsnips, pared and cut into chunks
8 cups chicken broth–*see page 262*
chopped parsley for garnish

- Melt butter in a heavy 5-quart saucepan. Sauté onion 3 minutes. Add coriander, pear and potatoes; cook 10 minutes over low heat.
- Add parsnips and chicken broth; simmer 45 to 50 minutes.
- Transfer mixture, 1 to 2 cups at a time, to a food processor and process until smooth, or push through a food mill.
- Return mixture to saucepan. Add additional chicken broth if necessary and heat. Garnish with parsley.

ZUCCHINI PESTO SOUP

Yield: 6 servings

1 cup fresh basil leaves
2 garlic cloves, minced
¼ cup freshly grated Parmesan cheese
3 tablespoons olive oil
2 tablespoons butter
2 tablespoons flour
6-7 cups chicken broth–*see page 262*
½ cup orzo pasta
2 small zucchini, diced
salt and pepper to taste

- Combine basil, garlic and Parmesan cheese in food processor bowl. With machine running, add oil and process until smooth. Reserve.
- In a medium saucepan, blend butter and flour and cook a minute or two. Whisk in broth and simmer about 15 minutes.
- Add orzo pasta and cook 4 minutes.
- Add zucchini and simmer 7 minutes.
- Whisk in basil paste and season with salt and pepper to taste.
- If soup is too thick, add a bit more broth.

CREAM of CAULIFLOWER SOUP

Yield: 4 to 6 servings

1 medium cauliflower, broken into florets
¼ cup chopped onion
⅓ cup chopped celery and leaves
6 tablespoons butter *or* margarine, divided
¼ cup flour
salt to taste
¼ cup milk, more if needed
chopped fresh parsley *or* chives

- In a medium saucepan, cook cauliflower in boiling water until just tender. Drain, reserving 2 cups cooking water. Set aside.
- Lightly sauté onion and celery in 2 tablespoons of butter in a small skillet.
- In a food processor, finely chop cauliflower, onion and celery.
- Over low heat, melt remaining 4 tablespoons of butter in saucepan. Add flour and whisk until mixture is bubbly, not brown. Add 2 cups of reserved cooking water slowly, still whisking; simmer until thickened. Add chopped vegetable mixture, salt and milk. Still whisking, bring to simmering point; do not boil.
- When serving, garnish with parsley or chives.

–Cornell Cooperative Extension Service

Cook's Notes

To keep *cauliflower* white, add 1 tablespoon of vinegar, 2 tablespoons of lemon juice or 1 cup of milk to cooking water. Cooking cauliflower in milk sweetens the flavor and the milk can be used in the soup.

CHEESE BROCCOLI BISQUE

Yield: 8 servings

- 1 cup sliced leeks, white and part of green
- 1 cup sliced mushrooms
- 3 tablespoons unsalted butter
- 2 tablespoons flour
- ½ teaspoon freshly ground white pepper
- 3 cups chicken broth-*see page 262*
- 1 cup fresh broccoli florets
- 1 cup light cream
- 1 cup shredded Swiss cheese *or* ½ cup shredded Swiss cheese mixed with ½ cup ricotta cheese

- In a large saucepan, sauté leeks and mushrooms in butter; do not brown. Add flour and whisk over low heat until bubbling. Season with pepper and remove from heat.
- Gradually blend in broth and return to heat. Stir and cook until smooth and thickened.
- Add broccoli, reduce heat and simmer about 10 to 15 minutes, until broccoli is tender but not mushy.
- Blend in cream and cheeses. Simmer until heated through and cheese is melted.

ASPARAGUS and LEEK SOUP

Yield: 4 servings

- 1 cup finely chopped leek, white and part of pale green
- 1 garlic clove, minced
- 2 tablespoons unsalted butter
- 1 pound asparagus, trimmed and cut into 1-inch pieces
- 1¾ cups chicken broth-*see page 262*
- ½ cup water
- ⅓ cup sour cream, regular *or* fat free
- salt and pepper to taste

- Cook leek and garlic in butter over moderately low heat, stirring until leek is softened, about 5 minutes.
- Add asparagus, broth and water; simmer for 10 to 12 minutes, until asparagus is very tender.
- Purée ⅔ of mixture until smooth. Stir purée back into remaining mixture and whisk in sour cream; season to taste. Cook until heated, but do not boil.

FENNEL SOUP

Yield: 8 servings

- 8 medium fennel bulbs, trimmed, reserving some of the ferny leaves
- 4 tablespoons olive oil
- 6 shallots, chopped
- 2 garlic cloves, mashed
- leaves from 6 sprigs of fresh thyme
- 6 cups chicken broth–*see page 262*
- 1 teaspoon salt, *or* to taste
- ¼ teaspoon freshly ground white pepper, *or* to taste
- juice of 1 lemon

- Remove tough outer leaves of fennel bulbs and cut bulbs into large cubes.
- In a large pot, heat olive oil. Add fennel, shallots, garlic and thyme; toss to thoroughly coat with oil. Cook gently about 5 minutes or until soft.
- Add broth and seasonings. Bring to a boil, lower heat and simmer until fennel is very tender, about 20 to 30 minutes.
- Transfer mixture to a blender and purée in batches until very smooth. Pour through a fine strainer into a clean saucepan. Stir in lemon juice and correct seasoning if necessary.

✓ *Recipe can be prepared ahead and reheated just before serving.*

- Serve with reserved leaves for garnish. You could also serve with a splash of dry sherry, croutons or a dollop of sour cream.

Cook's Notes

Fennel usually is available September through April. *Fennel* bulbs should be firm and smooth without cracks and brown spots. Stalks should be crisp, and the leaves should be bright green and fresh-looking.

Store fennel in a plastic bag in the refrigerator up to 4 days.

CREAM of CARROT SOUP

Yield: 4 servings

- 2 cups sliced carrots
- 1 cup water
- 2½ cups milk, skim *or* whole
- 2 chicken bouillon cubes
- 5 tablespoons butter *or* margarine
- 2 tablespoons flour
- freshly ground pepper to taste
- ⅓ cup orange juice

- Simmer carrots in 1 cup water for 10 minutes, or until tender. Pour carrots and water into blender jar.
- Add milk to saucepan and bring to simmer. Add bouillon cubes and stir until dissolved.
- In another small saucepan, melt butter and whisk in flour. Remove from heat and add 1 cup of milk mixture, stirring until smooth. Add this mixture to carrots and water in blender. Blend until smooth.
- Pour back into second saucepan; add remaining milk, pepper and orange juice. Over low heat, simmer gently for 30 minutes, stirring occasionally.

SHERRIED TOMATO SOUP

Yield: 4 to 6 servings

- 1 medium onion, chopped
- 1 medium carrot, coarsely shredded
- 3 tablespoons butter *or* margarine
- ¼ cup flour
- dash of freshly grated nutmeg
- 1 32-ounce can tomato juice
- 2 cups beef broth
- ½ cup dry sherry
- 1 tablespoon minced fresh parsley
- 1 tablespoon honey

- In a saucepan, cook onion and carrot in butter until tender.
- Stir in flour and nutmeg. Add tomato juice and broth. Cook and stir until slightly thickened and bubbly.
- Add sherry, parsley and honey. Simmer until vegetables are tender, about 5 to 10 minutes.

TORTELLINI and SAUSAGE SOUP

Yield: 8 to 10 servings

3 garlic cloves, minced
4 leeks, white part only, chopped
6 medium mushrooms, sliced
2 tablespoons olive oil
6 cups chicken broth-*see page 262*
1 28-ounce can crushed tomatoes
2 teaspoons chopped fresh oregano
2 teaspoons chopped fresh parsley
2 tablespoons chopped fresh basil
3-4 links mild Italian sausage, casing removed
2 9-ounce packages cheese tortellini
freshly grated Parmesan cheese

- In a large pot, sauté garlic, leeks and mushrooms in olive oil until soft. Add chicken broth, tomatoes and herbs. Simmer over low heat 1 hour.

- In a sauté pan, cook Italian sausage meat, breaking it into small pieces as it cooks. Add to broth.

- In another pot, boil tortellini in water until al dente.

- Just before serving, add cooked tortellini to soup. Serve with Parmesan cheese.

✓ *The flavor of the soup improves if made the day before serving. However do not add tortellini until ready to serve.*

Cook's Notes

To clean *leeks*, cut off the root and the tough green part of the stalk. Split the leek almost to the bottom, spread the layers and wash well under running water.

Leeks are available year-round. Look for healthy-looking leeks with crisp, green leaves. Avoid leeks that are larger than 1½ inches in diameter because they will be less tender.

ALABAMA SHRIMP GUMBO

Yield: 4 to 6 servings

1 large frying chicken, cut up
2 quarts water
2 garlic cloves, minced
2 onions, sliced
½ green pepper, thinly sliced
¼ cup butter
2 tablespoons flour
2½ cups canned tomatoes with their juice
1 package frozen okra
3 beef bouillon cubes
4 teaspoons Worcestershire sauce
¼ teaspoon ground cloves
½ teaspoon chili powder
pinch of dried basil
1 bay leaf
1½ teaspoons salt *or* to taste
¼ teaspoon freshly ground black pepper
1½ pounds medium raw shrimp, peeled and deveined
cooked white rice

- Boil chicken in 2 quarts water for 20 minutes, or until done. Let chicken cool in broth. Remove meat from bone, dice and set aside. Save broth.
- In a large heavy kettle, sauté garlic, onions and green pepper in butter until wilted. Stir flour into vegetable mixture and cook over low heat until vegetables are tender, stirring constantly.
- Add 4 cups reserved broth to kettle along with remaining ingredients except shrimp and rice. Simmer, partially covered, for 45 minutes.
- Just before serving, add shrimp and diced chicken to simmering mixture. Cook, uncovered, for 5 minutes or until shrimp are pink and tender. Remove bay leaf and serve over cooked rice.

Cook's Notes

To cook *white rice*, measure desired amount of rice and twice that amount of water into a saucepan; salt to taste. Bring to boil and stir with a fork. Cover, turn heat to medium-low and cook 14 minutes.

GUMBO YA YA

Yield: 8 servings

1 large roasting chicken, cut into serving-sized pieces
salt, cayenne pepper and garlic powder to taste
2½ cups flour
1 cup vegetable oil
2 cups coarsely chopped onion
1½ cups coarsely chopped celery
2 cups coarsely chopped sweet green pepper
6 cups chicken broth, warmed–*see page 262*
1½ teaspoons minced fresh garlic
1 pound andouille sausage, *or* any spicy smoked sausage, such as kielbasa
cooked white rice

- Refer to page 262 for information regarding making brown roux. Have all ingredients ready before starting to cook.
- Season chicken with salt, cayenne and garlic powder and set aside at room temperature for 30 minutes.
- Measure flour into a large paper bag. Add chicken pieces and shake until well coated. Remove chicken and reserve flour.
- In a large skillet, brown chicken in medium-hot oil; remove and set aside. Stir oil remaining in skillet with a wire whisk to loosen brown particles from bottom and sides of pan. Lower heat.
- Whisk in 1 cup of reserved flour and stir constantly until mixture of oil and flour *(roux)* becomes dark brown. Remove from heat and add onion, celery and green pepper, stirring constantly so they do not burn. Transfer roux and vegetables to a large, heavy saucepan.
- Add warm broth to roux and vegetables and bring to a boil, stirring. Lower heat to a quick simmer and add garlic, sausage and chicken. Continue cooking until chicken is tender, 1¾ to 2 hours.
- Adjust seasonings and serve over cooked white rice. This thick soup could serve as an entrée.

AZTEC SOUP

Preheat oven to 350°F

Yield: 4½ quarts

- vegetable cooking spray
- 2 pounds russet potatoes
- seasoned salt
- coarsely ground black pepper
- freshly grated Parmesan cheese
- vegetable oil for frying
- 10 small corn tortillas, cut into thin strips
- 1 large onion, chopped
- 2 garlic cloves, minced
- 1 28-ounce can whole tomatoes
- 6 cups chicken broth–*see page 262*
- 1 teaspoon ground coriander
- 1 teaspoon ground cumin
- 1 teaspoon dried oregano
- 1 tablespoon chili powder
- 4 chicken breast halves, skinned and boned
- 1 pound fresh spinach, stemmed and cut into ¼-inch strips
- freshly grated Monterey Jack cheese

- Line a 10x15-inch roasting pan with foil and coat with vegetable spray.
- Cut potatoes into irregular chunks up to ¾ inch thick. Place potatoes in roasting pan and coat with vegetable spray. Sprinkle liberally with seasoned salt, pepper and Parmesan cheese. Roast 1 hour in preheated oven, turning every 15 minutes. Set aside.
- While potatoes are roasting, heat oil in a medium saucepan and fry tortilla strips until crisp. Drain on paper towels and set aside.
- Coat a small nonstick skillet with vegetable spray and sauté onion and garlic until soft over medium heat. Combine them in a food processor with tomatoes and their juice. Process until smooth.
- Place mixture in a large stock pot and add broth, seasonings and chicken. Cook until chicken is done, about 30 minutes.
- Remove chicken, cool and cut crosswise into ¼-inch strips; return to pot. Add potatoes to soup and heat through. Add spinach just before serving.
- To serve, crumble a few tortilla strips in bowl, add soup and a sprinkling of Monterey Jack cheese and additional Parmesan.
- Potatoes can also be served as a side dish on their own.

HEARTY VEGETABLE SOUP

Yield: 6 generous servings

1½ pounds ground beef
1 tablespoon vegetable oil
4 large carrots, sliced on diagonal
3 ribs of celery, sliced on diagonal
2 medium onions, sliced
3 medium potatoes, pared and chunked
1 quart home-canned tomatoes *or* equivalent
1 quart water
1 bay leaf
chopped parsley, freshly ground pepper and garlic powder to taste
1 teaspoon browning sauce, optional
1½ cups fresh *or* frozen corn
12 ounces fresh *or* frozen green beans

- Brown ground beef in oil in a 5-quart stock pot.
- Add carrots, celery, onions and potatoes to ground beef. Toss and cook about 3 minutes over medium-high heat.
- Add tomatoes, water, bay leaf, seasonings and browning sauce. Stir until blended. Cook about 1 hour, uncovered, over low heat until vegetables are tender.
- Add corn and beans; cook about 10 minutes more.
- Serve in soup crocks with crusty Italian or French bread and, if you like, a sprinkling of freshly grated Parmesan cheese.

Cook's Notes

Drop a cold lettuce leaf into a pot of homemade soup to absorb the *excess fat* from the top.

If you have excess or leftover soup broth, freeze it in ice cube trays. Use it to flavor rice, pasta or vegetables.

BEEF BORSCHT

Yield: 8 servings

3 pounds shin beef
1 large marrow bone
1 tablespoon salt
2 quarts water
1 28-ounce can chopped tomatoes
1 medium onion, peeled and quartered
1 rib of celery, chopped
4 parsley sprigs
6 whole peppercorns
1 bay leaf
2 16-ounce cans sliced beets
3 cups coarsely shredded cabbage, about 1 pound
1½ cups thickly sliced carrots
1 cup chopped onion
2 tablespoons snipped fresh dill
¼ cup cider vinegar
2 tablespoons sugar
1 teaspoon salt
sour cream

- The day before serving, in a deep 6-quart kettle, place beef, marrow bone, 1 tablespoon salt and water. Cover and bring to boiling. Skim foam from surface, reduce heat, cover and simmer 1 hour.
- Add tomatoes, onion, celery, parsley, peppercorns, and bay leaf. Simmer, covered, 2 hours longer, or until beef is tender. Remove from heat.
- Lift out beef, dice and set aside. Remove and discard marrow bone. Strain soup and skim off fat; return broth and beef to kettle. You should have about 9 cups of liquid.
- Add beets and their juice, cabbage, carrots, onion, dill, vinegar, sugar and 1 teaspoon salt. Bring to a boil. Reduce heat, cover and simmer 30 minutes, or until beef and vegetables are tender. Remove from heat and refrigerate overnight.
- To serve, reheat and top with a dollop of sour cream.

COUNTRY CHICKEN BARLEY SOUP

Yield: 4 servings

4 chicken thighs,
skinned and excess fat removed
½ cup barley
5½ cups chicken broth–*see page 262*
1 rib of celery, chopped
3 small carrots, sliced
1 large tomato, peeled and chopped
2 garlic cloves, peeled
1 tablespoon soy sauce
½ teaspoon dried basil
dash of dried oregano
dash of dried thyme
dash of cayenne pepper
2 tablespoons minced fresh parsley

- Place all ingredients except parsley in a large saucepan or stock pot. Bring to a boil, cover and reduce heat. Simmer 1¼ hours, stirring occasionally.
- Remove chicken thighs. When cool, cut meat from bone into bite-sized pieces and return to soup. Simmer 15 minutes more.
- Add parsley and serve.

SARAH'S ZUCCHINI SOUP

Yield: 4 servings

4 green onions, sliced
1 tablespoon butter
2 medium zucchini, cubed
4 cups chicken broth–*see page 262*
2 tablespoons red wine vinegar
1 teaspoon farina
½ cup sour cream
salt and pepper to taste
1½ teaspoons chopped fresh dill
or ½ teaspoon dried

- In a soup pot, sauté green onions in butter until soft, about 4 minutes.
- Add zucchini, broth and vinegar; bring to a boil. Add farina and simmer about 20 minutes. Cool.
- Blend sour cream into soup; season to taste. Garnish with dill. Serve hot or cold.

MUSHROOM VEGETABLE SOUP

Yield: 8 servings

1 teaspoon diced shallots
2 tablespoons diced carrots
1½ cups sliced mixed wild mushrooms
½ cup sliced button mushrooms
4 cups vegetable *or* chicken broth
¼ cup chopped Savoy cabbage
1 teaspoon chopped fresh chives
1 teaspoon chopped fresh parsley
¼ cup cooked wild rice
2 drops hot seasoning oil, optional
salt and pepper to taste

- Coat medium saucepan with vegetable spray. Sauté shallots and carrots until lightly colored. Add mushrooms and cook, covered, over low heat for about 10 minutes.
- Add broth and remaining ingredients and continue to cook for 5 minutes. Taste and correct seasoning if necessary.

ROASTED RED PEPPER SOUP

Yield: 8 servings

1½ cups diced onions
1½ tablespoons minced garlic
¼ cup olive oil
2 cups Roasted Red Peppers-*see page 16*
2 tablespoons chopped jalapeño peppers, *or* to taste
¾ teaspoon dried thyme
2 cups chicken broth-*see page 262*
2 tablespoons white wine vinegar
¾ teaspoon salt
2 cups heavy cream *or* half-and-half

- In a medium saucepan over moderate heat, cook onions and garlic in olive oil until translucent.
- Add red peppers and jalapeños; cook several minutes.
- Purée mixture in a blender or processor and return to saucepan. Add remaining ingredients to purée and mix well.
- This soup can be served hot or cold.

Daniel Lombardo, Chef
–Mendon House Restaurant

COLD PEACH SOUP

Yield: 4 to 6 servings

10 very ripe peaches, peeled and pitted
2 cups fresh orange juice
½ teaspoon ground ginger
1 tablespoon confectioners' sugar, more if needed
1 cup sour cream
ground cinnamon

- In a blender, purée peaches with orange juice, ginger and sugar in batches until smooth. Reserve a few slices to garnish each bowl.
- Remove to a large bowl and stir in sour cream. Taste and add more sugar if needed.
- Chill thoroughly before serving.
- At serving time, dust each bowl of soup lightly with cinnamon. Make a swirling pattern in surface with handle of wooden spoon. Garnish with peach slices.

CHLODNIK

Yield: 6 to 8 servings

1 quart buttermilk
16 ounces sour cream
1 cup chopped cooked shrimp
1 large cucumber, pared, seeded and chopped
½ cup chopped green onions, white part and a little of the green
2 tablespoons chopped fresh dill
½ teaspoon ground fennel seed
1 garlic clove, crushed
salt and freshly ground pepper

- In a large bowl, beat buttermilk and sour cream until smooth.
- Add shrimp, cucumber, green onions, dill, fennel seed and garlic; stir gently but thoroughly. Chill.
- Before serving soup, season to taste. Cold soup can stand more salt than hot soup can.

TWO-MELON SOUP

Yield: 6 servings

- 1 small very ripe cantaloupe, pared, seeded and chopped
- 2 tablespoons fresh lemon juice
- ½ very ripe honeydew, pared, seeded and chopped
- 3 tablespoons fresh lime juice
- 2 tablespoons minced fresh mint leaves
- mint sprigs for garnish

- In processor or blender, purée cantaloupe with lemon juice in batches until very smooth. Place in a pitcher.
- Purée honeydew with lime juice and minced mint; place in another pitcher. Chill both pitchers at least 3 hours.
- Using 2 pitchers, pour into serving bowl at same time from opposite sides of bowl. Soups will meet in center of bowl to give 2-color effect.
- Garnish each serving with an additional sprig of mint.

ANY TIME GAZPACHO

Yield: 10 to 12 servings

- 1 medium onion, finely chopped
- 2 teaspoons chopped fresh parsley
- ½ teaspoon garlic powder
- freshly ground black pepper to taste
- 1 46-ounce can tomato juice
- 2 tablespoons olive oil
- 1 tablespoon Worcestershire sauce
- ½ cup red wine vinegar
- ¼ cup white wine vinegar
- ¼ cup dry sherry
- 3 dashes red pepper sauce
- 2 large cucumbers, pared and cubed
- 2 large firm tomatoes, cubed
- 1 large sweet green pepper, finely chopped

- Add onion, parsley, garlic powder and black pepper to tomato juice. Stir well.
- In a bowl, mix together olive oil, Worcestershire sauce, vinegars, sherry and red pepper sauce. Add to tomato juice and combine thoroughly.
- Chill at least 4 hours before serving.
- Stir in chopped vegetables at serving time.

SPINACH BASIL SALAD

Yield: 8 servings

6 cups fresh spinach, washed, stemmed and dried
2 cups fresh basil, washed, stemmed and dried
½ cup olive oil
3 garlic cloves, sliced
½ cup pine nuts
4 ounces prosciutto, slivered
freshly grated Parmesan cheese
pimiento strips for garnish

- Toss spinach and basil.
- Heat oil over medium heat; add garlic and pine nuts. Sauté until golden. Discard garlic.
- Stir in prosciutto and sauté for 1 minute.
- Toss spinach with warm dressing and sprinkle with Parmesan cheese. Garnish with pimiento strips

STILTON CHEESE and WALNUT SALAD

Yield: 8 servings

1 cup olive oil
⅓ cup red wine vinegar *or* 3 tablespoons balsamic vinegar
1 tablespoon Dijon mustard
1 teaspoon minced shallot
1 garlic clove, crushed
1 teaspoon dried fines herbes
½ teaspoon sugar
¼ teaspoon salt
4 heads Boston lettuce, torn
½ cup coarsely chopped walnuts
8 ounces Stilton cheese, crumbled
freshly ground black pepper to taste

- Whisk olive oil, vinegar, mustard, shallot, garlic, fines herbes, sugar and salt until thoroughly blended.
- Toss lettuce and walnuts in a large bowl with just enough dressing to coat the greens. Sprinkle salad with cheese and pepper.

SPINACH SALAD with PANCETTA and CARAMELIZED WALNUTS

Yield: 6 to 8 servings

- ⅓ pound pancetta *or* bacon, diced
- ½ cup coarsely chopped walnuts
- 1½ tablespoons sugar
- 8 cups spinach, washed, stemmed and torn into pieces
- 6 green onions, sliced
- Mustard Vinaigrette–*see page 88*

- In a skillet, cook pancetta until crisp. Drain on paper towels.
- In second skillet, cook walnuts and sugar over medium heat. Stir until caramelized and slightly brown. Cool and separate.
- To serve, toss spinach, pancetta, walnuts and green onions with enough dressing to make spinach glisten.

Dick and Ginger Howell
–The Seasonal Kitchen

GRILLED VEGETABLE SALAD

Yield: 4 servings

- 4 tablespoons olive oil
- 2 garlic cloves, crushed
- 1 teaspoon chopped fresh sage
- 1 teaspoon chopped fresh rosemary
- 1 teaspoon fresh thyme leaves
- 1 small eggplant
- 1 small zucchini
- 1 small yellow squash
- 1 sweet red pepper, quartered
- 2 slices red onion, ½ inch thick
- 4 cups mixed tender baby greens
- Balsamic Dressing–*see page 87*

- Several hours before serving, combine oil, garlic and herbs.
- Cut 4 slices on the diagonal, ¼ inch thick, from the eggplant, zucchini and yellow squash.
- Brush all vegetables with the oil and herb mixture and let stand for at least 2 hours.
- Grill vegetables until tender-crisp. Serve at room temperature.
- Place 1 cup of mixed greens on each of 4 large salad plates. Arrange grilled vegetables over greens and spoon a little Balsamic Dressing on top.

MARIE'S MANGO SALAD

Yield: 4 servings

- 2 medium *or* 1 large mango, peeled, seeded and cut into chunks
- ½ sweet onion, such as Vidalia, diced
- ½ cup chopped fresh cilantro
- ½ small hot pepper, diced *or* to taste
- juice and grated zest of 1 lime
- 1 teaspoon honey
- salt to taste

- Combine all ingredients in a bowl and stir gently. Refrigerate.

Kathy Lindsley, Food Editor
–Democrat & Chronicle/Times-Union

BRUTUS SALAD

Yield: 6 generous servings

- 2 heads romaine lettuce, torn into bite-sized pieces
- 1 small red onion, sliced
- ¾ pound fresh mushrooms, sliced
- ½ cup pine nuts, toasted until golden brown
- Anchovy Dressing–*see page 87*
- ½ cup freshly grated Parmesan cheese
- 1 loaf French or Italian bread, cubed and baked until toasted
- freshly ground black pepper

- Wash romaine, wrap in a towel and refrigerate while preparing other ingredients.
- Place romaine in wooden bowl and toss with onion, mushrooms and pine nuts. Add dressing and toss again. Mix lightly with Parmesan cheese and bread cubes.
- Serve immediately with freshly ground black pepper.

ROASTED PEPPER SALAD

Yield: 12 servings

3 sweet green peppers
2 sweet red peppers
2 6-ounce jars marinated artichoke hearts, drained and patted dry, reserving marinade
olive oil
½ pound feta cheese, patted dry and crumbled
½ cup sliced green onions
2 6-ounce cans pitted black olives, drained
¾ cup sliced fresh mushrooms
6 tablespoons minced fresh parsley
2 teaspoons minced garlic
1½ tablespoons dried oregano *or* ¼ cup chopped fresh
juice of 2 lemons
salt and freshly ground pepper
toasted sesame seeds *or* additional feta cheese for garnish

- Broil peppers on baking sheet, turning several times, until skins are black and peppers soft. Place in paper bag, close loosely; cool. Remove skins. Halve peppers; discard stems and seeds; thinly slice. Transfer to large glass serving bowl.
- Combine reserved artichoke marinade with olive oil to equal ¾ cup. Pour over peppers. Add remaining ingredients, except garnish; toss well. Refrigerate at least 24 hours.

✓ *This can be prepared up to 1 week ahead and kept refrigerated.*

- Serve at room temperature; garnish with sesame seeds or cheese.

ORANGE and ROMAINE TOSS

Yield: 6 servings

1 head romaine lettuce, torn
3 kiwi fruits, pared and sliced
1 11-ounce can mandarin orange sections, drained
1 small red onion, sliced
Orange Lime Dressing–*see page 84*
croutons, preferably homemade
⅓ cup pecan halves
3 ounces blue cheese, crumbled

- Combine first 4 ingredients in large bowl.
- Toss salad with dressing just before serving. Top with croutons, pecans and blue cheese.

SUMMER SALAD with GORGONZOLA

Yield: 4 servings

2 large tomatoes, thinly sliced
4 whole fresh green onions, diced
2 cucumbers, pared and thinly sliced
2 celery ribs with leaves, minced
¼ cup virgin olive oil
2 tablespoons red wine vinegar
juice of ½ lemon
½ teaspoon salt
½ teaspoon freshly ground black pepper
1 teaspoon dried oregano
8 fresh parsley sprigs, coarsely chopped
2 hard-cooked eggs, mashed with a fork
1 garlic clove, mashed
4 slices Gorgonzola cheese

- Place tomatoes, onions, cucumbers and celery in a bowl.
- Mix oil, vinegar, lemon juice, salt, pepper and oregano. Add parsley, eggs and garlic. Pour over salad and toss.
- Serve a slice of cheese on each salad plate and accompany salad with a loaf of fresh Italian bread.

BROCCOLI SLAW

Yield: 4 to 6 servings

peeled stalks from 1 bunch broccoli
1 carrot, pared
1 red *or* green sweet pepper
1 small onion
Celery Seed Dressing-*see page 88*

- In a food processor, chop broccoli stalks, carrot, sweet pepper and onion.
- Pour as much dressing as desired over slaw and chill.

BROCCOLI CAULIFLOWER SALAD

Yield: 8 or more servings

- ½ pound bacon, diced
- 2 bunches broccoli, florets chopped
- 1 head cauliflower, chopped
- 1 cup freshly grated Cheddar cheese
- 1 small onion, chopped
- 1 cup mayonnaise
- ¼ cup sugar
- 4 tablespoons white wine vinegar

- Fry diced bacon until crisp; drain.
- In a large bowl, mix broccoli, cauliflower, bacon, cheese and onion.
- In a small bowl, blend mayonnaise, sugar and vinegar. Pour over salad and mix well. Chill.

SWEET POTATO SALAD

Yield: 10 to 12 servings

- 3 pounds sweet potatoes, cooked, peeled and cubed
- ½ cup chopped onion
- 1 cup chopped sweet red pepper
- ½ cup chopped celery
- ¾ cup mayonnaise
- ½ cup low-fat sour cream *or* yogurt
- 1½ teaspoons salt
- ½ teaspoon freshly ground black pepper
- ¼ teaspoon hot pepper sauce

- In a large bowl, mix potatoes, onion, sweet pepper and celery.
- In a small bowl, blend remaining ingredients; add to potato mixture and toss to coat. Chill.

Cook's Notes

You can make your own *wine vinegar* by adding 1 part of wine to 3 parts of vinegar. Use white wine with white vinegar and red wine with cider vinegar.

NEW POTATOES VINAIGRETTE

Yield: 4 servings

1 pound new potatoes, washed and sliced
2 tablespoons white wine vinegar
2 tablespoons water
2 tablespoons chopped red *or* green onion
1 tablespoon chopped chives
2 tablespoons chopped parsley
salt and freshly ground pepper
3 tablespoons olive oil *or* to taste

- Cover and cook potatoes in boiling water just until tender, about 3 to 5 minutes. Drain and toss with vinegar, water, onion, chives, parsley, salt and pepper. Chill.
- Before serving, add oil and correct seasoning. This can be served chilled or at room temperature.

Dick and Ginger Howell
–The Seasonal Kitchen

MARINATED VEGETABLE SALAD

Yield: 6 to 8 servings

1 sweet green pepper
1 sweet red pepper
1 sweet yellow pepper
1 6-ounce jar marinated artichokes, drained, rinsed and sliced
1 6-ounce can pitted black olives, drained and sliced
1 15-ounce can chick peas, drained
1½ cups cherry tomatoes, halved
1 cup cubed Cheddar cheese
Italian Salad Dressing–*see page 86*

- Slice peppers into thin strips and place in a large bowl with remaining vegetables and cheese.
- Add enough Italian Salad Dressing to moisten. Cover and chill overnight.

CUCUMBER SALAD

Yield: 4 to 6 servings

- 3 cups pared, seeded and sliced cucumbers
- 1 cup finely julienne-cut carrots
- ⅔ cup finely julienne-cut sweet red peppers
- ⅓ cup thinly sliced red onion
- 1 tablespoon sugar
- ½ teaspoon salt
- ½ teaspoon freshly ground pepper
- 4 tablespoons Champagne vinegar
- 1½ tablespoons chopped fresh mint leaves
- 1½ teaspoons chopped fresh cilantro

- Place cucumbers, carrots, peppers and onion in a large bowl.
- Whisk together sugar, salt, pepper and vinegar. Pour over vegetables and sprinkle with mint leaves and cilantro.
- Serve salad on your choice of leaf lettuce or mixed greens.

Toby TenEyck, Executive Chef
–The Clark House Restaurant

BROCCOLI WALDORF SALAD

Yield: 4 to 6 servings

- 3 cups fresh broccoli florets
- 3 cups unpared Empire apple chunks, about 3 medium apples
- 1 cup raisins
- ¼ cup chopped pecans, toasted
- ¼ cup frozen orange juice concentrate, thawed
- ¼ cup vegetable oil
- 1 tablespoon sugar
- 1 tablespoon plus 1 teaspoon vinegar
- ¼ teaspoon dry mustard
- ⅛ teaspoon salt
- ⅛ teaspoon hot pepper sauce

- In a large salad bowl, combine broccoli, apples, raisins and pecans.
- Mix together orange juice concentrate, oil, sugar, vinegar, mustard, salt and hot pepper sauce. Add dressing to salad and toss.

–Cornell Cooperative Extension Service

FRESH GREEN BEAN SALAD

Yield: 6 servings

1½ pounds fresh green beans, washed and ends removed
1 sweet red pepper, cut into strips
1 sweet yellow pepper, cut into strips
Citrus Vinaigrette-*see page 85*

- Cook beans in boiling water about 8 minutes or until still slightly crunchy. Drain; put in bowl of ice water to refresh. Drain on paper towel.
- Combine beans with pepper strips in a large bowl.
- Spoon enough dressing onto beans to coat. Refrigerate salad before serving.

MIXED GREEN SALAD with BALSAMIC VINAIGRETTE

Yield: 4 servings

2 cups radicchio leaves, rinsed and torn
2 cups arugula, rinsed and torn
1 cup shredded carrots
½ cup fresh mint leaves
Warm Balsamic Vinaigrette-*see page 88*

- Combine radicchio, arugula, carrots and mint; toss.
- Divide among 4 serving bowls.
- Top with 3 tablespoons of Warm Balsamic Vinaigrette. Serve immediately.

Toby TenEyck, Executive Chef
–The Clark House Restaurant

RHUBARB SALAD

Yield: 8 servings

4 cups diced fresh rhubarb
1½ cups cold water, divided
¾ cup sugar
6 ounces raspberry *or* strawberry gelatin
1 tablespoon grated fresh orange rind
½ cup finely chopped celery
½ cup chopped nuts

- In a medium saucepan, cook rhubarb, ½ cup water and the sugar until a sauce forms, about 8 minutes. Remove from heat, add gelatin and stir until dissolved.
- Add orange rind, celery, nuts and remaining water. Mix well.
- Pour into a lightly greased 4 to 6-cup mold, cover and chill until set. Unmold to serve.

SPICED CRANBERRY RING

Yield: 12 servings

6 ounces raspberry gelatin
¼ teaspoon salt
¼ teaspoon ground cinnamon
dash of cloves
2 cups boiling water
1 16-ounce can whole cranberry sauce
2 tablespoons grated fresh orange rind
1 cup diced orange sections
1 cup chopped apple

- Dissolve gelatin, salt, cinnamon and cloves in boiling water. Add cranberry sauce and orange rind. Chill until thickened.
- Fold in orange and apple.
- Pour into a lightly greased 6-cup mold and chill until firm, about 4 hours. Unmold to serve and garnish as desired.

Cook's Notes

Select *rhubarb* with crisp, young stalks. If rhubarb is wilted or has thick stalks, do not buy it. Do not eat the green leaves as they are poisonous.

WILD RICE PASTA SALAD

Yield: 4 to 6 servings

½ cup uncooked wild rice
1½ cups chicken broth–*see page 262*
½ cup uncooked orzo pasta
½ sweet red *or* green pepper, chopped
½ cup pitted ripe olives, sliced
½ cup chopped tomatoes, drained
2 tablespoons capers, drained
2 ounces feta cheese, crumbled
¼ cup toasted pine nuts, optional
¼ cup olive oil
⅓ cup balsamic vinegar
2 tablespoons snipped fresh basil
1 tablespoon chopped green onion
2 garlic cloves, minced
freshly ground pepper to taste

- Simmer wild rice in chicken broth, covered, for 45 minutes, or until tender.
- Cook pasta in boiling water for 8 minutes or until al dente.
- Mix all salad ingredients in a large bowl.
- Whisk together oil, vinegar, basil, green onions, garlic and pepper. Stir well; mix with rice-pasta salad. Chill at least 4 hours before serving.

STRAWBERRY CHICKEN SALAD

Yield: 6 servings

1 whole skinless and boneless chicken breast, cooked and cut into chunks
2 cups strawberries, halved if large
2 cups honeydew melon, cubed
1 cup brie cheese, cubed
1 large avocado, peeled and diced
1 Vidalia onion, sliced
3 cups romaine lettuce, torn into bite-sized pieces
Orange Poppy Seed Dressing–*see page 87*

- Combine and gently toss all salad ingredients. Prepare dressing and drizzle over salad, using as much as needed. Toss gently again.

Dick and Ginger Howell
–*The Seasonal Kitchen*

TUNA SALAD VINAIGRETTE

Yield: 2 luncheon servings

4 cups torn mixed greens
6 green onions, chopped
½ large sweet red pepper, chopped
½ cup sliced mushrooms
1 6-ounce can solid white water-packed tuna, drained
¼ cup crumbled blue cheese
1 tablespoon vegetable oil
3 tablespoons red wine vinegar
pinch of red pepper flakes
salt and freshly ground pepper to taste
sliced tomato

- In a medium bowl, combine all ingredients except tomato. Let stand 5 minutes to blend flavors.
- Place half on each plate and decorate with sliced tomato.
- Serve with crusty sourdough bread and sliced fruit on the side.

ANTIPASTO PASTA SALAD

Yield: 10 servings

1 pound small shell macaroni, cooked
¼ pound pepperoni, chopped
¼ pound salami, chopped
¼ pound provolone cheese, grated
2 large sweet green peppers, diced
2 medium onions, diced
1 6-ounce jar marinated artichokes, drained
1 6-ounce can sliced black olives, drained
1 7-ounce jar sliced green olives, drained
3 tomatoes, diced
1 tablespoon dried oregano
1 teaspoon freshly ground pepper
1 teaspoon salt
2 tablespoons brown sugar
¾ cup vegetable oil
½ cup vinegar
2 tablespoons freshly grated Parmesan cheese

- Combine macaroni and next 9 ingredients in a large bowl.
- Blend oregano, pepper, salt, brown sugar, oil, vinegar and Parmesan. Pour over salad; toss. Serve at room temperature.

BASIL CHICKEN and PASTA SALAD

Yield: 2 servings

¾ cup water
¼ cup dry white wine
¼ teaspoon dried basil
6 black peppercorns
1 bay leaf
1 garlic clove, halved
½ pound skinned and boned chicken breasts
2 tablespoons nonfat mayonnaise
2 tablespoons plain nonfat yogurt
1 tablespoon red wine vinegar
1 tablespoon olive oil
½ teaspoon spicy brown mustard
⅛ teaspoon salt
⅛ teaspoon freshly ground pepper
1 cup cooked rotini pasta
1 cup cherry tomatoes, halved
¼ cup thinly sliced green onions
red leaf lettuce leaves

- In a large saucepan, combine water, wine, basil, peppercorns, bay leaf and garlic; bring to a boil.
- Add chicken, cover and reduce heat. Simmer for 13 minutes, or until chicken is done.
- Remove chicken from saucepan. Strain cooking liquid, reserving 2 tablespoons of liquid; discard solids. Chop chicken and set aside.
- In a large bowl, combine reserved cooking liquid, mayonnaise, yogurt, vinegar, olive oil, mustard, salt and pepper. Stir well. Add chicken, pasta, tomatoes and onions; toss gently to coat. Chill.
- Serve salad on lettuce-lined plates.

Cook's Notes

When cutting *chicken* or any raw meat or fish, use a plastic cutting board which can be washed thoroughly with soap. Harmful bacteria can lodge in improperly cleaned wooden cutting boards.

PAELLA SALAD

Yield: 8 generous servings

- 1 pound of one of the following:
  - cold poached scallops,
  - cubed broiled chicken,
  - cubed cooked ham *or*
  - cubed broiled swordfish
- 1 pound cooked, peeled and deveined large shrimp
- 1 cup olive oil, divided
- 2 cups raw long-grain rice
- 5 cups chicken broth-*see page 262*
- 1 teaspoon salt, divided
- ¼ teaspoon saffron
- ⅓ cup red wine vinegar
- 2 garlic cloves, minced
- 1 sweet red pepper, cut into narrow strips
- 1 sweet green pepper, cut into narrow strips
- 1 cup frozen peas, thawed
- ⅓ cup chopped green onion
- 1 14-ounce can artichoke hearts, quartered
- romaine lettuce leaves
- 3 tablespoons chopped fresh parsley

- Heat ¼ cup olive oil in a heavy saucepan. Add rice and stir to coat, 2 to 3 minutes.
- Remove from heat and stir in broth, ½ teaspoon salt and saffron. Bring to boil, stir and cover. Cook over low heat until rice is done and broth is absorbed, about 30 minutes.
- Uncover and cool to room temperature.
- In a glass cup or bowl, whisk vinegar, ½ teaspoon salt, garlic and ¾ cup olive oil.
- In a large bowl, mix rice with oil and vinegar mixture. Stir well. Add remaining ingredients except romaine and parsley. Chill several hours to blend flavors.
- To serve, line a large serving bowl with romaine leaves, spoon on salad; sprinkle with parsley. Serve at room temperature or slightly chilled.

ORIENTAL CHICKEN RICE SALAD

Yield: 6 servings

6 ounces water
2 cups chicken broth-*see page 262*
1 cup uncooked rice, not instant
Sesame Ginger Dressing-*see page 84*
2 cups diced cooked chicken
¼ pound fresh bean sprouts
¼ pound fresh mushrooms, sliced
4 green onions with tops, sliced
½ medium sweet red pepper, julienned

- Combine water and chicken broth in a medium saucepan; bring to a boil. Add rice, stir with a fork, cover and cook for 14 minutes or until done. Transfer to a large bowl.
- Stir dressing into hot cooked rice. Cover and chill for 2 to 3 hours.
- Stir remaining ingredients into rice just before serving.

ASCOT CHICKEN SALAD

Yield: 6 servings

1 4-pound chicken, cooked
4 ounces slivered almonds
2 sweet green peppers, finely shredded
1 pound grapes, seeded if necessary
¼ cup sliced pimiento-stuffed olives
French Dressing-*see page 84*
Sour Cream Dressing-*see page 84*
lettuce leaves

- Skin and bone chicken and cut into bite-sized pieces. Add almonds, peppers, grapes and olives but do not mix. Pour French Dressing over salad but do not toss until serving time.
- Serve on lettuce leaves with Sour Cream Dressing.

ORANGE LIME DRESSING

Yield: 1 cup

½ cup olive oil
¼ cup fresh lime juice
2 tablespoons red wine vinegar
3 tablespoons orange marmalade
salt and freshly ground pepper

- In a small bowl, whisk together all ingredients, seasoning to taste. Mix well.

FRENCH DRESSING

Yield: About ½ cup

3 tablespoons white wine vinegar
2 teaspoons prepared mustard
½ teaspoon salt
6 tablespoons olive oil

- Mix vinegar, mustard and salt in a small bowl. Whisk in oil. Refrigerate, covered, until needed.

SOUR CREAM DRESSING

Yield: About ¾ cup

6 tablespoons white wine vinegar
10 ounces sour cream
2 teaspoons sugar
½ teaspoon salt
½ teaspoon freshly ground pepper

- Slowly beat vinegar into sour cream. Add sugar, salt and pepper. Adjust seasoning to taste.

SESAME GINGER DRESSING

Yield: ¾ cup

¼ cup vegetable oil
¼ cup sesame oil
2 tablespoons soy sauce
1 tablespoon vinegar
½ teaspoon ground ginger
2 tablespoons toasted sesame seeds

- Whisk together all ingredients until well blended.

FRUIT SALAD DRESSING

Yield: About 2 cups

- 1 egg
- ½ cup sugar
- 2 tablespoons flour
- 1 cup pineapple juice

- Combine ingredients in a small saucepan. Cook over low heat, stirring constantly, until mixture thickens. Chill.
- Use over fresh fruit such as oranges, grapefruit, grapes, etc.

CITRUS VINAIGRETTE

Yield: 1½ cups

- 1 cup olive oil
- 2 tablespoons grated fresh orange rind
- ¼ cup fresh orange juice
- ¼ cup fresh lemon juice
- 1½ teaspoons coarsely ground mustard
- 2 teaspoons chopped fresh chives
- ½ teaspoon salt
- ½ teaspoon freshly ground pepper

- Whisk all ingredients in a small bowl. Excess dressing can be refrigerated for another salad.

ITALIAN SALAD DRESSING

Yield: 1 cup

- ½ cup olive oil
- ⅓ cup red wine vinegar
- 2 tablespoons water
- ¼ teaspoon dried basil
- ¼ teaspoon dried oregano
- ½ teaspoon salt
- 1 garlic clove, crushed
- pinch of tarragon
- freshly ground black pepper
- dash of red pepper flakes, optional

- Place all ingredients in a jar with a tight cover. Shake well. Allow to sit for at least 1 hour before using.
- Shake again and toss with salad greens.

TOMATO GARLIC SALAD DRESSING

Yield: 3 cups

- 1 cup mayonnaise
- 1 cup plain yogurt
- 1 teaspoon freshly squeezed lemon juice
- 1 large garlic clove, chopped
- 2 tomatoes, peeled, seeded and chopped

- Put all ingredients into a food processor or blender and blend thoroughly. Chill.
- Serve on tossed salad.

BALSAMIC DRESSING

Yield: About 1½ cups

- ¼ cup balsamic vinegar
- 2 teaspoons Dijon mustard
- ½ cup olive oil
- 2 shallots, minced
- 2 plum tomatoes, diced
- ⅓ cup pitted Kalamata olives, chopped
- 1 tablespoon capers, drained

• In a small bowl, whisk together balsamic vinegar and mustard; slowly whisk in olive oil. Stir in remaining ingredients. Store refrigerated, but use at room temperature or warmed.

ORANGE POPPY SEED DRESSING

Yield: 1 cup

- ½ cup vegetable oil
- ¼ cup rice wine vinegar
- 1 tablespoon sugar
- 2 teaspoons minced onion
- 1 teaspoon salt
- 1 teaspoon dry mustard
- 1 tablespoon poppy seeds
- 2 tablespoons orange juice

• Process all ingredients in blender until smooth. Store in tightly lidded jar and shake well before using.

Dick and Ginger Howell
– *The Seasonal Kitchen*

ANCHOVY DRESSING

Yield: 1¼ cups

- 1 cup nonfat mayonnaise
- 1 tablespoon low-sodium soy sauce
- 2 garlic cloves, minced
- 3 tablespoons balsamic vinegar
- 2 tablespoons anchovy paste

• Whisk together all ingredients.

MUSTARD VINAIGRETTE

Yield: ½ cup

- 3 tablespoons red wine vinegar
- 1 teaspoon sugar
- salt and pepper to taste
- 1 garlic clove, minced
- ½ teaspoon Dijon mustard
- ¼ cup vegetable oil

- In a bowl, mix well the vinegar, sugar, salt and pepper. Mix in garlic and mustard. While whisking, slowly drizzle in the oil. Store in a screw-top jar and shake well before using.

WARM BALSAMIC VINAIGRETTE

Yield: About 1 cup

- ½ cup olive oil
- 4 large garlic cloves, thinly sliced
- ¼ cup balsamic vinegar
- 2 tablespoons red wine vinegar
- 2 tablespoons brown sugar
- ¼ teaspoon salt
- ¼ teaspoon freshly ground black pepper

- Combine oil and garlic in a medium saucepan. Cook until garlic is golden brown but not burned. Remove garlic with a slotted spoon and discard. Let oil cool for a few minutes.
- Carefully add vinegars to hot oil, starting slowly so oil doesn't boil over. Add brown sugar, salt and pepper. Boil gently for 1 minute to caramelize sugar and develop flavors.

Toby TenEyck, Executive Chef
–The Clark House Restaurant

CELERY SEED DRESSING

Yield: 1 cup

- ⅓ cup sugar
- ⅓ cup vinegar
- ¾ teaspoon celery seed
- ¾ teaspoon salt
- ⅓ cup vegetable oil

- In a saucepan, mix sugar, vinegar, celery seed and salt; bring to boil. Add oil, return to boiling and cook until sugar dissolves. Leftover dressing will keep for the next preparation.

Vegetables & Side Dishes

The kitchen, where families cook and eat together

Vegetables

Potatoes & Grains

Vegetarian Entrées

Accompaniments

HONEY CARROTS

Preheat oven to 375°F Yield: 4 servings

1 pound carrots, pared and thinly sliced on the diagonal
¼ cup raisins
¼ cup butter *or* margarine
3 tablespoons honey
1 tablespoon fresh lemon juice
¼ teaspoon ground ginger
¼ cup sliced almonds

- Cook carrots, covered, in ½ inch boiling water for 8 minutes; drain.
- Place carrots in a 1-quart baking dish. Stir in raisins, butter, honey, lemon juice and ginger.
- Bake, uncovered, in preheated oven for 35 minutes, stirring occasionally.
- Spoon into serving bowl and sprinkle with almonds.

BEANS and GREENS

Yield: 4 to 6 servings

1 bunch of escarole, about 1 pound
1 large garlic clove, minced
1 tablespoon olive oil
1 15-ounce can Great Northern *or* cannellini beans, drained
1 chicken bouillon cube
¼ cup hot water

- Wash and trim escarole. Chop coarsely. Place greens in a pot of rapidly boiling water. Bring back to a boil and cook 1 minute. Drain and press out excess liquid.
- In a skillet, cook garlic in olive oil over low heat 1 minute. Add greens and beans and toss 2 minutes.
- Dissolve the bouillon cube in the hot water; add liquid to skillet. Cover and simmer over low heat for 5 minutes.

Nella Neeck
–Wegmans Produce Department

BROCCOLI STIR-FRY

Yield: 5 servings

3½ cups broccoli florets and stems
1 tablespoon corn *or* safflower oil
1½ teaspoons pared and finely chopped fresh ginger
1 garlic clove, minced *or* crushed
1 tablespoon water
1 teaspoon sugar
½ teaspoon salt
toasted sesame seeds *or* toasted chopped nuts

- Drop broccoli into rapidly boiling water; cook until tender when pierced with a fork, about 3 to 4 minutes. Drain broccoli and cool quickly in cold water. Drain again and set aside.
- Prepare all remaining ingredients and have them within reach of the range.
- Heat a 10-inch or larger frying pan or wok over high heat; add oil. As soon as oil is hot enough to ripple when the pan is tipped, add ginger and garlic. Quickly stir with a spatula until browning starts, about 30 seconds.
- Add broccoli, water, sugar and salt. Keep turning with a spatula until heated through, about 1 to 2 minutes.
- Turn out onto a warm serving dish and garnish with seeds or nuts.

–Cornell Cooperative Extension Service

ASPARAGUS TARRAGON

Yield: 3 to 4 servings

1 pound fresh asparagus
salt
3 tablespoons butter
2 teaspoons tarragon vinegar
¼ cup chopped pecans

- Cut tough ends from asparagus, trim scales and wash well.
- In a skillet with a small amount of water, cook asparagus, covered, until tender-crisp, about 5 minutes. Salt to taste and keep warm.
- In another small skillet, melt butter until hot but not brown. Add vinegar all at once. When foam and steam have subsided, add nuts. Pour over asparagus.

PEAS WITH SAVORY SAUCE

Yield: 3 to 4 servings

- 2 tablespoons olive oil
- 2 tablespoons vinegar
- 1 small tomato, chopped
- ½ teaspoon dried basil
- 1 tablespoon chopped onion
- freshly ground pepper to taste
- 1 12-ounce package frozen peas *or* 1½ cups fresh peas

- In a medium saucepan, simmer all but peas for 10 minutes.
- Cook fresh or frozen peas and dress with tomato mixture. Serve hot.

SQUASH STICKS

Yield: 4 servings

- 1 small yellow summer squash, cut in julienne strips
- 1 small zucchini, cut in julienne strips
- ½ cup chopped shallots
- 1 tablespoon olive oil
- 1 tablespoon butter
- 8 cherry tomatoes
- 1 teaspoon fresh lemon juice
- salt and pepper to taste
- chopped fresh parsley *or* dill

- Microwave squash sticks with a splash of water for 2 minutes; drain.

✓ *Squash can be cooked ahead, covered and chilled.*

- In a heavy skillet, cook shallots in oil and butter until just soft. Add squash sticks, cherry tomatoes and lemon juice. Cook until heated through.
- Season to taste and sprinkle with parsley or dill.

FALL VEGGIE ROAST

Preheat oven to 425°F — Yield: 4 servings

6 carrots, pared and cut in half lengthwise, then in half again
8 new potatoes, scrubbed and quartered
2 turnips, pared and cubed, optional
3 medium onions, quartered
1 whole head of garlic, peeled
3-4 tablespoons olive oil
1 teaspoon herbes de Provence *or* rosemary
salt and pepper to taste

- Place carrots, potatoes, turnips, onions and garlic cloves in a baking dish large enough to hold them in a single layer. Drizzle with oil, herbs, salt and pepper.
- Roast in preheated oven about 45 minutes, or until tender, stirring every 15 minutes to brown evenly.

Dick and Ginger Howell
–The Seasonal Kitchen

SUMMER VEGETABLE MEDLEY

Yield: 6 to 8 servings

1 medium onion, chopped
1 garlic clove, chopped
3 tablespoons olive *or* vegetable oil
1 large *or* 2 small zucchini, diced
1 bunch broccoli, cut into florets
3 carrots, pared and diced
3 tomatoes, cut into chunks
salt and pepper to taste
¼ cup freshly grated Parmesan cheese
½ cup seasoned bread crumbs

- Sauté onion and garlic in oil over moderate heat for about 5 minutes. Add zucchini, broccoli and carrots. Continue cooking for 15 minutes, or until vegetables are just crisp.
- **Preheat oven to 350°F.**
- Add tomatoes and cook 5 minutes more. Season to taste.
- Pour into 9x13-inch glass baking dish. Sprinkle with grated cheese and then top with crumbs. Bake for 25 to 30 minutes.

CAULIFLOWER with BALSAMIC VINEGAR

Yield: 6 to 8 servings

2 tablespoons olive oil
4 ounces bacon, diced
1 large cauliflower, cut into florets
2 garlic cloves, minced
5 ripe tomatoes, peeled and cut into eighths
⅓ cup balsamic vinegar
½ cup chicken broth-*see page 262*
1 teaspoon sugar
1 teaspoon anchovy paste, optional
salt and freshly ground pepper
3 tablespoons minced fresh parsley

- Heat oil in a large skillet over medium-high heat. Add bacon and cook until softened but not browned, about 3 minutes. Add cauliflower and sauté, stirring frequently, until lightly browned, 5 to 7 minutes.
- Add garlic and tomatoes to skillet; cook 2 minutes more. Stir in vinegar, broth, sugar and anchovy paste.
- Cover, reduce heat to low and simmer until cauliflower is tender-crisp, about 5 minutes.
- Uncover, increase heat again; cook until liquid is reduced to a glaze. Season to taste with salt and pepper. Sprinkle with parsley and serve.

SWEET and SOUR VIDALIA ONIONS

Preheat oven to 350°F

Yield: 4 servings

4 medium Vidalia onions, peeled and sliced
½ cup boiling water
½ cup melted butter
¼ cup cider vinegar
½ cup brown sugar

- Place onions in an 8x8-inch baking pan. Mix together remaining ingredients and pour over onion slices.
- Bake, uncovered, for 1 hour in preheated oven.

ONIONS BRAISED in RED WINE

Yield: 6 to 8 servings

6 large yellow onions, peeled
3 tablespoons butter
2 whole cloves
salt and pepper to taste
1 cup Burgundy wine

- Cut onions into ¼-inch slices; separate into rings.
- Melt butter in a large skillet. Add onions and cook until well coated. Add cloves, salt and pepper. Sauté until golden brown.
- Add Burgundy, cover and simmer about 15 minutes.
- Discard cloves and cook, uncovered, until wine is reduced almost to a glaze.

FRENCH ONION CASSEROLE

Preheat oven to 350°F

Yield: 4 servings

4 medium onions, sliced
3 tablespoons butter
2 tablespoons flour
freshly ground pepper
¼ cup dry sherry
1 cup beef broth
1½ cups plain croutons
¼ cup shredded Swiss cheese
2 tablespoons freshly grated Parmesan cheese

- Cook onions in butter until tender. Blend in flour and a dash of pepper. Add sherry and broth; stir until thick.
- Place in a 1-quart casserole dish.

✓ *Recipe can be prepared ahead to this point; cover and chill until ready for final preparation.*

- Bake, covered, in preheated oven for 30 minutes.
- Sprinkle with croutons, Swiss and Parmesan cheeses. Bake, uncovered, 10 minutes more.

PENNSYLVANIA DUTCH CABBAGE

Yield: 6 servings

- 8 cups shredded white cabbage
- 4 slices bacon, chopped
- 1 small onion, minced
- 2 tablespoons brown sugar
- 2 tablespoons flour
- ½ cup water
- ⅓ cup vinegar
- ½ teaspoon salt
- ⅛ teaspoon freshly ground pepper

- Cook cabbage in boiling salted water until tender, about 5 to 7 minutes. Drain.
- Meanwhile, cook bacon until crisp. Remove from skillet.
- Add onion to bacon drippings and cook until tender. Blend in brown sugar and flour. Add water and vinegar and cook, stirring constantly, until thickened. Season to taste.
- Add sauce and bacon to drained cabbage; heat thoroughly.

–Cornell Cooperative Extension Service

BRAISED LEEKS

Yield: 4 servings

- 8 leeks
- 2 tablespoons olive oil
- 1 garlic clove, minced
- ½ teaspoon salt
- ¼ teaspoon freshly ground pepper
- ½ cup chicken broth–*see page 262*
- juice of 1 lemon

- Cut off tough green ends of leeks. Split leeks almost in half and wash out sand which lodges inside.
- Heat oil over medium heat. Cook garlic and leeks gently until golden. Add salt, pepper and chicken broth. Cover and cook briskly for 10 minutes.
- **Reduce heat**, add lemon juice and simmer until tender.
- Serve hot as a vegetable or cold with additional olive oil and lemon juice.

POTATOES au GRATIN

Preheat oven to 375°F — Yield: 4 to 5 servings

4 large potatoes, pared
salt and freshly ground pepper
freshly grated nutmeg
6 tablespoons heavy cream
4 ounces shredded Gruyère cheese
4 tablespoons freshly grated Parmesan cheese
2 tablespoons butter

- Butter a large au gratin dish.
- Thinly slice potatoes and pat dry in a towel. Arrange ⅓ of potatoes in dish, overlapping each slice by one half. Sprinkle layer with salt, pepper, nutmeg, 2 tablespoons of cream, 4 tablespoons of Gruyère and 2 tablespoons of Parmesan cheese.
- Repeat process with another ⅓ of potatoes, seasonings, cream and cheeses.
- Add remaining potatoes and top with salt, pepper, nutmeg and cream Dot with butter.
- Bake, uncovered, in preheated oven for 1 hour or until potatoes are soft.

SWEET POTATOES MANDARIN

Yield: 8 to 12 servings

5 fresh sweet potatoes
***or* two 16-ounce cans, drained**
1 11-ounce can mandarin oranges
¼ teaspoon ground ginger
¼ teaspoon freshly ground pepper
½ teaspoon salt
2 tablespoons butter *or* margarine
¼ cup slivered almonds

- Cook sweet potatoes if using fresh.
- **Preheat oven to 350°F.**
- Reserve ½ cup of juice from mandarin oranges. In a saucepan, simmer juice with ginger, pepper, salt and butter until hot. Heat sweet potatoes in this mixture.
- Mash potatoes and gently fold in drained oranges. Place in a 7x11-inch baking dish and sprinkle top with almonds. Bake 15 minutes, or until hot.

TWICE-BAKED POTATOES

Preheat oven to 375°F | Yield: 8 generous servings

- 8 **baking potatoes**
- 4-6 **tablespoons butter**
- ½ **cup sour cream *or* as needed**
- 1 **cup chopped green onions, white part only**
- 4 **tablespoons diced green chilies**
- 8 **ounces Cheddar cheese, grated**
- ¼ **teaspoon salt**
- **freshly ground pepper to taste**

- Wash potatoes, pierce in several places with a sharp fork and bake 1 hour, or until tender.
- Cool just enough to handle and cut off top third with a sharp knife. Scoop out insides and mash with butter. Add enough sour cream to get a nice consistency. Stir in green onions, chilies, cheese, salt and pepper.
- Scoop back into shells, place on a baking sheet and return to preheated oven until hot and lightly browned, about 20 to 30 minutes.

Dick and Ginger Howell
–*The Seasonal Kitchen*

POTATO and CARROT MASH

Yield: 4 servings

- 6 **medium potatoes, pared and cubed**
- 1 **large onion, peeled and chopped**
- 6 **large carrots, scraped and cubed**
- 4 **tablespoons butter**
- ½ **cup milk**
- ½ **teaspoon salt**
- **dash of freshly ground white pepper**
- 1 **cup grated sharp Cheddar cheese**

- Boil potatoes, onion and carrots until tender, about 30 minutes. Drain and mash slightly.
- **Preheat oven to 375°F.**
- Whip vegetables with electric beater, adding butter, milk, salt and pepper.
- Place in a buttered baking dish and top with cheese. Heat in oven until cheese melts.

MUSTARD-GLAZED TOMATOES

Preheat oven to 425°F

Yield: 4 servings

1 tablespoon sharp and creamy mustard
3 tablespoons mayonnaise
1 tablespoon chopped fresh chives
1 tablespoon chopped fresh parsley
2 medium *or* large tomatoes
1 tablespoon freshly grated Parmesan cheese
freshly ground pepper

- Mix together mustard, mayonnaise, parsley and chives.
- Slice tomatoes in halves if medium or thirds if large. Place on baking pan, cut side up.
- Just before baking, divide mustard mixture among tomatoes, spreading to cover. Sprinkle with Parmesan cheese and then with pepper.
- Bake in preheated oven about 10 minutes until hot. Run under broiler for a minute or so until bubbling. Serve immediately.

COUSCOUS with APPLES and GREEN ONIONS

Yield: 4 servings

2 cups chicken broth–*see page 262*
4 tablespoons unsalted butter
1 cup couscous
6 green onions, thinly sliced, white part and some green
1 large red apple, finely diced
salt to taste

- In a medium saucepan, combine broth and butter. Bring to a boil. Remove from heat and add couscous and green onions. Cover and let stand for 5 minutes.
- Add apples and toss to mix. Season with salt and serve hot.

Dick and Ginger Howell
–The Seasonal Kitchen

WILD RICE with CARROTS and ONIONS

Yield: 2 servings

- ⅓ cup wild rice, rinsed and drained
- 1 cup chicken broth–*see page 262*
- ⅓ cup finely diced carrot
- 2 tablespoons unsalted butter
- ⅓ cup chopped onion
- 1 teaspoon fresh lemon juice *or* to taste
- 2 tablespoons minced fresh parsley

- Place wild rice and chicken broth in a small saucepan and bring to a boil. Reduce heat, cover pan and simmer until rice is tender; about 40 to 50 minutes. Drain rice if all liquid has not been absorbed.
- In a skillet, cook carrot in butter over moderately low heat, stirring, for 5 minutes. Add onion and cook, still stirring, for 5 minutes, or until all are tender.
- Remove from heat. Stir in cooked rice, lemon juice and parsley.

WILD RICE with ARTICHOKE HEARTS

Yield: 6 servings

- 1 cup uncooked wild rice, rinsed
- 3 cups chicken broth–*see page 262*
- ¼ cup butter *or* margarine
- 1½ cups sliced mushrooms
- 1½ cups chopped celery
- 1 10-ounce package frozen artichoke hearts, thawed
- ¼ cup chopped green onions, white part and some green
- 1 tablespoon fresh lemon juice
- ½ teaspoon dried *or* 1 tablespoon fresh thyme
- salt and pepper to taste

- In a medium saucepan, combine wild rice and chicken broth; bring to a boil. Reduce heat, cover and simmer for 30 minutes. Do not drain. Rice will be undercooked.
- In another saucepan, melt butter; sauté mushrooms and celery for 5 minutes, or until tender-crisp. Halve artichoke hearts; add to mushroom and celery mixture along with green onions, lemon juice, thyme, salt and pepper.
- Preheat oven to 325°F.
- Put undercooked wild rice into a 2-quart casserole. Stir in mushroom and celery mixture. Cover and bake for 60 minutes.

BROWN RICE MEDLEY

Yield: 4 servings

- 2 tablespoons butter
- 2 tablespoons olive oil
- ¾ cup chopped onion
- 3 green onions, chopped, white and green parts
- ¾ cup chopped sweet green and red peppers
- ¾ cup sliced mushrooms
- ½ teaspoon salt
- ¼ teaspoon freshly ground pepper
- ½ teaspoon dried thyme
- 1 cup brown rice
- 1½ cups chicken broth–*see page 262*
- ½ cup dry white wine *or* additional broth
- chopped tomato and parsley, optional

- Place butter and oil in a saucepan. On medium heat, sauté onion, green onions, peppers and mushrooms until vegetables are tender but not brown, about 7 minutes.
- Add salt, pepper and thyme. Add rice; sauté 1 to 2 minutes.
- Add broth and wine; stir to combine. When mixture comes to simmer, cover and cook over low heat for 45 minutes. Do not uncover until time is up.
- Add chopped tomato and parsley for garnish.

Cook's Notes

Brown rice is the entire grain with only the inedible outer husk removed. Brown rice takes at least twice as long to cook as regular white long-grain rice.

NUTTY BROWN RICE

Preheat oven to 400°F | Yield: 8 servings

1 pound mushrooms, sliced
4 green onions, cut into ½-inch pieces, including green parts
1 garlic clove, minced
4 tablespoons unsalted butter
2 cups uncooked brown rice
½ teaspoon dried thyme
¼ teaspoon ground turmeric
freshly ground pepper
6 cups beef broth
1½ cups chopped pecans
whole pecans and chopped green onion tops for garnish

- In an ovenproof casserole, sauté mushrooms, onions and garlic in butter for 5 to 7 minutes.
- Stir in rice and cook for 3 minutes.
- Add seasonings and broth, heat to boiling and bake, uncovered, in preheated oven for 45 minutes.
- Stir in pecans and bake another 15 minutes. Test rice and cook a little longer if not done.
- To serve, garnish with whole pecans and green onion tops.

DOUBLE JASMINE RICE with MUSHROOMS

Yield: 4 servings

2 cups water
¼ cup jasmine tea leaves
1 cup uncooked jasmine rice *or* other long-grain rice
½ pound fresh button mushrooms
¼ pound fresh shiitake mushrooms
¼ pound fresh oyster mushrooms
2 tablespoons butter
2 tablespoons finely chopped shallots
2 teaspoons minced garlic
2 green onions, thinly sliced
2 teaspoons oyster sauce
pinch of salt
¼ cup chopped walnuts for garnish

- Bring 2 cups of water to boil in a 2-quart pan. Turn off heat and add tea. Cover and steep 10 minutes. Pour tea through a strainer and reserve the liquid.
- Return 1½ cups of tea liquid to pan and add rice. Bring to boil, reduce heat to medium-high and cook, uncovered, until water is reduced to level of rice. Reduce heat to low, cover and simmer until rice is tender, about 15 minutes. Turn off heat and let stand, covered, 5 minutes.
- While rice is cooking, slice button mushrooms, cut off shiitake mushroom stems and quarter caps. Cut large oyster mushrooms in half; leave small oyster mushrooms whole.
- Heat a wok over medium heat until hot. Add butter, shallots and garlic; stir-fry 30 seconds. Add mushrooms and stir-fry 1 minute. Add cooked rice, green onions, oyster sauce and salt; toss to mix well. Garnish with walnuts.

Martin Yan
–Yan Can Cook, Inc.

Cook's Notes

Oyster mushrooms have a fan-shaped cap that varies in color from pale gray to dark brownish gray. *Shiitake mushrooms* have a brown floppy cap, usually 3 to 6 inches in diameter. Only the caps are used.

MUSHROOM NOODLES with CRISPY SHALLOTS

Yield: 4 servings

vegetable oil for frying
½ pound large shallots, peeled, sliced and separated into rings
¼ pound mushrooms, thinly sliced
2 tablespoons butter
½ pound medium egg noodles
salt and pepper to taste

- In a heavy skillet, heat ½ inch of oil over medium high heat until it is hot but not smoking.
- Fry shallots in small batches, stirring occasionally, for 2 to 3 minutes, or until they are golden. Move quickly, as they go from golden to well done very fast. Remove with slotted spoon to paper towels and drain. Cover and keep warm.
- Sauté mushrooms in butter until golden.
- In a deep saucepan of boiling salted water, cook noodles 7 to 9 minutes or until tender. Drain.
- Toss noodles with mushrooms. Add more softened butter and seasoning to taste. Place noodles and mushrooms in a heated serving bowl and sprinkle with shallots.

BARLEY CASSEROLE

Preheat oven to 350°F

Yield: 4 servings

1 cup pearl barley, not quick-cooking
2 cups beef broth, divided
2 tablespoons butter
¾ pound fresh mushrooms, minced
5 garlic cloves, minced, *or* to taste
1 medium onion, chopped
1½ cups peeled, seeded and chopped tomatoes
salt and freshly ground pepper to taste

- Grease a 1-quart casserole.
- Place barley and 1 cup of broth in casserole. Cover and bake for 30 minutes.
- Add second cup of broth and bake until liquid is absorbed, about 20 minutes.
- Melt butter in a medium saucepan. Add mushrooms, garlic and onion; cook until onion is soft. Add to barley along with tomatoes and seasonings.
- Bake until warmed through and flavors are well blended.

OAXACA STEW

Yield: 4 servings

1 medium zucchini
1 medium yellow squash
12 baby carrots, pared
1 large sweet cubanella pepper, cored and seeded
1 medium onion
1 8-ounce can yellow corn
1 14-ounce can whole tomatoes
¼ cup water
1 package taco seasoning mix

- Pare zucchini and yellow squash unless they are young and tender. Cut all vegetables into large chunks.
- Place all ingredients in a 1-quart pot. Cover and cook over medium heat, stirring frequently, for about 15 minutes, or until vegetables are tender-crisp. Add water if necessary so that stew does not get too dry. Serve with rice and tortillas.

ONION TART

Preheat oven to 350°F

Yield: 8 to 12 servings

8 cups sliced onions
2 cups sliced sweet red peppers
⅓ cup olive oil
1 teaspoon Cajun seasoning
¾ teaspoon dried savory
¼ teaspoon freshly ground black pepper
1 large pizza crust, purchased *or* freshly made

- Sauté onions and peppers in oil over medium heat until soft but not brown. Stir often to prevent burning.
- Add seasonings and mix well.
- Brush pizza shell with a little more oil. Top with onion and pepper mixture.
- Bake in preheated oven for 20 to 25 minutes. Serve hot.

ASPARAGUS QUICHE

Preheat oven to 400°F Yield: 4 to 6 servings

2 cups asparagus slices, 1 inch long
1½ cups sliced fresh mushrooms
¼ cup diced onion
2 tablespoons butter *or* margarine
½ cup diced bacon
1 9-inch unbaked pie crust-*see page 263*
4 eggs
½ cup milk
8 ounces Swiss cheese, shredded
1 tablespoon chopped fresh parsley

- Place asparagus in a skillet with ½ inch of water. Cover and steam 3 to 4 minutes, or until tender-crisp.
- Sauté mushrooms and onion in butter until tender. Toss steamed and drained asparagus with mushrooms and onion.
- Cook bacon until crisp and reserve for topping.
- Bake pie crust 10 minutes in preheated oven. Meanwhile beat eggs until frothy and stir in milk.
- When crust has baked 10 minutes, remove from oven and fill with vegetable mixture. Sprinkle cheese over vegetables. Pour egg and milk mixture over cheese and top with parsley and bacon. Bake 15 minutes.
- **Lower oven temperature to 350°F** and continue baking 20 minutes longer, until knife inserted in center comes out clean. Let stand 5 minutes before cutting.
- This makes an elegant spring luncheon dish, served with a garden salad and fresh rolls.

Cook's Notes

Select firm, bright green *asparagus* spears with tight tips. Snap off the thick ends when ready to use. To store stand in about 1 inch of water in a bowl in refrigerator, covered with plastic wrap.

EGGPLANT PIE

Preheat broiler — Yield: 4 servings

- 1 medium eggplant, pared and cut into ½-inch slices
- ¾ teaspoon salt
- ⅛ teaspoon freshly ground pepper
- 2 medium tomatoes, peeled and thinly sliced
- 1 medium sweet green pepper, cored and thinly sliced
- 1 small onion, peeled and thinly sliced
- 2 tablespoons olive oil
- ¼ teaspoon garlic powder
- ½ teaspoon dried oregano
- ½ teaspoon dried basil
- 4 ounces shredded part-skim mozzarella cheese
- ½ cup freshly grated Parmesan cheese

- Arrange eggplant slices on foil-covered baking sheet or broiler pan. Sprinkle with salt and pepper. Broil 6 inches from heat for 8 minutes, or until lightly browned.
- Heat oven to 375°F.
- Line a 10-inch pie plate with eggplant slices, browned side down, overlapping in a circular pattern. Arrange consecutive layers of tomato, pepper and onion over eggplant.
- Drizzle with oil and sprinkle with garlic powder, oregano and basil. Sprinkle mozzarella cheese over top, followed by Parmesan.
- Bake 40 minutes, or until cheese is golden.
- Cut into wedges to serve.

Cook's Notes

Salting before sautéing or stir-frying helps to keep *eggplant* from absorbing too much oil. Slice or dice eggplant. Sprinkle with ½ teaspoon salt per pound. Place in colander in sink and let stand at least 1 hour. Rinse lightly and press with paper towels to remove moisture.

SPANAKOPITA

Preheat oven to 375°F Yield: 48 pieces

1 package phyllo pastry, thawed
2 medium onions, chopped
2 teaspoons butter
1 bunch flat-leaf Italian parsley
2 10-ounce packages frozen chopped spinach, thawed and liquid squeezed out
1 pound Monterey Jack cheese, grated
¼ pound feta cheese, crumbled
6 eggs, beaten
2 teaspoons dried dill
salt and freshly ground pepper to taste
½ pound unsalted butter, melted
¼ teaspoon freshly grated nutmeg

- Refer to page 261 for information on handling phyllo.
- Sauté onions in 2 teaspoons of butter until soft and translucent. Add parsley and spinach, cheeses, eggs and seasonings.
- Lightly grease a large roasting pan, 17x11x2 inches, with a little butter.
- Unfold phyllo and cut to fit pan. Cover phyllo with a damp towel to keep it from drying out.
- Place 1 sheet of phyllo on bottom of pan and brush with melted butter. Continue this process until half the sheets have been used. You can also spread the trimmed pieces of phyllo every fourth layer or so.
- Spread spinach and cheese mixture evenly over buttered phyllo. Continue layering remaining phyllo over spinach mixture, buttering each sheet.
- With a sharp knife, cut through the top layers of phyllo, making 48 squares.
- Cover with foil and bake 35 to 40 minutes in preheated oven.

✓ *If you wish to prepare ahead, spanakopita can be cooled and frozen at this point. Thaw before continuing.*

- Cut through to bottom layers of dough, and continue baking, uncovered, 20 to 30 minutes, or until lightly browned.

SPINACH QUICHE

Preheat oven to 425°F — Yield: 6 servings

- pastry for a 9-inch pie–*see page 263*
- ¼ cup chopped onion
- 1 garlic clove, minced
- 1 cup sliced mushrooms
- 2 tablespoons butter
- 4 eggs
- 1 cup low-fat milk
- ½ teaspoon dried oregano
- ½ teaspoon salt
- ¼ teaspoon dried thyme
- 5 cups fresh spinach, washed and stemmed
- 1 cup grated sharp Cheddar cheese

- Prepare pastry and place in 8 or 9-inch pie pan or quiche dish.
- Sauté onion, garlic and mushrooms in butter until onion is soft.
- In a medium bowl, beat eggs. Add milk, oregano, salt and thyme; mix well. Add onions, garlic and mushrooms.
- Tear spinach into pieces and place in pie shell.
- Pour egg mixture over spinach and sprinkle with grated cheese.
- Bake for 25 minutes in preheated oven. Let cool 10 minutes before cutting to serve.

Cook's Notes

To transfer *pie crust* to pie pan, roll the dough around your rolling pin and gently lay it on the pan. Ease the dough into the pan without stretching. Prick the bottom of a shell to be pre-baked. Do not prick a shell which will be filled before baking. The crust will be soggy.

EXOTIC MUSHROOM CHEESE BAKE

Yield: 4 to 6 servings

1 ounce dried porcini mushrooms
1 cup boiling water
¼ cup unsalted butter
10 ounces fresh imported mushrooms, such as portobello, shiitake, *or* Italian brown
¼ cup minced shallots
2 tablespoons brandy
2 tablespoons chopped fresh herbs of your choice, divided
2 tablespoons flour
¼ teaspoon dry mustard
1 cup milk
3 eggs, lightly beaten
2 cups shredded Gruyère cheese, divided

- Rinse dried porcini in a sieve under running water. Place in a small bowl and add boiling water. Let stand 30 minutes.
- Remove porcini, pressing as much liquid as possible from mushrooms, reserving liquid. Coarsely chop porcini.
- Melt butter in a heavy skillet. Sauté fresh mushrooms and porcini until golden, about 10 minutes. Add shallots and sauté 2 minutes. Add brandy and reserved porcini liquid. Boil until almost all liquid is absorbed, about 5 minutes. Mix in 1 tablespoon of herbs. Cool.
- Mix together flour, dry mustard and 1 tablespoon of herbs. Slowly whisk in milk and then eggs.
- **Preheat oven to 375°F.** Coat a 9-inch pie plate with vegetable spray.
- Place 1½ cups cheese in pie plate, spreading evenly. Add cooled mushroom mixture. Pour egg and milk mixture over all. Sprinkle with remaining ½ cup cheese.
- Bake for 40 to 45 minutes, or until custard is set.

RASPBERRY APPLESAUCE

Yield: 8 servings

- 3 pounds Cortland *or* other firm apples
- 2 tablespoons sugar
- ½ cup water *or* cider
- ¼ teaspoon ground cinnamon
- 1½ cups frozen raspberries
- 2 tablespoons applejack *(apple brandy)*

- Pare and core apples; cut into large chunks.
- In a saucepan, combine apples, sugar and water. Cook, covered, until tender, about 15 minutes.
- Add cinnamon and cook 5 minutes, uncovered. Add frozen raspberries, stirring to defrost.
- Stir in applejack; simmer 5 minutes more. Cool. Purée or leave chunky. Serve warm or cold.

OVEN APPLESAUCE

Preheat oven to 300°F

Yield: About 4 quarts

- 12 20-ounce apples
- ½ cup sugar, *or* more to taste
- ½ teaspoon ground cinnamon
- ¼ teaspoon salt
- dash of freshly grated nutmeg
- ¼ cup water
- 2 tablespoons butter, cut into bits

- Lightly butter a large roasting pan.
- Pare, core and cut apples into chunks. Place in roasting pan.
- Mix dry ingredients and sprinkle over apples. Add water and butter.
- In preheated oven, bake 1 to 1¼ hours, or until as tender as desired. Stir occasionally.

APPLE CHUTNEY

Yield: 6 to 8 cups

8 cups pared and chopped apples, about 3 pounds
4 cups sugar
½ cup cider vinegar
1 cup currants
½ cup chopped walnuts
zest of 1 small navel orange
¼ teaspoon ground cloves

- Combine all ingredients in a saucepan and cook for 25 minutes, or until apples are tender and chutney has turned a warm caramel color.
- This can also be served as an appetizer with slices of Cheddar cheese and crackers.

Dick and Ginger Howell
–*The Seasonal Kitchen*

CHERRY HONEY RELISH

Yield: 2½ cups

1 14-ounce can pitted tart cherries with their juice
½ cup raisins
½ cup honey
¼ cup cider vinegar
¼ cup brown sugar, packed
½ teaspoon ground cinnamon
⅛ teaspoon ground cloves
½ cup pecans, coarsely chopped
1 tablespoon cold water
1 tablespoon cornstarch

- In a 2-quart saucepan, combine cherries and juice, raisins, honey, vinegar, sugar, cinnamon and cloves. Cook slowly, uncovered, 30 minutes. Stir in pecans.
- Combine cold water and cornstarch and gradually stir into cherry mixture. Cook, stirring constantly, until mixture thickens.
- This is a good accompaniment to turkey, pork or ham.

–*New York Cherry Growers Association*

CRANBERRY RELISH IN A SHELL

Preheat oven to 350°F

Yield: 6 servings

1 small cooking pumpkin, about 8 inches in diameter
1 cup chopped apples
1 cup fresh cranberries
1 cup raisins, mixed light and dark
½ cup chopped walnuts
⅓ cup sugar
1 teaspoon fresh lemon juice
¼ teaspoon freshly grated nutmeg
½ teaspoon ground cinnamon

- Cut top from pumpkin and set aside. Remove seeds, wash pumpkin and place on cookie sheet.
- Combine remaining ingredients and fill pumpkin.
- Bake, uncovered, for 30 to 35 minutes in preheated oven. Cover with pumpkin top and continue to bake for 20 minutes.
- Serve warm or cold as a dinner accompaniment.

SALSA

Yield: About 5 cups

2 28-ounce cans tomatoes
1 16-ounce can stewed tomatoes
2 jalapeño peppers, fresh *or* canned
6 green onions, coarsely chopped, white and part of green
1 heaping tablespoon chopped fresh parsley *or* cilantro

- Drain tomatoes and stewed tomatoes in colander.
- Put peppers in blender jar. Add tomatoes and blend for a few seconds. Taste and add more peppers if desired. Stir in onions and parsley.
- Place in a covered jar and refrigerate. This will keep for 2 to 3 weeks.

A safe corner for tiny tots

Pastas

Sauces

Pastas

WILD MUSHROOM, CHICKEN and GREEN FETTUCCINE GRATIN

Yield: 8 to 10 servings

- **6** **chicken breast halves, skinned and boned**
- **1½** **pounds assorted fresh wild mushrooms, washed and sliced**
- **6** **tablespoons butter**
- **2** **garlic cloves, minced**
- **2** **tablespoons flour**
- **1** **cup chicken broth**–*see page 262*
- **1** **cup heavy cream *or* half-and-half**
- **salt and freshly ground pepper**
- **1** **pound fresh *or* dried green fettuccine**
- **dash of dry sherry**
- **1½** **cups freshly grated Parmesan cheese**

- Butter a 9x13-inch au gratin dish or other ovenproof baking dish.
- Broil chicken on baking sheet or grill outdoors. Slice and reserve.
- In a large saucepan, sauté mushrooms in butter over medium heat until they soften slightly, about 3 minutes. Add garlic; cook 2 minutes. Stir in flour and cook 2 to 3 minutes.
- Gradually stir in chicken broth and then cream. Add salt and pepper to taste. If sauce seems too thick add more cream. Cook on very low heat 10 to 15 minutes.
- While sauce is simmering, cook pasta 8 to 10 minutes in a large pot of boiling water. Drain.
- When cream sauce has finished cooking, stir in sherry and cooked chicken. Add drained pasta to the mixture and spread in au gratin dish. Sprinkle with Parmesan cheese.
- Broil for 2 to 3 minutes until golden, or make ahead and bake in a 400°F oven for 20 minutes, or until hot.

Dick and Ginger Howell
–The Seasonal Kitchen

FETTUCCINE with MUSHROOMS and FRESH TOMATOES

Yield: 4 servings

½ cup boiling water
½ ounce dried porcini mushrooms
2 tablespoons olive oil
1 small onion, finely chopped
½ pound fresh button mushrooms, diced
½ teaspoon salt
⅛ teaspoon freshly ground pepper
2 garlic cloves, minced
1 cup dry white wine
8 ounces fettuccine *or* other pasta
1½ pounds fresh plum tomatoes, peeled, seeded and chopped
⅓ cup chopped fresh parsley
1 tablespoon chopped fresh tarragon *or* basil
freshly grated Romano cheese

- Pour ½ cup boiling water over porcini mushrooms in a small bowl and soak until soft, about 30 minutes. Drain, reserving soaking liquid, and cut mushrooms into small pieces.
- Heat oil in a large skillet over medium heat. Add onion and sauté until soft, about 4 minutes.
- Add porcini, fresh mushrooms, salt and pepper. Cook about 5 minutes.
- Add garlic and wine and cook mixture until liquid is reduced to 2 tablespoons, about 10 minutes.
- Pour reserved mushroom liquid into skillet, leaving any sediment in bottom of bowl, and cook until liquid is reduced to ¼ cup, about 15 minutes. Stir in tomatoes and cook 5 minutes more.
- Cook fettuccine in a large kettle of boiling water for 8 to 10 minutes.
- Drain pasta and add to skillet along with parsley and tarragon or basil. Toss well and serve immediately with grated cheese.

FETTUCCINE with PINE NUTS and PROSCIUTTO

Yield: 6 servings as a first course;
3 as an entrée

- 12 ounces fresh *or* dried fettuccine
- 4 tablespoons butter
- 1 garlic clove, minced
- 1½ tablespoons fresh lemon juice
- 4 ounces prosciutto, thinly sliced and torn into 2-inch-long strips
- 1 cup finely chopped fresh parsley
- ⅓ cup pine nuts, lightly toasted
- salt and freshly ground pepper to taste
- thin lemon wedges as accompaniment
- freshly grated Parmesan cheese

- In a large kettle of boiling water, cook fettuccine 8 to 10 minutes, or until it is al dente. Drain.
- While fettuccine is cooking, heat butter in a skillet over moderately high heat, swirling it, until butter is golden brown. Sauté garlic lightly.
- Remove skillet from heat and stir in lemon juice, prosciutto, parsley and pine nuts.
- In a large bowl, toss fettuccine with butter sauce and season to taste. Serve with lemon wedges and Parmesan cheese.

Cook's Notes

Pine nuts should be refrigerated to prevent them from turning rancid. They can also be frozen so that they are ready when needed.

TORTELLINI di MAGGIO

Yield: 6 servings

- 1 tablespoon unsalted butter
- 2 tablespoons extra virgin olive oil, divided
- 1 chicken breast, skinned, boned and cut into 4 pieces
- 2 shallots, chopped
- 1 carrot, pared and cut into 4 parts and then into thin strips
- 1 cup chicken broth–*see page 262*
- 1 teaspoon tomato paste
- 1 16-ounce can tomato purée
- ½ cup heavy cream *or* half-and-half, optional
- 1 ½-inch-thick slice prosciutto di Parma, cut into thin strips
- 1 pound tortellini, preferably fresh
- 1 pound asparagus, cleaned and cut into 1-inch pieces
- 8 ounces mozzarella cheese, cubed
- freshly grated Parmesan cheese

- In a skillet, heat butter and 1 tablespoon of oil. Lightly sauté chicken on both sides about 10 minutes, turning often. Remove chicken to a plate.
- Add remaining oil to skillet along with shallots and carrot. Sauté for a few minutes and add broth. Cover and bring to a boil, reduce to simmer and cook until broth is reduced by half. Add tomato paste and purée. Simmer, covered, about 20 minutes. Add cream.
- Shred chicken and add to sauce with prosciutto. Keep warm.
- Cook tortellini and asparagus in rapidly boiling water until both are al dente. Drain and place in shallow bowl.
- Just before serving, toss mozzarella cubes with sauce and add to tortellini and asparagus. Serve with a bowl of Parmesan cheese.

✓ *This dish can be prepared ahead and heated in a buttered baking dish 30 to 40 minutes at 325°F.*

Anna Teresa Callen
–Food Writer and Teacher

SPINACH BEEF LASAGNA

Preheat oven to 350°F   Yield: 6 to 8 servings

- 1 pound lean ground beef
- 1 tablespoon vegetable oil
- ⅔ cup chopped onion
- 2 garlic cloves, crushed
- 1 15-ounce can tomato sauce
- 1 teaspoon dried oregano
- ½ teaspoon salt
- 3 lasagna noodles
- 2 10-ounce packages frozen chopped spinach, thawed and squeezed dry
- 1½ cups low-fat cottage cheese
- 1 egg, lightly beaten
- ⅓ cup freshly grated Parmesan cheese
- ⅛ teaspoon freshly grated nutmeg

- Brown ground beef in oil in a large skillet. Remove beef with a slotted spoon and discard all drippings except 1 teaspoonful.
- Add onion and sauté until soft. Add garlic and continue cooking for 1 minute. Return beef to skillet.
- Add tomato sauce, oregano and salt; heat to boiling. Reduce heat to low, cover and simmer 15 minutes. Remove from heat and set aside.
- Cook noodles for 10 minutes in a large pot of boiling water; drain.
- Mix together spinach, cottage cheese, egg, Parmesan cheese and nutmeg. Spread spinach mixture evenly in a greased 9x13-inch baking pan. Top with noodles. Spread meat sauce over all.
- Cover with foil and bake in preheated oven for 40 to 45 minutes, removing foil for the last 5 minutes. Let stand 10 minutes before cutting.

SPINACH GNOCCHI

Yield: 4 servings

Tomato and Cream Sauce-*recipe follows*
2 tablespoons finely chopped onion
2 tablespoons butter *or* margarine
1 10-ounce package frozen chopped spinach, thawed and squeezed dry
salt and pepper to taste
¾ cup ricotta cheese, regular *or* low-fat
⅔ cup flour
2 eggs
1 cup freshly grated Parmesan cheese
¼ teaspoon freshly grated nutmeg

- Make Tomato and Cream Sauce and set aside.
- In a medium saucepan over medium-low heat, sauté onion in butter, stirring, until onion is golden. Add spinach, salt and pepper and sauté over medium heat for 5 to 6 minutes, stirring frequently. Transfer mixture to a large bowl.
- Stir in ricotta cheese and flour; add eggs, cheese and nutmeg, mixing thoroughly.
- Break off small chunks of dough and, on a floured board, roll into long ropes ½ inch in diameter. With a sharp knife, cut off 1-inch segments. With well-floured hands, shape into little pillows. With a finger, press an indentation into each little pillow or press with tines of a fork. Dough will be moist; keep flouring your hands. Lay gnocchi out on a tray in one layer.

✓ *If desired, gnocchi can be frozen at this point and stored in a sealable bag. Cook frozen.*

- Cook gnocchi, a handful at a time, in moderately boiling water until they float to the top. This will take only a few minutes. Remove with a slotted spoon to a serving bowl and continue until all are cooked. Toss with heated Tomato and Cream Sauce.

TOMATO and CREAM SAUCE

Yield: About 5 cups

4 tablespoons butter *or* margarine
¼ cup chopped onion
¼ cup chopped carrot
¼ cup chopped celery
1 28-ounce can chopped tomatoes with juice
½ teaspoon salt, *or* to taste
½ cup heavy cream *or* half-and-half

- Put all ingredients except cream into a heavy saucepan and simmer over low heat for 1 hour, uncovered. Stir occasionally.
- Purée contents of pan through food mill or fine sieve; return to pan and bring to simmer. Add cream and cook 1 minute. Correct seasoning.

PASTA with PROSCIUTTO, PEPPERS and HERBS

Yield: 4 servings

1 small red onion, finely chopped
1 sweet yellow pepper, finely chopped
2 tablespoons extra-virgin olive oil, divided
11 ounces roasted red peppers, drained and finely chopped
3 ounces finely chopped prosciutto
½ pound spiral pasta
⅔ cup finely chopped fresh basil
⅓ cup mixed, finely chopped fresh parsley and mint
salt and pepper to taste
lemon wedges
freshly grated Parmesan cheese

- In a heavy skillet, cook onion and yellow pepper in 1 tablespoon of olive oil over moderately low heat, stirring, until softened; stir in red peppers and prosciutto.
- In a kettle of boiling water, cook pasta for 10 minutes, or until al dente.
- Drain pasta and place in a large serving bowl. Toss pasta with pepper mixture and remaining tablespoon of oil, herbs and seasoning to taste.
- Serve pasta with lemon wedges and Parmesan cheese.

TURKEY-FILLED LASAGNA ROLLS

Yield: 6 to 8 servings

- 1 medium onion, chopped
- 3 tablespoons olive oil, divided
- 1 35-ounce can plum tomatoes, including liquid
- 1½ teaspoons sugar
- 2 teaspoons salt, divided
- ½ teaspoon freshly ground pepper, divided
- 1 pound ground turkey
- 12 lasagna noodles
- 16 ounces ricotta *or* cottage cheese
- 2 tablespoons freshly grated Parmesan cheese
- 1 cup frozen peas
- 1 tablespoon chopped fresh parsley
- 1 egg
- 8 ounces shredded mozzarella cheese, divided

- Cook onion in 1 tablespoon olive oil until tender. Add tomatoes with liquid, sugar, 1½ teaspoons salt and ¼ teaspoon pepper. Heat to boiling, stirring to break up tomatoes. Reduce heat and simmer for 15 minutes, stirring occasionally.
- While tomatoes are cooking, place 2 tablespoons of olive oil in a 12-inch skillet over medium heat. Cook ground turkey, stirring frequently, until all pan juices evaporate and meat is browned, about 10 minutes. Remove from heat.
- Cook lasagna noodles for 10 minutes in a large pot of boiling water; drain.
- Preheat oven to 375°F.
- Spoon half of sauce into a 9x13-inch baking dish.
- Stir ricotta cheese, Parmesan cheese, peas, parsley, egg, half of mozzarella cheese, ½ teaspoon salt and ¼ teaspoon pepper into meat.
- Spoon 2 heaping teaspoons of filling on the end of each lasagna noodle; roll up. Arrange seam side down in sauce.
- Spoon remaining sauce over noodles. Top with remaining mozzarella cheese.
- Cover loosely with foil and bake 20 minutes. Remove foil and bake another 5 minutes.

FRESH APPROACH LASAGNA

Preheat oven to 350°F Yield: 8 servings

- 1 cup ricotta cheese
- ¾ cup mozzarella cheese, divided
- ¼ cup freshly grated Parmesan cheese, divided
- 2 tablespoons chopped fresh basil *or* to taste
- 1 6-ounce can tomato paste
- 1 8-ounce can tomato sauce
- 11 lasagna noodles, uncooked
- 1 small zucchini, sliced
- 1 medium onion, chopped
- 1 sweet green pepper, chopped
- 3 medium tomatoes, sliced

- Mix ricotta with half the mozzarella and Parmesan cheeses. Add basil and set aside.
- Blend tomato paste and tomato sauce. Spread half the mixture in a 7x11-inch glass baking dish. Place 5 noodles on top. Place a layer of zucchini on noodles, sprinkle with onion and green pepper. Add a layer of tomato slices.
- Top with 3 more noodles. Spread the ricotta mixture over noodles. Top with 3 more noodles. Spread with remaining tomato mixture. Add a layer of tomato slices on top.
- Cover with foil and bake lasagna in preheated oven for 50 minutes. Uncover, sprinkle with remaining mozzarella and Parmesan cheeses and bake 15 minutes more.

Cook's Notes

Fresh *basil* can be available most of the year by growing it in pots in a sunny window or in your garden. Basil can also be easily dried in the microwave by spreading about ¼ cup leaves on a paper towel. Microwave at 100% power 1 to 3 minutes. Cool before storing in a jar with a tight lid.

GRAMA'S MANICOTTI

Yield: 4 to 6 servings

Topping:

Marinara Sauce-*see page 134*
freshly grated Parmesan cheese

Pancakes:

1 tablespoon butter *or* margarine
1 cup sifted flour
1 cup milk
½ teaspoon salt
2 eggs *or* ½ cup egg substitute

Filling:

¼ cup chopped fresh parsley
1½ pounds ricotta cheese
2 eggs *or* ½ cup egg substitute
¼ cup freshly grated Parmesan cheese
salt and pepper to taste
3 ounces cubed *or* shredded mozzarella cheese, optional

- Prepare Marinara Sauce and set aside.
- To make pancakes, melt butter and mix with remaining ingredients until smooth. Let stand about 1 hour before using.
- Mix together filling ingredients, seasoning to taste.
- Heat a 5 to 6-inch frying pan until hot. Oil bottom lightly.
- Add 2 to 3 tablespoons of pancake batter to pan, tip until batter covers bottom and cook to a delicate brown. Turn and cook second side until brown. Repeat until all 12 pancakes are cooked. Stack them between sheets of wax paper as they are cooked.
- **Preheat oven to 350°F.**
- Spoon a thin layer of Marinara Sauce over bottom of 9x13-inch baking dish.
- Spoon equal portions of filling on pancakes, roll and place in baking dish. Pour additional sauce on top, sprinkle with Parmesan cheese and bake 20 to 25 minutes, or until hot and bubbly.

SHRIMP with PASTA

Yield: 4 servings

1 pound medium shrimp, peeled and deveined
2 medium zucchini, approximately 1 pound
6 tablespoons olive oil, divided
1 tablespoon finely minced garlic
1 teaspoon finely chopped green chili peppers *or* ½ teaspoon dried hot pepper flakes
1½ pounds ripe tomatoes, peeled, seeded and chopped
20 small pitted black olives
½ pound fusilli pasta
2 tablespoons finely chopped fresh basil, *or* 1 tablespoon dried
freshly grated Parmesan cheese

- Cut shrimp in half lengthwise.
- Trim and discard ends of zucchini. Cut each zucchini crosswise into 2-inch lengths. Cut each piece lengthwise into 6 equal wedges.
- Heat 4 tablespoons olive oil in a large skillet over low to medium heat. Add zucchini and cook 2 minutes, stirring; remove to a bowl.
- Add garlic and cook 2 minutes, stirring often.
- Stir in chilies, tomatoes and black olives and cook 5 minutes, stirring often.
- Add shrimp and zucchini and cook 1 minute. Cover and hold over low heat until ready to serve.
- Bring 3 quarts of water to boil in a large pot. Add fusilli and cook 10 minutes, or until al dente. Drain, reserving ¼ cup of liquid, and place pasta in a large bowl. Add remaining 2 tablespoons of olive oil to pasta if desired.
- Stir basil and reserved liquid into sauce and pour over fusilli. Toss and serve with Parmesan cheese.

MEDITERRANEAN PASTA

Yield: 4 servings

48 littleneck *or* Maine clams, well scrubbed
2 cups water
1 pound fusilli *or* linguine pasta
1 tablespoon butter *or* margarine
1 tablespoon olive oil
24 medium shrimp, shelled and deveined
2 garlic cloves, minced
1 bunch broccoli, cut into florets, *or* asparagus cut into 1-inch lengths
24 medium pitted black olives
juice of 1 lemon
⅓ cup freshly grated Parmesan cheese
4 tablespoons chopped fresh parsley
red pepper flakes, optional

- In a large kettle, steam clams in 2 cups of boiling water, tightly covered, for 5 to 10 minutes or until clams have opened. Discard any that do not open. Remove clams from shells and reserve 1 cup of broth.
- In a large pot of boiling water, cook pasta 8 to 10 minutes or until al dente.
- While pasta is cooking, heat butter and olive oil in a large nonstick pan. Sauté shrimp, garlic and broccoli until shrimp are pink, about 3 minutes.
- Add clams with broth, black olives, lemon juice and Parmesan cheese. Simmer for about 2 minutes.
- Drain pasta and place in a large serving bowl. Pour simmering sauce over pasta and stir well.
- Serve in individual bowls topped with more Parmesan cheese, parsley and red pepper flakes.

Cook's Notes

To remove sand from *clams* soak in cold salted water for 1 hour. Discard any which float to top.

SHRIMP and BROCCOLI with BOW TIES

Yield: 4 servings

4 slices of bacon, diced
4 cups broccoli florets
1 pound bow tie pasta
1½ pounds large shrimp, peeled and deveined
¼ cup olive oil
4 garlic cloves, minced
1 large jalapeño pepper, seeded and minced
½ cup chopped onions
2 tablespoons oil-packed sun-dried tomatoes, minced
3 tablespoons capers
1 cup sliced black olives
1 16-ounce can tomatoes, partially drained and chopped
salt to taste
freshly grated Parmesan cheese

- Cook bacon until crisp, drain and set aside.
- In a pot of boiling water, blanch broccoli for 1 minute, or until tender-crisp. Refresh in cool water and set aside.
- Cook pasta in a pot of boiling water for 8 to 10 minutes, or until al dente.
- While pasta cooks, quickly sauté shrimp in olive oil in a large skillet for about 30 seconds. Add garlic, jalapeño and onions. Toss for 1 minute.
- Add the sun-dried tomatoes, capers, olives, canned tomatoes and broccoli. Cook for 2 minutes, tossing.
- Drain pasta, add to skillet and toss everything together for 2 minutes. Salt to taste.
- Sprinkle with reserved bacon and Parmesan cheese.

Dick and Ginger Howell
–The Seasonal Kitchen

BAKED ZITI

Yield: 6 to 8 servings

- 3 tablespoons olive oil
- 1 large onion, chopped
- 1 garlic clove, minced
- 1 pound ground beef
- 2 32-ounce cans Italian plum tomatoes in purée
- 1 6-ounce can tomato paste
- 1 cup white wine
- 1 teaspoon salt
- 2 teaspoons dried oregano
- 1 teaspoon dried basil
- 1 bay leaf
- 2 tablespoons chopped fresh parsley
- 8 ounces ricotta cheese
- 8 ounces shredded mozzarella cheese
- ½ cup freshly grated Parmesan cheese
- 2 eggs
- 1 pound ziti pasta

- In a large pan or Dutch oven, heat oil and lightly sauté onion, garlic and ground beef until meat is no longer pink.
- Add tomatoes, tomato paste, white wine, salt and herbs. Cover and simmer for 2 hours.
- Make filling by mixing together ricotta, mozzarella, Parmesan and eggs.
- Cook ziti in a large pot of boiling water for 12 to 14 minutes, or until al dente; drain.
- **Preheat oven to 350°F.** Grease a 4-quart casserole dish.
- Spread some meat sauce, a layer of ziti and a layer of cheese filling in dish. Repeat, ending with meat sauce on top.
- Bake 40 to 45 minutes. Do not overcook.

SHRIMP with CLAM SAUCE and ANGEL HAIR PASTA

Yield: 4 servings

- 2 tablespoons butter
- 4 tablespoons olive oil
- 4 large garlic cloves, minced
- 4 shallots, minced
- 1 8-ounce jar clam juice
- 2 6-ounce cans chopped clams with their juice
- 2 tablespoons chopped fresh basil
- ¼ cup chopped fresh parsley
- freshly ground pepper to taste
- 1 pound shrimp, peeled and deveined
- 2 tablespoons olive oil mixed with juice of 1 lemon
- unflavored bread crumbs
- 8 ounces angel hair pasta
- freshly grated Parmesan cheese

- In a large saucepan, heat butter and 4 tablespoons olive oil together. Gently sauté garlic and shallots until soft. Add clam juice and simmer 5 minutes.
- Add chopped clams with juice, basil, parsley and pepper. Stir well and cook, uncovered, 8 to 10 minutes so liquid will reduce a little.

✓ *Recipe can be prepared ahead to this point.*

- Line a cookie sheet with foil; place shrimp on foil. Brush shrimp with half of oil and lemon mixture; sprinkle with bread crumbs. Broil 2 minutes. Turn shrimp and brush with remaining oil and crumbs; broil for 2 minutes longer.
- While shrimp are broiling, cook angel hair in a large pot of boiling water for 5 minutes or until al dente. Drain.
- Put shrimp into hot clam sauce and heat 1 minute.
- Serve shrimp and sauce over hot angel hair pasta and pass Parmesan cheese.

PASTA with BAY SCALLOPS

Yield: 4 servings

1 lemon
1 pound bay scallops,
or quartered sea scallops
4 tablespoons olive oil
8 tablespoons butter, divided
8 shallots, finely sliced
½ cup white wine
1¼ cups canned puréed plum tomatoes
3 tablespoons chopped sun-dried tomatoes
8 ounces clam juice
¼ teaspoon fennel seeds
salt and freshly ground pepper to taste
½ pound angel hair pasta
½ cup chopped fresh parsley

- With a fine grater, remove zest of lemon and set aside. Squeeze juice from lemon. Marinate scallops in lemon juice for up to 30 minutes.
- While scallops are marinating, heat olive oil and 4 tablespoons of butter in a skillet. Sauté shallots until transparent.
- Add wine, puréed tomatoes, sun-dried tomatoes, clam juice, fennel seeds, salt and pepper. Bring to boil and simmer 15 to 20 minutes. Add more clam juice or tomato purée if thinner sauce is desired.
- In a large pot of boiling water, cook pasta for 5 minutes or until al dente.
- Drain scallops and sauté in 2 tablespoons of butter over high heat for 3 minutes. Stir in 1 tablespoon lemon zest. Do not add scallops to the sauce until the last minute.
- Drain pasta and toss with scallops, sauce and remaining 2 tablespoons butter. Sprinkle with parsley.

ELBOWS, CHICK PEAS and ESCAROLE

Yield: 4 servings as an entrée,
6 as a first course

- 1 head escarole, well-washed and chopped
- 1 cup water
- 1 tablespoon minced garlic
- 1 tablespoon olive oil
- 5 tablespoons chicken broth–*see page 262*
- 1 tablespoon tomato paste
- 1 can chick peas, drained and rinsed
- ½ teaspoon salt
- ¼ teaspoon pepper
- 2 cups elbow macaroni
- freshly grated Parmesan cheese

- Simmer escarole in 1 cup water for 20 minutes, covered. Do not drain.
- In a saucepan, sauté garlic in oil and broth until soft; stir in tomato paste. Add chick peas and mash about half of them. Season to taste and add cooked escarole.
- Cook macaroni in a large pot of boiling water for 12 minutes, or until al dente. Drain, reserving 1 cup of cooking liquid.
- Mix all ingredients, adding cooking liquid if necessary. Add cheese at the table.

Cook's Notes

Escarole can be very sandy. Wash each leaf individually under cold running water to remove grit. Soak in clean cold water 10 minutes. Drain and rinse again.

PARTY PASTA

Yield: 6 to 8 servings

- 4 tablespoons olive oil
- 1 pound mushrooms, cleaned and sliced
- 6 garlic cloves, minced
- 1 pound Italian *or* poultry sausage, casing removed
- 1 4-ounce jar roasted red peppers
- ¼ cup dry white wine
- salt and pepper
- dried oregano
- chopped fresh parsley
- 1 pound penne *or* other pasta
- freshly grated Parmesan cheese

- Heat oil in a large nonstick skillet. Add mushrooms and garlic; sauté lightly. Set aside.
- Place sausage in skillet, break up with a fork and cook until browned; drain. Add roasted peppers, mushrooms and wine. Season to taste with salt, pepper, oregano and parsley.
- In a large pot of boiling water, cook pasta 10 minutes or until al dente; drain.
- On a platter, combine pasta with sausage mixture and sprinkle with cheese.

PASTA with SPINACH and ALMONDS

Yield: 4 servings

- 8 ounces penne *or* corkscrew pasta
- 2 tablespoons sliced almonds
- 1 teaspoon olive oil
- 1 garlic clove, minced
- 1 large bunch spinach, about 1 pound, well-washed and coarsely chopped
- 3 tablespoons dried cherries *or* golden raisins
- ½ teaspoon instant chicken bouillon
- 2 medium plum tomatoes, peeled, seeded and diced
- 3 tablespoons freshly grated Parmesan cheese

- Cook pasta in a large pot of boiling water for 10 minutes or until al dente.
- While pasta is cooking, toast almonds in a nonstick skillet until golden, stirring and shaking often. Remove almonds and set aside.
- In the same skillet, heat oil and cook garlic until golden. Increase heat to medium-high and add spinach, raisins or cherries, and bouillon, cooking until spinach just wilts.
- Drain penne and return to pot. Add spinach mixture and plum tomatoes; heat through. Add 2 tablespoons Parmesan cheese and toss.
- Spoon penne mixture into a large serving bowl and sprinkle with toasted almonds and remaining Parmesan cheese.

ANGEL HAIR PASTA with SHRIMP and SPINACH

Yield: 4 to 6 servings

- ½ pound medium shrimp, shelled and deveined
- ½ cup flour for dredging
- 4 tablespoons olive oil, divided
- 6 shallots, chopped
- 2 large garlic cloves, chopped
- 1 large sweet red pepper, diced
- 1 large sweet yellow pepper, diced
- ½ pound fresh mushrooms, sliced
- ½ cup dry white wine
- 1 cup chicken broth-*see page 262*
- ¼ cup chopped fresh parsley
- freshly ground black pepper
- 1 pound fresh spinach, stemmed
- ½ cup grated Asiago cheese
- 1 pound angel hair pasta, cooked

- Dredge shrimp in flour. Quickly brown shrimp in 2 tablespoons olive oil until lightly golden. Do not let shrimp overcook. Set aside.
- Add 2 tablespoons olive oil to same pan and lightly sauté shallots, garlic and peppers. Add mushrooms and sauté until golden.
- Add wine and quickly cook until reduced by half. Add chicken broth, parsley and pepper; simmer until thickened.
- Add spinach and shrimp, cover and cook until spinach is wilted, about 2 minutes.
- Just before serving, stir in Asiago cheese. Serve over cooked angel hair pasta.

WEST COAST PASTA

Yield: 2 servings

- 2 tablespoons butter *or* margarine
- 2 tablespoons olive oil
- 1 large onion, chopped
- 1 garlic clove, chopped
- 2 large fresh tomatoes, peeled, seeded and chopped
- ⅓ cup chopped fresh parsley
- ⅓ cup sliced, pitted black olives
- 4 ounces spaghetti
- salt and pepper to taste
- ¼ cup freshly grated Parmesan cheese

- In a large skillet, heat butter and oil. Sauté onion and garlic until golden, about 5 minutes. Add tomatoes and cook until just mushy. Stir in parsley and olives.
- Cook spaghetti in a pot of boiling water for 6 to 8 minutes, or until al dente; drain. Ladle sauce over spaghetti and toss to coat well. Season to taste. Sprinkle with Parmesan cheese.

PARSLEY and BASIL PESTO

Yield: 2 cups, enough for 2 pounds of pasta

- 1 cup lightly packed parsley sprigs
- 1 cup lightly packed basil leaves
- 3 garlic cloves
- ½ cup pine nuts
- 1 cup olive oil
- 2 tablespoons fresh lemon juice
- ¾ cup freshly grated Parmesan cheese
- ½ cup freshly grated Romano cheese
- ½ teaspoon freshly ground black pepper
- salt to taste

- Using a food processor with metal blade, chop parsley, basil, garlic and pine nuts until quite small.
- With machine running, slowly add oil and then lemon juice. Add cheeses and pepper.
- Remove pesto to a bowl and add salt to taste. Use at room temperature, tossing over hot cooked pasta.

MARINARA SAUCE

Yield: About 3 quarts

3 tablespoons extra virgin olive oil
3 garlic cloves, chopped
4 28-ounce cans chopped *or* crushed tomatoes
1 large onion, chopped
¼ cup chopped fresh basil leaves
½ teaspoon salt
½ teaspoon freshly ground pepper

- Heat oil in a very large pot. Over medium heat, sauté garlic for 1 to 2 minutes, taking care not to burn.
- Add tomatoes, onion, basil, salt and pepper. Simmer for 30 to 45 minutes.

FRESH BAKED TOMATO SAUCE

Preheat oven to 350°F

Yield: 3 cups

¼ cup olive oil
1 large onion, diced
5 garlic cloves, crushed in a garlic press
3 tablespoons fresh chopped basil *or* 1 tablespoon dried
1 tablespoon dried Italian seasoning
salt and pepper to taste
3 pounds plum tomatoes, peeled, seeded and chopped

- Heat olive oil in a large sauté pan. Add onion, garlic and seasonings; cook, stirring, for 3 minutes or until soft but not browned. Add tomatoes and mix well.
- Place mixture in a 9x12-inch baking pan and bake, uncovered, for 1½ hours in preheated oven. Stir several times during the baking.
- Serve over pasta or broiled fish.

A family unwinds by watching a movie

Meats

Beef & Game

Veal

Pork

Lamb

Sauces

Meats

TENDERLOIN TIPS in BURGUNDY SAUCE

Yield: 8 servings

4 tablespoons butter *or* margarine, divided
1 pound large onions,
peeled and cut into
½-inch cubes
2 cloves garlic, minced
1 teaspoon dried thyme
1 pound mushrooms, sliced
1 cup Burgundy wine
1 cup beef broth
1 teaspoon Worcestershire sauce
2 tablespoons cornstarch
½ cup water
2 teaspoons concentrated beef flavoring (optional)
salt and pepper to taste
2½ pounds beef tenderloin,
cut into 1 to 2-inch cubes
chopped fresh parsley

- In large skillet, melt 2 tablespoons butter over medium high heat. Add onions, garlic and thyme and sauté, stirring, until onions are softened and transparent. Stir in mushrooms and continue to cook, stirring, until mushrooms are lightly browned.
- In large saucepan, heat wine and beef broth over medium heat. Remove pan from heat, add Worcestershire sauce and stir in cornstarch blended with water. Return to heat and simmer, whisking, until slightly thickened. Add mushroom mixture, beef flavoring and seasonings.
- Melt 2 tablespoons butter in skillet over medium-high heat and sauté tenderloin tips until done to your taste. Add to mushroom mixture.

✓ *Dish can be prepared ahead to this point and reheated gently.*

- Sprinkle with chopped parsley and serve.
- **Suggestion**: For extra flavor, substitute portobello mushrooms for the button variety.

–Hill Top Inn, Elmira, NY

Cook's Notes

When slicing or *cutting meat* into chunks, cut across grain for more tender results.

TOURNEDOS of BEEF in TOMATO BRANDY SAUCE

Yield: 4 to 6 servings

4 tablespoons butter, divided
1 tablespoon flour
1 tablespoon vegetable oil
8 3-ounce center-cut tenderloin steaks
2 garlic cloves, minced
¼ cup oil-packed sun-dried tomatoes, chopped
2 cups sliced fresh mushrooms
¼ cup dry white wine
½ cup beef broth
salt and pepper to taste
¼ cup brandy
chopped fresh parsley

- Make a light roux by cooking 1 tablespoon of butter with 1 tablespoon of flour in a small saucepan over medium heat, stirring constantly until light brown. Set aside.
- Heat 1 tablespoon of butter with vegetable oil in a large heavy skillet. Sauté steaks to rare, about 3 minutes on a side, over medium-high heat. Remove to a plate and keep warm.
- Pour off fat and wipe skillet. Add 2 tablespoons of butter to same skillet and sauté garlic and tomatoes for about 2 minutes. Add mushrooms and stir-fry 2 minutes.
- Add wine, beef broth and roux, stirring until sauce thickens, about 5 minutes.
- Return meat to skillet and simmer just long enough to warm through. Season to taste, stir in brandy and remove to a serving plate.
- Pour sauce over meat and sprinkle with parsley.

BEEF STROGANOFF

Yield: 8 servings

2 pounds beef tenderloin, well trimmed
½ cup flour
1 teaspoon salt
⅛ teaspoon freshly ground pepper
8 tablespoons butter, divided
½ cup finely chopped onion
2 cups beef broth
½ pound mushrooms, sliced
1 cup sour cream
3 tablespoons tomato paste
1 teaspoon Worcestershire sauce
finely chopped parsley
cooked rice

- Cut beef into 2x¼x¼-inch strips. Combine flour, salt and pepper in a plastic bag, add beef in batches and shake to coat.
- Heat 5 tablespoons butter in a large skillet, add beef strips and chopped onion. Slowly brown beef and onions. When meat is browned on all sides, slowly add broth. Cover and simmer 10 to 20 minutes, or just until meat is tender.
- In another skillet, brown mushrooms in 3 tablespoons butter.
- Blend together sour cream, tomato paste and the Worcestershire sauce.
- When meat is tender, remove skillet from heat; add mushrooms. Add sour cream mixture in small amounts, stirring vigorously. Return to heat.
- Continue to simmer over low heat 3 to 5 minutes, stirring constantly; do not boil. Sprinkle with parsley and serve with cooked rice.

MARINATED FLANK STEAK

Yield: 4 to 6 servings

- ¼ cup soy sauce
- 3 tablespoons honey
- 2 tablespoons cider *or* wine vinegar
- ¾ cup vegetable oil
- 2 tablespoons fresh lemon juice
- 1¼ teaspoons garlic powder
- 1¼ teaspoons ground ginger
- 1 green onion, finely chopped
- 1½ to 2-pound flank steak

- Early in the day, prepare marinade. With a hand beater or a whisk, combine all ingredients except steak until well blended.
- Marinate flank steak in a large covered dish or resealable plastic bag, refrigerated, at least 4 hours. Turn steak in marinade occasionally.
- Remove steak from marinade and broil over charcoal or in an oven broiler for 8 minutes on first side and 5 minutes on second.
- Thinly slice steak on the bias.

Cook's Notes

Soy sauce comes in several varieties. Japanese and Chinese types differ greatly. They can range from light to dark in color and sweet to very salty. Some textures can differ as well from thin and watery to thick. Try different types to discover your own favorites.

VEGETABLE BEEF STIR-FRY

Yield: 2 servings

½ ounce dried shiitake mushrooms
2 tablespoons cornstarch, divided
4 tablespoons soy sauce, divided
1 teaspoon sugar
2 teaspoons pared and minced fresh ginger
1 medium garlic clove, minced
1 teaspoon Chinese hot chili paste, optional
½ pound flank steak
1 cup water
4 ounces fresh broccoli florets, cut into bite-sized pieces
1 medium carrot, pared and cut diagonally into ⅛-inch slices
1 medium onion, chunked and separated
2 tablespoons peanut oil, divided
1 teaspoon oriental sesame oil
hot boiled rice

- Prepare all ingredients before starting to stir-fry. Thinly slice beef on the bias. This is most easily done if beef is slightly frozen.
- Place dried mushrooms in small bowl, cover with boiling water and let sit 30 minutes. Drain and squeeze water from mushrooms. Cut off and discard stems; cut caps in half.
- In medium bowl, combine 1 tablespoon each of cornstarch and soy sauce with sugar, ginger, garlic and hot chili paste. Stir in beef and let stand 15 minutes.
- In small bowl, combine 1 tablespoon cornstarch with 3 tablespoons soy sauce and 1 cup water. Set aside.
- Put broccoli florets, carrot slices and onion chunks in another bowl.
- Heat 1 tablespoon peanut oil in a wok or large non-stick skillet over high heat. Add meat and stir-fry 1 minute or until beef is browned. Remove meat and set aside.
- Add to skillet 1 tablespoon peanut oil and 1 teaspoon sesame oil. Add mushrooms and stir-fry 2 minutes. Add broccoli, carrot and onion and stir-fry another 4 minutes or until vegetables are tender-crisp.
- Return meat to skillet. Stir up soy sauce mixture and add to skillet. Cook and stir until slightly thickened, about 30 seconds.
- Serve immediately with boiled rice.

HUNAN BEEF

Yield: 4 servings

1 pound round *or* flank steak
2 tablespoons soy sauce
4 teaspoons cornstarch
1 teaspoon sugar
1 tablespoon vegetable oil
3 tablespoons dry sherry
2 tablespoons soy sauce
1 tablespoon sugar
1½ teaspoons hoisin sauce
¾ teaspoon oriental sesame oil
8 green onions, including green part
2 sweet red peppers
1 teaspoon pared and minced fresh ginger, more *or* less to taste
3 teaspoons minced garlic
½ teaspoon cayenne pepper
2 tablespoons vegetable oil, divided
hot boiled rice

- Thinly slice beef on the bias. This is done most easily if beef is slightly frozen.
- Combine 2 tablespoons soy sauce, cornstarch, 1 teaspoon sugar and vegetable oil; add beef and marinate, refrigerated, for 2 hours.
- Combine dry sherry, 2 tablespoons soy sauce, 1 tablespoon sugar, hoisin sauce and sesame oil in a small bowl; set aside.
- Cut green onions into ½-inch lengths. Cut peppers into julienne strips. Combine ginger, garlic and pepper.
- Heat 1 tablespoon of oil in wok or large skillet over high heat. Remove meat from marinade and stir-fry 20 to 30 seconds, or until no longer red. Remove to a dish and set aside.
- Add 1 tablespoon of oil to wok and lower heat a little. Add garlic mixture and stir-fry 30 seconds, taking care not to let garlic brown.
- Add peppers and sauce; stir until sauce bubbles. Return meat to skillet along with green onions; stir briefly until meat is heated through.
- Serve with boiled rice.

DUTCH BEEF ROULADES

Yield: 8 servings

1 teaspoon prepared mustard
8 thin slices top round of beef, 8 ounces each
8 strips of bacon
4 large dill pickles, halved lengthwise
¼ teaspoon dried thyme
salt to taste
2 tablespoons vegetable oil
3 cups raw vegetables:
finely chopped carrots,
celery, onions, parsley
¼ cup tomato paste
¼ cup flour
freshly ground pepper to taste
1 12-ounce can dark beer
2 tablespoons vinegar
2 cups beef broth
½ bay leaf

- Spread mustard, evenly divided, on 8 slices of meat. Place strip of bacon and pickle slice on each slice of meat. Sprinkle with thyme and salt. Roll up meat around pickle slices and fasten with toothpicks.
- Heat oil in heavy saucepan and brown meat.
- Add vegetables and tomato paste; cook 10 minutes.
- Sprinkle with flour. Add pepper, beer, vinegar, broth and bay leaf. Simmer for 1 to 1½ hours.

Cook's Notes

Mustards can come mild or fiery hot, coarse and grainy or smooth. The flavors vary greatly as well. Always use the mustard that is called for to insure the proper taste and texture.

BEEF with BROCCOLI for TWO

Yield: 2 servings

- ½ pound lean boneless top round *or* sirloin steak
- ¾ ounce dry-packed sun-dried tomatoes, about 10
- ½ cup boiling water
- 2 teaspoons cornstarch
- ⅓ cup dry white wine
- ¼ cup low-sodium soy sauce
- 2 teaspoons olive oil
- 2 cups fresh broccoli florets
- ¼ cup sliced green onions, including a little green
- 2 garlic cloves, minced
- hot boiled rice

- Trim fat from steak; slice into thin strips.
- Combine sun-dried tomatoes and water; let stand 5 minutes. Drain and thinly slice; set aside.
- In a small bowl, combine cornstarch, wine and soy sauce; set aside.
- Coat a large skillet with cooking spray. Heat skillet and add steak. Stir-fry 2 minutes; remove and set aside.
- Add olive oil to skillet; heat. Add broccoli and stir-fry 5 minutes. Add tomatoes, green onions and garlic. Stir-fry 2 minutes.
- Stir up cornstarch mixture and add to skillet along with beef. Stir-fry 2 minutes, or until sauce is thick and bubbly.
- Serve over rice.

MARINATED BEEF STEW

Yield: 6 to 8 servings

2 cups dry red wine
¼ cup olive oil
4 tablespoons vinegar
6 peppercorns
2 garlic cloves, crushed
1 bay leaf, crushed
3 pounds good stew beef, trimmed and cut into 2-inch cubes
4 tablespoons flour
¼ pound salt pork, diced
3 cups beef broth
2 teaspoons Worcestershire sauce
freshly ground pepper to taste
18 pearl onions, peeled
4 carrots, cut into 1-inch lengths
¼ pound sliced mushrooms, sautéed
4 potatoes, cut into 6 to 8 pieces each
½ cup dry sherry

- The day before, combine wine, olive oil, vinegar, peppercorns, garlic and bay leaf in a large glass bowl. Place meat in marinade, cover and refrigerate for 24 hours, turning meat once or twice during that time.
- Drain meat, reserving ¼ cup of marinade. Pat meat dry and dust lightly with flour.
- In a large skillet, sauté salt pork until golden. Add meat and brown on all sides.
- In a saucepan, bring to a boil the beef broth, reserved marinade and Worcestershire sauce.
- Pour off any fat drippings in skillet. Slowly add boiling broth mixture to meat, stirring to loosen flour bits sticking to bottom of pan. Season to taste.
- Add all vegetables and bring to boil. Cover, reduce heat and gently simmer for 1 hour, or until meat is tender; stir occasionally.
- Add sherry, stir and cover. Cook another 15 minutes.

MEXICAN TART

Yield: 6 servings

1 pound lean beef
1½ teaspoons paprika
¼ teaspoon chili powder
1 tablespoon vegetable oil
1 large onion, chopped
1 large garlic clove, minced
1 9-inch unbaked pie crust-*see page 263*
1 egg white, lightly beaten
1½ cups grated Cheddar cheese
1 cup sour cream
¾ cup chopped green onions
¼ cup chopped green chilies
3 eggs, beaten
freshly ground pepper
sour cream and salsa for garnish

- Cut beef into chunks and sprinkle with paprika and chili powder.
- Heat oil in large non-stick skillet with cover. Brown beef.
- Add onion and garlic to skillet. Cover and cook over low heat until tender, about 1 to 1½ hours.
- Remove cover and boil down accumulated liquid. Let meat cool, then shred with a fork.
- **Preheat oven to 400°F.**
- Prepare pie crust and brush with beaten egg white. Bake 5 minutes; cool.
- **Lower oven temperature to 325°F.**
- In large bowl, combine meat, Cheddar cheese, sour cream, green onions, chilies, eggs and pepper. Mix well. Pour into pie crust.
- Bake 55 to 60 minutes, until filling is set. Center should be firm when shaken. Cool 10 minutes before serving.
- Slice and serve with a dollop of sour cream and salsa.

SOMBRERO PIE

Preheat oven to 350°F

Yield: 6 or more servings

1 pound ground beef
¼ pound bulk pork sausage
1 small onion, chopped
1 garlic clove, finely chopped
1 16-ounce can whole tomatoes
1 16-ounce can whole kernel corn, drained
20 pitted black olives
1 tablespoon chili powder
1½ teaspoons salt
1 cup cornmeal
1 cup milk
2 eggs, well beaten
4 ounces Cheddar cheese, grated

- Cook and stir beef, sausage, onion and garlic until meat is brown; drain.
- Stir in tomatoes and their liquid, corn, olives, chili powder and salt. Heat to boiling.
- Pour into ungreased 9-inch baking dish or 2-quart casserole.
- Mix cornmeal, milk and eggs; pour over meat mixture. Sprinkle with cheese.
- Bake, uncovered, in preheated oven until golden brown.

TEXAS CHILI

Yield: 8 to 10 servings

1 pound lean pork,
  cut into ¼-inch pieces
1 pound lean beef,
  cut into ¼-inch pieces
2 tablespoons olive oil
2 large yellow onions, chopped
3 garlic cloves, minced
1 sweet green pepper,
  seeded and diced
1 jalapeño pepper,
  seeded and diced
1 28-ounce can whole tomatoes
1 6-ounce can tomato paste
1 4-ounce can green chilies, diced
10 ounces pineapple juice
2 tablespoons chili powder *or* more to taste
2 teaspoons ground cumin, optional
2 teaspoons salt *or* to taste
1 cup beef broth
1 tablespoon sugar
1 large bay leaf
2 16-ounce cans chili beans *or* kidney beans, optional
chopped green onions, shredded Cheddar cheese
  and sour cream for garnish

- In a large pot, brown meat on all sides in olive oil, a little at a time. Add onions and garlic and cook until onions are soft. Add green pepper and jalapeño; continue cooking for 2 minutes.
- Add all remaining ingredients except beans and garnish, cover and simmer 2 hours.
- Add beans and simmer another 15 minutes.
- Garnish with green onions, Cheddar cheese and sour cream. Serve with hot corn bread.

Cook's Notes

To quench the heat of a *too-spicy* mouthful, chew on something starchy, such as bread. Water only spreads the fire.

SPICY BEEF and GREEN BEANS

Yield: 4 servings

1 teaspoon sugar
1 teaspoon Chinese chili paste with garlic *or* more to taste
1 teaspoon hoisin sauce
1 tablespoon soy sauce
1 tablespoon dry sherry *or* rice wine
1 teaspoon vegetable oil
1 garlic clove, minced
1 tablespoon pared and minced fresh ginger
1 sweet red pepper, seeded and cut into thin strips
1 medium onion, peeled, cut in half lengthwise and sliced
1 pound lean ground beef *or* poultry
1 10-ounce package frozen whole green beans
1 teaspoon vinegar
1 teaspoon oriental sesame oil
hot boiled rice

- Make sauce by mixing sugar, chili paste, hoisin sauce, soy sauce and sherry in a small bowl; set aside.
- Heat oil in large non-stick skillet or wok over high heat. Add garlic, ginger, sweet red pepper and onion. Stir-fry quickly until vegetables begin to soften slightly.
- Stir sauce ingredients and add to skillet, mixing well.
- Add ground beef and beans. Continue to stir-fry, breaking meat apart and cooking until meat is done, beans are hot and everything is coated with sauce.
- Sprinkle with vinegar and sesame oil. Serve with boiled rice.

Kathy Lindsley, Food Editor
–Democrat & Chronicle/Times-Union

Cook's Notes

Fresh *ginger* can be stored in refrigerator, tightly wrapped, for up to 3 weeks or frozen for 1 year. If frozen, slice off what you need and refreeze the remainder.

PICCADILLO

Yield: 8 servings

- 2 medium onions, diced
- 2 large sweet green peppers, diced
- 4 tablespoons olive oil, divided
- 1½ pounds ground beef
- ¼ teaspoon freshly ground pepper
- ½ teaspoon celery seed
- ¼ teaspoon dried oregano
- ½ teaspoon garlic powder
- ½ teaspoon paprika
- 2 tablespoons Worcestershire sauce
- 1 28-ounce can tomato sauce
- 1 3-ounce jar capers, undrained
- 1 5-ounce jar stuffed olives with ¼ cup of their juice
- 8 ounces seedless raisins

- Sauté onions and peppers in 2 tablespoons olive oil. Set aside.
- In large saucepan, sauté meat in 2 tablespoons olive oil until cooked. Drain fat from meat.
- Place next 5 seasonings in small bowl and stir with fork to mix. Add to meat. Stir in Worcestershire sauce and tomato sauce, mixing well. Add capers, stuffed olives, ¼ cup olive juice, raisins and sautéed onions and peppers.
- Cover and cook 40 minutes over low heat.

✓ *This can be made ahead and frozen.*

Cook's Notes

When *raisins* are stuck together, they can be separated by placing in the microwave for a few seconds, heating in the oven at 300°F or freezing them and rubbing apart between your palms.

VENISON STEAK STRIPS

Preheat oven to 275°F

Yield: 6 servings

1½ cups seasoned bread crumbs
½ cup freshly grated Parmesan cheese
½ teaspoon garlic powder
½ teaspoon freshly ground black pepper
2 large eggs
½ cup milk
¼ cup vegetable oil
1½ pounds venison steaks, sliced into ½-inch-thick strips
4 medium onions, sliced into rings
1½ pounds fresh mushrooms, sliced
flour
2 cups water
5 beef bouillon cubes
cornstarch *or* flour for gravy

- In medium bowl, mix bread crumbs, cheese, garlic powder and pepper.
- In another bowl, beat eggs and milk.
- Place oil in large non-stick skillet and heat on medium-high.
- Dip steak strips into egg/milk mixture, then roll in bread crumb mixture.
- Brown steak strips quickly in hot skillet.
- In a medium-sized roaster, layer the steak strips, onions and mushrooms. Dust lightly with flour. Repeat layering until steaks, onions and mushrooms are used up.
- Add water mixed with bouillon cubes. Bake 2 hours in preheated oven.
- Just before serving, gently drain liquid from roaster into a large saucepan. Make gravy with cornstarch or flour. Pour over steaks and serve.
- This dish is very good served with wild rice or mashed potatoes and comes to us from the Seneca Indian Reservation.

VEAL CACCIATORE

Yield: 2 servings

2 veal cutlets, ¼-inch thick, about ½ pound
2 tablespoons olive oil, divided
2 garlic cloves, chopped
1 cup crushed Italian plum tomatoes
1 small onion, chopped
1 cup sliced fresh mushrooms
1 cup thinly sliced sweet red and green peppers
½ teaspoon salt *or* to taste
½ teaspoon crushed red pepper flakes
1 tablespoon chopped fresh parsley
¼ cup medium dry sherry

- Cut each veal cutlet into 3 serving-sized medallions. Place between 2 sheets of plastic wrap and pound to ⅛-inch thickness.
- Heat 1 tablespoon olive oil in a 12-inch sauté pan and brown cutlets quickly over medium-high heat about 30 seconds on each side. Set aside and keep warm.
- Add remaining 1 tablespoon olive oil to sauté pan and cook garlic until it sizzles. Add crushed tomatoes, onion, mushrooms and peppers. Cook 4 minutes over high heat.
- Return veal to pan and add seasonings, parsley and sherry. Cook 10 minutes over medium heat. Cover and simmer 4 minutes. Serve immediately.
- This recipe can also be used with skinless and boneless chicken breasts, seafood or other meat.

Nate Cianciola
–Nate's Brown Derby

PARMESAN VEAL

Yield: 3 to 4 servings

½ cup freshly grated Parmesan cheese
1 pound veal round steak, trimmed well
salt and pepper to taste
2 tablespoons olive oil
2 garlic cloves, minced
½ cup beef broth
2 tablespoons fresh lemon juice
½ teaspoon dried marjoram
¼ teaspoon dried thyme
½ cup dry white wine
½ pound sliced mushrooms, optional
2 tablespoons butter, optional

- Pound cheese into both sides of meat. Keep pounding until cheese is used up and meat is about ¼ inch thick. Season to taste.
- Cut meat into 3-inch medallions and sauté briefly in olive oil.
- Add garlic, beef broth, lemon juice, herbs and white wine. Cover and simmer 30 minutes. Add mushrooms sautéed in butter.

VEAL with LEMON SAUCE

Yield: 4 servings

4 veal scallops, about 1 pound
3 tablespoons butter, divided
salt and pepper
¼ cup minced shallots
2 teaspoons flour
½ cup heated chicken broth–*see page 262*
juice from ½ lemon
lemon slices and sprigs of parsley for garnish

- Cut scallops in half and flatten between sheets of wax paper.
- Sauté 4 at a time in 2 tablespoons butter for 1 minute on each side. Sprinkle with salt and pepper and remove to a warm platter.
- Add 1 tablespoon of butter to pan and sauté shallots.
- Add flour and cook for 3 minutes, stirring constantly.
- Pour heated chicken broth into skillet; simmer until sauce thickens. Season with lemon juice, salt and pepper.
- Pour sauce over veal; garnish with lemon slices and sprigs of parsley.

PORK TENDERLOIN with PEAR BRANDY

Yield: 4 servings

- 2 pork tenderloins, approximately 12 ounces each
- flour
- 2 tablespoons butter
- 2 tablespoons chopped shallots
- ¼ teaspoon curry powder
- ½ cup chicken broth-*see page 262*
- ½ cup bottled pear juice *or* natural juice from canned pears
- ½ cup heavy cream
- ⅜ cup pear brandy
- 1 pear, pared and cut into ¼-inch slices
- salt and pepper

- Slice pork tenderloins across the grain into 1-inch medallions. Flatten between 2 sheets of wax paper with a mallet or a small heavy skillet. Flour lightly.
- Melt butter in a large non-stick skillet over medium-high heat. Sauté pork until cooked through, about 3 minutes. Turn to ensure even browning. Remove and keep warm.
- In the same skillet, sauté shallots with curry powder over medium-low heat. Cook until tender but not browned. Stir in broth, pear juice, cream, brandy and sliced pear.
- Cook over medium heat until sauce thickens. Pears should be tender but not mushy. Season to taste with salt and pepper.
- To serve, arrange medallions on warmed serving plates and cover with pear sauce.

PORK TENDERLOIN with CHARCUTERIE SAUCE

Yield: 4 servings

- 1 pound or more pork tenderloin
- 2 tablespoons corn oil
- 2 tablespoons fresh lemon juice
- 2 teaspoons ground cumin
- salt and freshly ground black pepper
- Charcuterie Sauce-*recipe follows*

- Cut pork tenderloin into 1-inch crosswise slices and pound slightly; do not break fibers.
- In a flat glass dish, combine corn oil, lemon juice, cumin and a pinch of salt and pepper. Place tenderloin slices in marinade, turning to be sure marinade is on both sides. Leave in marinade at room temperature for about 10 minutes.
- Prepare Charcuterie Sauce.
- Grill tenderloin slices for about 10 minutes. Serve with Charcuterie Sauce.

CHARCUTERIE SAUCE

Yield: About 1 cup

- 3 tablespoons butter, divided
- ⅔ cup finely chopped onion
- ½ teaspoon finely minced garlic
- 2 tablespoons red wine vinegar
- ½ cup chicken broth-*see page 262*
- 1 tablespoon catsup
- salt and pepper
- 1 small bay leaf
- 1 sprig fresh thyme *or* ½ teaspoon dried
- 1 tablespoon Dijon mustard

- Melt 1 tablespoon butter in small skillet. Add chopped onions and garlic; cook over low heat until lightly browned. Add vinegar and cook briefly. Add chicken broth, catsup, salt and pepper to taste. Bring to boil, add bay leaf and thyme and simmer 5 minutes.
- Just before serving, remove bay leaf and stir in mustard and remaining butter.

GRILLED PORK TENDERLOIN

Yield: 4 servings

2 boneless pork tenderloins
1 cup beer
½ cup honey
½ cup prepared mustard
¼ cup vegetable oil
2 tablespoons onion powder
3 teaspoons chopped fresh rosemary leaves *or* 1 teaspoon dried
1 teaspoon garlic powder
freshly ground black pepper

- Place pork in a heavy plastic bag. Combine remaining ingredients and pour over pork. Seal bag tightly and marinate, refrigerated, for 1 hour.
- Remove pork from marinade and place on hot grill. Grill, covered, until meat has an internal temperature of 160°F, approximately 30 minutes. Do not overcook or meat will become dry.
- Simmer leftover marinade in saucepan for 5 minutes.
- Slice pork into ½-inch medallions. Serve with cooked marinade as sauce.
- Juice and zest of an orange can replace beer.

Cook's Notes

P*ork Tenderloin:* Lean pork cuts such as tenderloin or boneless pork roast are good choices for calorie-and-fat-conscious people. A 3-ounce serving contains about 130 calories and 4 grams of fat.

ROAST PORK TENDERLOIN with SWEET POTATOES

Preheat oven to 475°F Yield: 6 servings

1 tablespoon minced garlic
1½ teaspoons salt, divided
½ teaspoon freshly ground pepper
½ teaspoon ground ginger
1½ pounds pork tenderloin
4 small sweet potatoes pared and cut into ½-inch-wide sticks
2 tablespoons olive oil, divided
¼ cup firmly packed brown sugar
¼ cup balsamic vinegar
¼ cup soy sauce
1 tablespoon chopped fresh parsley

- Mash garlic with ¾ teaspoon salt, the pepper and ginger to form a paste. Place pork in jellyroll pan or large roasting pan; rub all over with garlic mixture.
- Toss sweet potatoes with 1 tablespoon oil and ¾ teaspoon more salt in large bowl. Arrange potatoes in jellyroll pan with pork.
- Combine brown sugar, vinegar, soy sauce and remaining 1 tablespoon oil in small saucepan; brush some of the mixture over pork tenderloin. Roast pork and potatoes 10 minutes.
- Meanwhile, bring remaining soy sauce mixture to boil over high heat. Boil until sauce is thickened, 5 minutes; remove from heat.
- Brush half the sauce over pork and turn sweet potatoes. Roast 5 minutes more until sweet potatoes are tender and meat thermometer inserted in thickest part of pork registers 155°F.
- Cut pork into ¾-inch slices. Arrange on platter with sweet potatoes. Pour any pan drippings and remaining sauce over pork. Sprinkle sweet potatoes with parsley.

PORK CUTLETS NORMANDY

Yield: 4 servings

1 tablespoon vegetable oil
1 tablespoon butter *or* margarine
salt and pepper
4 boneless pork cutlets, well trimmed
6 tablespoons applejack *(apple brandy)*
½ cup apple cider, more if needed
2 apples, pared, cored and cut into 8 wedges each
½ cup half-and-half

- Heat oil and butter in a deep heavy skillet. Season cutlets and brown; drain fat.
- Warm applejack and pour over pork, ignite and shake pan until flames die. Add cider and apples.
- Cover skillet and simmer over low heat 40 minutes or until cutlets are cooked through. Check periodically and add more cider if needed.
- Remove pork and apples to warm plate and add cream to skillet. Boil over high heat until sauce thickens slightly. Pour sauce over pork and apples and serve.

Cook's Notes

To *flame liqueur or brandy,* warm first and light with a long-handled match. Pour it carefully over the dish to be flamed and shake the pan until flames subside.

PORC à l'ORANGE

Preheat oven to 325°F

Yield: 12 servings

1 6 to 7-pound pork loin roast
1 garlic clove, thinly sliced
1 teaspoon dried rosemary, crushed
½ teaspoon salt
¼ teaspoon freshly ground pepper
2 tablespoons Dijon mustard
2 tablespoons orange marmalade
1 tablespoon light brown sugar
⅔ cup orange juice, divided
2 navel oranges, thinly sliced, optional
fresh parsley, optional
2 tablespoons orange-flavored liqueur

- Have butcher saw across backbone of roast to separate ribs from backbone.
- Cut slits in fat of loin and insert slivers of garlic. Combine rosemary, salt and pepper and rub on roast.
- Place meat, fat side up, on rack in open roasting pan. In preheated oven, roast 30 to 35 minutes per pound, to 170°F on meat thermometer.
- Combine mustard, marmalade, brown sugar and 2 tablespoons of the orange juice, mixing well. About 15 minutes before roast is done, brush with mustard mixture to glaze.
- When roast is finished, remove to serving platter. Garnish with orange slices and parsley. Keep warm.
- Skim fat from roasting pan. Add to pan juices the remaining orange juice and orange-flavored liqueur. Boil until slightly reduced and thickened. Pass sauce separately.

GARLIC PORK

Yield: 6 to 8 servings

1 cup water
½ cup garlic cloves, peeled
2 sprigs fresh thyme, leaves picked from stems
½ teaspoon cayenne pepper
2 teaspoons salt
3 tablespoons fresh lemon juice
¼ cup cider vinegar
½ cup olive oil
3-4 pounds boneless pork loin *or* tenderloin

- In a small saucepan, bring water to boil and blanch garlic 4 to 5 minutes. Drain and chop.
- Mix garlic, thyme, cayenne pepper, salt, lemon juice, vinegar and oil in a large ceramic or glass bowl.
- Cut pork into 1-inch-thick slices, place between sheets of plastic wrap and pound to approximately ¼-inch thickness.
- Place pork in marinade, cover and refrigerate at least 4 hours.

✓ *It can be left up to 36 hours.*

- Grill the meat over medium-hot coals for 3 to 4 minutes on each side, or broil the meat about 2 inches from heat for 3 to 4 minutes a side. Serve hot.
- Cubans serve this dish with corn bread, black beans and rice.

Cook's Notes

When choosing *pork,* look for pale pink meat and very white fat.

MUSHROOM PORK TENDERLOIN

Preheat oven to 400°F Yield: 4 to 6 servings

- 2 pork tenderloins, about 1½ pounds total
- 1½ teaspoons chopped fresh oregano *or* ½ teaspoon dried
- 1 medium onion, sliced and separated into rings
- 1 garlic clove, minced
- 2 tablespoons butter
- 10 ounces fresh mushrooms, sliced
- 2 cups dry red wine

- Place pork tenderloins, oregano, onion and garlic in an open casserole just large enough to hold meat. Cut butter into bits and scatter on top of meat. Bake for 40 minutes in preheated oven.
- Add sliced mushrooms and red wine. **Reduce heat to 300°F** and bake 1 hour or until tender.
- Slice meat and serve with sauce.

BARBECUED HAM

Preheat oven to 250°F Yield: 9 to 12 servings

- 3 pounds shaved, cooked ham
- 1 cup catsup
- ½ cup brown sugar
- ½ cup water
- 1 teaspoon dry mustard
- 1 tablespoon vinegar
- ¼ teaspoon freshly grated nutmeg

- Spread ham in 9x13-inch pan.
- Mix together remaining ingredients. Pour over ham. Cover and bake 45 minutes in preheated oven.

BARBECUED SPARERIBS OVEN STYLE

Preheat oven to 350°F — Yield: 6 to 8 servings

6 pounds pork spareribs, cut into 1-rib sections

Barbecue Sauce:

1 6-ounce can tomato paste
½ cup water
¼ cup brown sugar
¼ cup honey
¼ cup cider vinegar
2 tablespoons vegetable oil
1 tablespoon grated onion
2½ teaspoons salt
2 teaspoons chili powder
¼ teaspoon garlic powder

- Arrange spareribs in large roasting pan. Cover and bake ½ hour in preheated oven.
- While ribs are cooking, combine remaining ingredients for glaze.
- Remove ribs from oven and drain grease. Brush with glaze and continue baking, uncovered, for another ½ hour or more, basting occasionally.
- This sauce is excellent for any kind of barbecue. Save excess for later use.

SOUTHWESTERN PEACHY PORK

Yield: 4 to 6 servings

1½ pounds cubed boneless pork, all fat removed
1 tablespoon taco seasoning mix
2 teaspoons vegetable oil
1 8-ounce jar chunky salsa: hot, medium *or* mild
⅓ cup peach preserves
1 cup peeled and sliced peaches, fresh *or* canned

- Dust pork with taco seasoning mix.
- Heat oil in a large skillet and brown pork.
- Add salsa and preserves, lower heat, cover and simmer 15 to 20 minutes.
- During last 5 minutes, add sliced peaches. Serve over rice.

PORK BARBECUE

Yield: 10 to 12 servings

3 pounds boneless pork, cut into 1-inch cubes
2 cups water
1 teaspoon salt
1 cup chopped onion
3 tablespoons vegetable oil
4 teaspoons paprika
1 teaspoon freshly ground pepper
2 teaspoons dry mustard
dash of cayenne pepper *or* more to taste
1 teaspoon salt
⅓ cup vinegar
⅓ cup sugar
⅓ cup Worcestershire sauce
2 garlic cloves, minced
2 6-ounce cans tomato paste

- In a large pot, bring pork, water and salt to boil. Reduce heat, cover and simmer 2 hours, or until meat is very tender. Do not drain. In the pot, shred meat coarsely with 2 forks.
- Make sauce while meat is cooking. In a skillet, sauté onion in the oil about 5 minutes, until wilted but not brown. Add remaining ingredients and cook over low heat 20 minutes.
- Add shredded meat and mix well. Cover and cook over low heat for up to 30 minutes more. If mixture becomes too dry, add water.
- Taste and add salt and more cayenne if needed. Serve on buns.

Dick and Ginger Howell
–The Seasonal Kitchen

PORK LOUISIANNE

Preheat oven to 350°F — Yield: 4 servings

4 pork chops, with *or* without bones
2 sweet potatoes, pared and sliced ¼-inch thick
2 large white potatoes, pared *or* not, sliced ¼-inch thick
1 sweet green pepper, sliced
1 garlic clove, minced
1 onion, sliced
½ cup frozen orange juice concentrate, thawed
½ cup water
1 tablespoon cornstarch
1 teaspoon Worcestershire sauce
hot pepper sauce to taste
1 teaspoon curry powder, optional
1 tablespoon minced fresh rosemary

- Trim fat from pork and place in an ungreased baking dish with cover. Arrange vegetables over pork.
- In a small saucepan, mix orange juice concentrate, water, cornstarch, Worcestershire sauce, hot pepper sauce and curry powder. Stirring constantly, cook until thickened and bubbly. Pour sauce over vegetables. Sprinkle with rosemary.
- Cover and bake 60 to 90 minutes in preheated oven until meat and vegetables are tender and casserole is hot and bubbly.
- You can substitute chicken for pork.

Kathy Lindsley, Food Editor
–Democrat & Chronicle/Times-Union

Cook's Notes

Select *pork chops* about 1 inch thick. Thin chops are drier and tougher even when cooked in sauces.

ITALIAN SAUSAGE and VEGETABLE SAUTÉ

Yield: 6 to 8 servings

1 garlic clove, crushed
8 fresh parsley sprigs, leaves only
1 pound cabbage, sliced or shredded
¼ cup olive oil
2 ounces diced salt pork, optional
⅓ pound onions, peeled and diced
2 pounds mild Italian sausage, cut into chunks
6 medium sweet green *or* red peppers, cut into ½-inch strips
2 large ripe tomatoes, thinly sliced
1 teaspoon crumbled dried rosemary
pinch of freshly ground black pepper
¼ pound prosciutto, diced

- Chop garlic and parsley together.
- Steam cabbage with a little boiling water until just tender. Drain and keep warm.
- Combine olive oil and salt pork in a saucepan and cook until pork is crisp. Add onions and brown slowly. Remove onions and salt pork; set aside.
- Add sausage to pan and cook slowly 20 minutes.
- Add green peppers, tomatoes, rosemary, black pepper, onions, salt pork and garlic-parsley mixture. Stir in diced prosciutto and cooked cabbage.
- Cover and cook slowly 10 minutes to blend flavors.

KIELBASA and KRAUT

Preheat oven to 325°F

Yield: 4 servings

1 pound sauerkraut
1 large onion, thinly sliced
2 tablespoons butter *or* margarine
1 large apple, quartered and sliced
2 tablespoons brown sugar
½ teaspoon caraway seeds
½ teaspoon dried marjoram
½ cup dry white wine
1 pound kielbasa, regular *or* light

- Drain sauerkraut and rinse under cold water.
- Sauté onion in butter until translucent. Stir in drained sauerkraut, apple, brown sugar, caraway seeds, marjoram and wine. Bring to boil.
- Make thin, shallow cuts, 1 inch apart, in sausage. Transfer sauerkraut mixture to casserole and place sausage on top.
- Cover and bake 1½ hours in preheated oven, stirring occasionally and adding more wine if necessary, until sauerkraut is delicately browned.
- Slice sausage and serve with freshly boiled potatoes and spicy mustard.
- Instead of baking, you could cook this all day on low in a crock pot.

Cook's Notes

To reduce the salty taste of *sauerkraut,* rinse under cold water in a sieve for a few seconds. Drain well.

ROAST RACK of LAMB with MUSHROOM SAUCE

Preheat oven to 500°F

Yield: 4 servings

2 racks of lamb, well trimmed
1 garlic clove
½ teaspoon salt
½ teaspoon dried thyme
3 tablespoons Dijon mustard
3 tablespoons olive oil
½ cup fresh bread crumbs
Mushroom Sauce–*recipe follows*

- Score racks lightly and place in an open roasting pan. Roast 10 minutes in preheated oven.
- While racks are roasting, mash garlic and salt together to form a paste. Mash in thyme. Beat in mustard and oil.
- When racks have roasted 10 minutes, paint them with mustard mixture and sprinkle with bread crumbs.
- **Reduce oven heat to 400°F** and roast 8 minutes longer for pink meat.
- While meat is roasting for the second time, make sauce.
- When lamb has finished roasting, place it under broiler for another minute for a crisper crust. Remove from oven and let stand 5 minutes.
- Slice chops apart and arrange on warmed serving plates. Spoon a little Mushroom Sauce around chops and pass the rest.

MUSHROOM SAUCE

Yield: About 2 cups

1⅓ cups dry white wine
2 cups beef broth
1 teaspoon crumbled dried rosemary
6 tablespoons minced shallots
2 tablespoons butter, cut into small pieces
2 teaspoons concentrated liquid beef flavoring
½ pound portobello mushrooms, sliced and sautéed in a little butter

- In a small saucepan, combine wine, broth, rosemary and shallots. Bring to boil and reduce to 1 cup. Add butter and beef extract, swirling pan. Stir in mushrooms and keep warm.

✓ *Sauce can be made earlier in the day.*

BUTTERFLIED LEG of LAMB

Yield: 8 servings

¼ cup vegetable oil
¼ cup fresh lemon juice
¼ cup dry white wine
1 tablespoon Dijon mustard
2 tablespoons vinegar
1 tablespoon Worcestershire sauce
4 garlic cloves, chopped *or* slivered
1 tablespoon chopped fresh parsley
1 tablespoon chopped fresh basil
salt and pepper to taste
1 4-pound leg of lamb, butterflied
Honey Mint Sauce–*recipe follows*

- Mix together all ingredients except lamb and sauce. Pour marinade over lamb and refrigerate up to 24 hours, turning often.
- Grill lamb 30 to 45 minutes, until rare or pink. Slice diagonally across the grain.
- Serve with Honey Mint Sauce.

HONEY MINT SAUCE

Yield: 2½ cups

1 tablespoon vinegar
½ cup water
1 cup honey
¼ cup chopped fresh mint

- Heat vinegar and water. Add honey and mix well. Add mint and cook 5 minutes on low heat.

Dick and Ginger Howell
–*The Seasonal Kitchen*

Cook's Notes

Lamb is best when it is light red to pink in color. Domestic lamb is grain fed and is often meatier and milder in flavor than imported varieties.

BRAISED LAMB SHANKS

Yield: 4 servings

4 lamb shanks
¼ cup olive oil
1 red *or* white onion, sliced
2 large carrots, cut into ¼-inch rounds
5 garlic cloves, chopped
2 16-ounce cans Italian plum tomatoes, drained and chopped
1½ cups dry white wine
1 tablespoon freshly grated lemon peel
salt and pepper to taste

- In a large saucepan or deep kettle, brown shanks in oil for about 5 minutes on each side. Remove to a plate.
- Place onion, carrots and garlic in pot and cook until light brown.
- Add remaining ingredients; bring to a boil. Reduce heat to medium-low and return shanks to pot. Cover and cook until meat is tender, 2 hours or more.

Families stay together in comfortable bedrooms

Poultry

Chicken

Turkey

MEDITERRANEAN CHICKEN

Yield: 2 servings

- 2 boneless chicken breast halves, skinned
- salt and freshly ground pepper
- 1 tablespoon olive oil
- ⅓ cup finely chopped shallots
- ¼ cup dry white wine
- 1 16-ounce can Italian plum tomatoes, drained and chopped
- 1 tablespoon chopped fresh basil, *or* 1 teaspoon dried
- pinch of thyme, fresh *or* dried
- 6 Greek black olives, pitted and quartered
- 1 tablespoon drained capers
- chopped fresh parsley

- Pound chicken breasts between pieces of plastic wrap to flatten slightly. Season to taste.
- Heat oil in medium skillet; sauté chicken quickly over medium-high heat until lightly browned. Remove to a plate.
- Add shallots to skillet; cook over medium heat until golden. Add wine, tomatoes and herbs; simmer 5 minutes, stirring occasionally.
- Stir olives and capers into tomato mixture. Return chicken to pan along with accumulated juices. Cover and simmer about 10 minutes, or until chicken is done.
- Season to taste. Serve with sauce and sprinkle with parsley.

PEANUT CHICKEN BAKE

Preheat oven to 400°F

Yield: 4 to 5 servings

- ¾ cup chopped peanuts, divided
- 2½ cups cubed cooked chicken
- 1 small onion, chopped
- 2 teaspoons Dijon mustard
- 1½ cups cooked rice
- ¾ cup mayonnaise
- 1 cup plain yogurt *or* sour cream
- 1 cup sliced mushrooms
- 4 ounces Cheddar cheese, shredded
- salt and freshly ground pepper to taste

- Mix all ingredients, reserving ¼ cup peanuts for garnish.
- Place in 2-quart baking dish and sprinkle with peanuts.
- Bake about 20 minutes in preheated oven. Serve hot.

CHICKEN and PEANUT STIR-FRY

Yield: 4 servings

4 boneless and skinless chicken breast halves
4 green onions
1 1-inch piece of ginger, pared and minced
1½ tablespoons vegetable oil, divided
3 tablespoons soy sauce
¾ cup water
3 tablespoons cornstarch mixed into ½ cup water
1 cup dry-roasted unsalted peanuts
cooked rice

- Cut chicken into bite-sized pieces.
- Chop white part of onion. Cut green part of onion into 1-inch pieces.
- Stir-fry chicken, onion and ginger in 1 tablespoon of oil until chicken is no longer pink.
- Add soy sauce and ¾ cup water.
- Reduce heat and simmer, uncovered, until chicken is tender, about 5 minutes.
- Recombine cornstarch mixture and stir into chicken. Continue to simmer until thickened. Keep chicken warm over low heat while you prepare peanuts.
- In a small pan, sauté peanuts in ½ tablespoon of oil, stirring constantly, until lightly browned.
- Serve chicken over cooked rice and sprinkle with peanuts.

CHICKEN and SPINACH PILLOWS

Yield: 6 servings

2 tablespoons vegetable oil
3-4 cups chopped fresh spinach
¾ cup chopped onion
4 ounces mushrooms, chopped
3 ounces cream cheese, cubed and softened
¾ cup shredded mozzarella cheese
½ cup crumbled feta cheese
⅓ cup shredded Cheddar cheese
1 tablespoon flour
½ teaspoon freshly grated nutmeg
½ teaspoon ground cumin
6 skinned and boned chicken breast halves, pounded to ⅛-inch thickness
12 sheets of phyllo dough
½ cup butter *or* margarine, melted

- Refer to page 261 for information regarding handling of phyllo dough.
- Heat oil in a large skillet. Add spinach, onion and mushrooms. Sauté until onions are tender.
- Stir in cheeses, flour, nutmeg and cumin. Place mixture in a bowl and refrigerate 10 minutes.
- Divide filling evenly among chicken breast halves. Roll tightly into 6 rolls.
- Brush 1 sheet of phyllo with butter, top with another sheet and brush again. Place 1 chicken roll in center at bottom of narrow edge of the sheets. Fold both sides of phyllo over chicken. Begin rolling until entire sheet is used. A neat pillow should be formed. Moisten with water to seal end. Place seam side down in a 9x13-inch baking pan.
- Continue with remainder of rolls. Brush with butter.

✓ *Dish can be prepared to this point early in the day, covered with plastic wrap and refrigerated.*

- **Preheat oven to 350°F.**
- Sprinkle rolls with a little water to keep phyllo from flaking too much. Bake, uncovered, 35 minutes.

LEMON-GARLIC CHICKEN

Preheat oven to 350°F — Yield: 6 to 8 servings

4 ounces salted butter
8 garlic cloves, minced
1 cup bread crumbs, plain *or* flavored
1 cup freshly grated Parmesan cheese
¼ cup minced fresh parsley
8 skinless and boneless chicken breast halves
1-2 whole lemons, halved
paprika, optional

- In a small saucepan over medium heat, melt butter with minced garlic. Set aside.
- Combine crumbs, cheese and parsley on a plate; set aside.
- Pound each chicken breast between sheets of plastic wrap to flatten slightly. Dip in melted butter mixture, then coat well with crumbs.
- Roll each piece of chicken jellyroll fashion. Place chicken rolls, seam side down, in a glass 9x13-inch casserole dish that has been coated with vegetable spray.
- Pour any leftover butter and crumb mixtures over chicken. Squeeze lemon generously over entire surface. Sprinkle with paprika.
- Bake 1 hour, uncovered, in preheated oven.

✓ *This dish can be prepared the night before, covered and refrigerated. It can be cooked the following day.*

Cook's Notes

To make *bread crumbs*, use dry bread. Place in plastic bag and crush with a rolling pin.

1 slice=¼ cup dry crumbs. Store crumbs in freezer.

PECAN-BREADED CHICKEN

Preheat oven to 400°F — Yield: 8 servings

- 8 skinless and boneless chicken breast halves
- freshly ground pepper
- 6 tablespoons unsalted butter *or* margarine
- 6 tablespoons Dijon mustard, divided
- 2 cups pecans, very finely chopped
- 1 cup low-fat sour cream

- Flatten chicken breasts between sheets of plastic wrap and lightly pepper them.
- In a saucepan, melt butter and then remove pan from heat. Whisk in 4 tablespoons of mustard.
- Dip chicken into butter and mustard mixture and then into chopped pecans to coat.
- Lightly butter a 9x13-inch baking pan and place chicken breasts in it.

✓ *At this point you can refrigerate the chicken for up to 24 hours or proceed with the recipe.*

- In preheated oven, bake chicken 15 minutes, or until golden. Remove chicken from pan.
- Pour pan drippings into a bowl. Add sour cream and remaining 2 tablespoons of mustard; mix well.
- Divide sour cream mixture among dinner plates and cover with a chicken breast.

Cook's Notes

To prevent curdling when adding *sour cream* to hot sauces, mix it slowly a little at a time. Cook over low heat but do not boil.

GRILLED MUSTARD CHICKEN

Yield: 4 servings

- 2 tablespoons olive oil
- 4 tablespoons Dijon mustard
- 4 tablespoons barbecue sauce
- 2 teaspoons garlic powder
- 2 tablespoons chopped oil-packed sun-dried tomatoes
- 4 skinless and boneless chicken breast halves

- A day ahead, mix together all ingredients except chicken in a medium bowl. Add chicken pieces and turn to coat well. Cover and refrigerate overnight.
- Preheat grill.
- Grill chicken for 10 minutes on each side or until done.
- In a small saucepan, simmer leftover marinade 5 minutes.
- To serve, place chicken on a platter and cover with simmered marinade. Serve hot.

APRICOT CHICKEN BREASTS

Yield: 4 to 6 servings

- 2 tablespoons vegetable oil
- 3 chicken breasts with bone, split
- ¾ cup chicken broth–*see page 262*
- ⅓ cup apricot preserves
- 1 tablespoon chili sauce
- 2 teaspoons Dijon mustard
- salt and freshly ground pepper

- In a large skillet, heat oil over medium heat. Add chicken and cook, turning, until browned, about 10 minutes. Pour off fat.
- Add broth to pan, cover and simmer 30 minutes, until chicken is fork tender. Remove to a platter and cover with foil to keep warm.
- In a small bowl, combine preserves, chili sauce and mustard. Stir into liquid in pan and bring to a boil, stirring constantly. Season with salt and pepper to taste. Pour over chicken and serve.

CHICKEN BREASTS VERONIQUE

Preheat oven to 350°F   Yield: 4 to 6 servings

- 6 skinless and boneless chicken breast halves
- 1 cup fine dry bread crumbs
- ½ teaspoon salt
- ¼ teaspoon freshly ground pepper
- ½ teaspoon dried thyme
- 7 tablespoons butter, divided
- ½ cup finely chopped onion
- 1½ cups chicken broth–*see page 262*
- ¾ cup dry white wine
- ½ pound mushrooms, sliced
- 2 cups seedless green grapes

- Coat chicken breasts with a mixture of crumbs, salt, pepper and thyme.
- In a large skillet, brown chicken lightly on both sides in 4 tablespoons of butter. Remove to a shallow baking pan and set aside.
- Add onion to skillet and cook until tender. Pour in broth and wine and bring to a boil.
- Pour around chicken and bake 35 minutes, uncovered, in preheated oven.
- While chicken is baking, sauté mushrooms in remaining 3 tablespoons of butter and add to chicken along with grapes. Bake 10 minutes longer.

TANGERINE CHICKEN

Yield: 8 servings

2½ tablespoons crushed dried rosemary
⅔ cup dry vermouth
¼ cup water
8 skinless chicken breast halves
½ cup orange juice
⅔ cup flour
½ teaspoon ground ginger
salt and pepper to taste
2 tablespoons butter
2 tablespoons oil
2 cups long-grain rice
4 cups water
4 tablespoons butter, melted
1 6-ounce can frozen tangerine concentrate, thawed
2 tablespoons dry vermouth
6 green onions, sliced
1 16-ounce package frozen peas, thawed
1 4-ounce jar sliced pimientos, drained

- Mix rosemary, ⅔ cup dry vermouth and ¼ cup water; let stand at least 1 hour.
- Wash chicken pieces and pat dry. Dip in orange juice, and dredge in a mixture of flour, ginger, salt and pepper.
- In a large skillet, brown chicken in butter and oil. Add vermouth mixture and simmer 20 minutes.
- While chicken is cooking, prepare rice. Put rice and 4 cups water in medium saucepan. When water boils, stir with fork, cover and reduce heat to medium-low. Cook 14 minutes.
- **Preheat oven to 375°F.**
- Combine 4 tablespoons melted butter with tangerine concentrate, 2 tablespoons dry vermouth, salt and pepper to taste.
- Toss cooked rice with green onions, peas and pimientos. Add half of tangerine sauce and mix again. Spread in a 9x13-inch baking dish.
- Arrange chicken over rice and spread remaining tangerine sauce over chicken.

✓ *Recipe can be prepared ahead to this point and then baked later.*

- Cover and bake 20 minutes. Uncover and bake 10 minutes.

CHICKEN PROVENÇALE

Yield: 4 to 6 servings

- ¼ cup flour
- ¼ teaspoon freshly ground pepper
- 3 whole skinless and boneless chicken breasts, cut into 1½-inch chunks
- ¼ cup vegetable oil
- 1 large garlic clove, crushed
- 1 shallot, finely chopped
- 1 16-ounce can Italian plum tomatoes, well-drained
- ½ cup dry vermouth
- 1 cup chicken broth–*see page 262*
- 32 pitted Niçoise black olives
- 2 teaspoons dried tarragon leaves
- 2 teaspoons grated fresh orange peel
- ½ teaspoon dried thyme leaves
- ½ teaspoon dried basil leaves
- salt and pepper to taste
- julienned orange peel, optional

- Combine flour and pepper in a large plastic bag. Toss chicken in flour to coat.
- Heat oil in a heavy skillet over high heat. Add chicken and cook until golden, about 2 minutes.
- Reduce heat to medium; add garlic and shallot. Stir and cook until golden, about 1 minute. Add tomatoes, vermouth, chicken broth, olives, tarragon, grated orange peel, thyme and basil.
- Cover and cook until chicken is tender, 4 to 5 minutes. Using a slotted spoon, remove chicken from skillet and keep warm.
- Cook remaining sauce over medium-high heat until thickened, about 1 minute. Pour over chicken. Season with salt and pepper.
- Garnish individual servings with orange peel.

CHICKEN with BALSAMIC VINEGAR

Yield: 4 servings

4 shallots, chopped
2 garlic cloves, minced
2 tablespoons olive oil
2 large chicken breasts, skinned, boned and halved
½ teaspoon dried basil
freshly ground black pepper to taste
½ cup balsamic vinegar

- In a heavy skillet, lightly sauté shallots and garlic in oil.
- Add chicken breasts and brown completely. Sprinkle with basil and pepper.
- Add balsamic vinegar, cover and simmer over low heat for 10 minutes. Add more vinegar if needed.
- Serve chicken with pan juices.

UNFRIED CHICKEN

Preheat oven to 425°F

Yield: 4 servings

2 egg whites
1 teaspoon dried oregano
½ teaspoon onion powder
½ teaspoon salt
¼ teaspoon freshly ground pepper
1 cup crushed cornflakes
4-6 chicken pieces, skin removed
cherry tomato halves
lettuce leaves

- Generously coat a baking dish with vegetable cooking spray and set aside.
- In a medium bowl, combine egg whites, oregano, onion powder, salt and pepper. Beat lightly with a fork. Place crushed cornflakes on a large plate or sheet of wax paper.
- Dip chicken in egg mixture, roll in crushed cornflakes to coat completely. Place in one layer in pan, bone side up.
- Bake 25 minutes in preheated oven. With tongs, gently turn and bake 10 to 15 minutes longer until juices run clear when chicken is pierced with a fork.
- Place on serving plate and garnish with cherry tomato halves and lettuce leaves.

CHICKEN in RASPBERRY SAUCE

Yield: 2 servings

1 large whole chicken breast, skinned, boned and split
salt and pepper
1 tablespoon butter, more if needed
¼ cup finely chopped shallots
¼ cup raspberry vinegar
¼ cup chicken broth-*see page 262*
¼ cup nonfat sour cream
watercress and fresh raspberries for garnish, optional

- Pound chicken breasts between pieces of plastic wrap to flatten slightly. Season to taste.
- Melt butter in a large skillet over medium heat. Add chicken and cook 3 minutes. Turn and cook another 3 minutes. Remove from pan and set aside.
- Add shallots to pan, adding more butter if necessary. Cook over low heat 2 to 3 minutes until soft.
- Add raspberry vinegar, raise heat to medium-high; cook until liquid is almost evaporated and mixture is syrupy.
- Remove from heat; whisk in broth and sour cream. Return to lower heat and simmer 1 minute. Return chicken to skillet and simmer gently, basting, for 5 minutes.
- Remove to platter, baste with sauce and garnish with watercress and raspberries.

Cook's Notes

Shallots are in the onion family and are shaped like garlic. Store in a cool dry place. To cook peel like an onion.

COQ au VIN

Yield: 4 servings

1 2½-pound chicken, skinned and cut into serving-sized pieces
6 slices bacon, diced
2 tablespoons butter
8 whole mushrooms
8 white pearl onions
⅔ cup sliced green onions
1 garlic clove, crushed
2½ tablespoons flour
1 teaspoon salt
¼ teaspoon dried thyme
⅛ teaspoon freshly ground pepper
2 cups Burgundy wine
1 cup canned condensed chicken broth, undiluted
8 small new potatoes with skins
chopped fresh parsley

- Start preparation the day before serving.
- Wash chicken and dry on paper towels.
- In a Dutch oven, sauté bacon until crisp; remove from pan and set aside. Add butter to drippings and heat. Add chicken and brown well all over. Remove chicken from pan and set aside.
- Pour off all but 2 tablespoons of fat from Dutch oven. Add mushrooms and white onions; cook until browned. Remove and set aside with chicken.
- Sauté green onions and garlic in the same pot for 2 minutes. Remove from heat. Stir in flour, salt, thyme and pepper. Return to heat and cook, stirring constantly, until flour is browned, approximately 3 minutes.
- Gradually stir in wine and chicken broth; bring to boil, stirring. Remove from heat. Stir in bacon, chicken, onions and mushrooms. Cover and refrigerate overnight.
- Next day, **preheat oven to 400°F**.
- Add potatoes to chicken mixture, cover and bake 1¾ hours or until chicken and potatoes are tender. Garnish with parsley.

CHICKEN POTPIES

Yield: 4 servings

¾ cup chicken broth–*see page 262*
1 whole large chicken breast, skinned and boned
1 shallot, finely chopped
1½ tablespoons butter
1½ tablespoons flour
2 tablespoons heavy cream *or* sour cream
freshly ground black pepper
½ cup diced carrot
½ cup diced potato
½ cup frozen peas
pastry for a single-crust pie–*see page 263*

- Place broth and chicken breast in a saucepan and bring to boil. Cover, lower heat and simmer 10 to 15 minutes, or until chicken is tender. Drain, reserving broth, and cut chicken into bite-sized pieces.
- In same saucepan, sauté shallot in butter until soft but not browned, about 3 minutes. Add flour and cook, stirring, for 1 minute.
- Gradually add broth and cream; simmer, stirring constantly, for 1 minute. Season with pepper.
- Cook carrot and potato in water until barely tender; drain.
- Add chicken pieces, carrot, potato and peas to sauce and cool slightly.
- **Preheat oven to 425°F.**
- Pour chicken mixture into 4 individual baking dishes, about 1-cup size.
- Roll out pastry dough on a lightly floured board; cut circles a little larger than baking dishes. Place a pastry lid on each dish and crimp over rims. Cut steam vents in pastry tops and decorate with pastry cutouts if desired.
- Bake 30 minutes, or until pastry is golden brown.

✓ *This recipe can be frozen before baking. If frozen, increase baking time to 40 to 45 minutes.*

CHICKEN CURRY

Yield: 6 to 8 servings

1 3 to 4-pound chicken
2 quarts boiling water
1 teaspoon ground turmeric
1 teaspoon cumin seed
1 teaspoon ground cumin
1 2-inch cinnamon stick
4 whole cloves
2 whole cardamom pods, using seeds only
1 tablespoon crushed red pepper
½ teaspoon garlic powder
2 teaspoons salt
1½ cups chopped onion
3 large tomatoes *or* 28 ounces canned whole tomatoes

- Place chicken in a large pot and cover with boiling water. Return to boil, reduce heat, cover and simmer about 30 minutes, or until chicken is done. The time will vary with age of chicken. Cool chicken in cooking liquid, covered.
- Remove chicken, reserving broth. Shred or dice the meat.
- Place spices and red pepper in a cheesecloth bag and tie well.
- In a medium saucepan, combine spices, garlic powder and salt with 2 cups of reserved broth. Add onions, chicken and tomatoes. Bring to boil, reduce heat and simmer 1 hour. Curry will not be thick. Discard cheesecloth bag.
- Curry is a traditional Indian dish, usually served with cooked rice.

Cook's Notes

Curry powder is a blend of many spices usually including cumin, coriander, fenugreek, turmeric, red pepper and ginger. Toasting curry powder in a non-stick sauté pan for a few seconds intensifies the flavor.

GRILLED CHICKEN TERIYAKI

Yield: 8 servings

4 chicken breasts, split
with breast bones removed,
ribs left in
½ cup teriyaki sauce
or good quality soy sauce
2 tablespoons vegetable oil
2 tablespoons dry sherry
1½ tablespoons pared and grated fresh
ginger *or* ½ teaspoon dry ground
3 garlic cloves, finely chopped
1-2 teaspoons brown sugar
juice of ½ a lime

- Place chicken flat in one layer in a large dish.
- Combine remaining ingredients, mixing well; pour over chicken. Marinate 1 hour at room temperature or 2 hours refrigerated, turning frequently.
- Line broiler pan with foil and **preheat pan 4 to 5 inches from heat.**
- Place chicken in pan bone side up. Broil 12 minutes, brushing once or twice with marinade.
- Turn chicken and brush with marinade. Broil 12 to 14 minutes. If skin starts to burn, move broiler pan farther from heat.
- Chicken can also be grilled outdoors.

GRILLED LEMON CHICKEN

Yield: 6 to 8 servings

½ cup fresh lemon juice
¼ cup country Dijon mustard
1 tablespoon chopped fresh parsley
1 teaspoon dried oregano
½ teaspoon salt
¼ teaspoon freshly ground pepper
8 boneless chicken breast halves, skinned

- Combine first six ingredients in a shallow glass dish. Add chicken and turn to coat. Cover and refrigerate ½ to 1 hour.
- **Preheat grill.**
- Grill breasts 8 to 10 minutes per side, basting frequently.

PARMESAN CHICKEN

Preheat oven to 350°F Yield: 6 servings

½ cup fresh bread crumbs
⅓ cup freshly grated Parmesan cheese
2 tablespoons chopped fresh parsley
¼ teaspoon garlic salt
¼ teaspoon freshly ground pepper
1 teaspoon dried Italian seasoning
¼ cup low-fat mayonnaise
***or* more if needed**
6 boneless chicken breast halves, skinned

- Combine crumbs, cheese, parsley and seasonings in a pie plate; set aside.
- Spread mayonnaise over both sides of chicken pieces and dredge in bread crumb mixture. Place chicken in a 9x13-inch baking pan coated with vegetable spray.
- Bake, uncovered, in preheated oven for 45 minutes.

ROAST CHICKEN DIJON

Preheat oven to 400°F Yield: 6 to 8 servings

2 3½ to 4-pound whole chickens
¼ cup Dijon mustard
salt
1 teaspoon paprika
1 tablespoon chopped fresh tarragon
***or* 1 teaspoon dried**

- Dry chickens with paper towels. Tie legs together with string and tuck wings back and under.
- Rub chickens well with Dijon mustard and sprinkle with salt, paprika and tarragon.
- Place in roasting pan and slide into hot oven. **Immediately turn oven heat down to 375°F.** Roast 1½ hours, basting with juices after the first half hour, and then every 20 minutes. Chickens are done when legs move easily in their sockets or juices run clear when thigh is pierced.
- Remove from pan and cool. These can be served hot or cold.

Dick and Ginger Howell
–*The Seasonal Kitchen*

BAKED MARINATED CHICKEN

Yield: 3 to 4 servings

- 1 large onion, minced
- zest of 1 orange
- ⅓ cup fresh orange juice
- ⅓ cup fresh lemon juice
- 4 tablespoons soy sauce
- 3 tablespoons white wine vinegar
- 3 tablespoons honey
- 1 teaspoon minced *or* grated fresh ginger root
- 1½ tablespoons Dijon mustard
- 3 garlic cloves, minced
- 6 pieces of chicken, bone in

- The day before serving, combine all but chicken in a large non-metallic dish and stir well.
- Add chicken pieces, turning to coat, cover and refrigerate overnight.
- Bring chicken to room temperature before proceeding.
- Preheat oven to 375°F.
- Remove chicken from marinade, place in a baking dish and bake 30 to 45 minutes, basting occasionally.

DIJON-CRUSTED CHICKEN

Preheat oven to 350°F

Yield: 6 to 8 servings

- ⅓ cup butter *or* margarine, melted
- 1 tablespoon Dijon mustard
- ⅔ cup crushed wheat crackers
- ⅓ cup freshly grated Parmesan cheese
- ½ teaspoon garlic powder *or* to taste
- 4 whole chicken breasts, boned and halved

- In one bowl, stir together melted butter and mustard. In a second bowl, mix crushed crackers, cheese and garlic powder.
- Dip chicken first in butter mixture, then in crackers. Place in uncovered 9x13-inch baking dish and bake 20 to 30 minutes in preheated oven.

WHITE CHICKEN CHILI

Yield: 6 to 8 servings

- 2 pounds chicken breasts
- 6 cups water
- 1 tablespoon olive oil
- 2 medium onions, chopped
- 4 garlic cloves, minced
- ¼ cup peperoncini peppers, minced
- 2 teaspoons ground cumin
- 1½ teaspoons oregano
- ¼ teaspoon ground cloves
- ¼ teaspoon cayenne pepper
- 2 cans Great Northern white beans
- chicken broth if needed
- 2 cups grated Cheddar cheese

Garnish:

- sour cream
- salsa
- grated Cheddar cheese
- chopped green onions
- chopped tomatoes
- chopped black and green olives

- Cook chicken in a large pot, with at least 6 cups water, enough to completely cover chicken. Bring to boil and skim. Simmer partly covered until tender, 2 to 3 hours. Cool chicken and shred. Save cooking broth.
- In large pot, heat oil. Add onions and sauté for 10 minutes, stirring often. Stir in garlic, peperoncini and seasonings. Sauté 2 minutes.
- Add beans, shredded chicken, and 6 cups broth. If necessary, add chicken broth to make 6 cups. Simmer for 1 hour.
- Just before serving, stir in Cheddar cheese.
- Serve in bowl. Garnish with a large dollop of sour cream. Top with a spoonful of salsa. Sprinkle with grated Cheddar cheese and chopped vegetables. Serve with tortilla chips.

GRILLED TURKEY BREAST

Yield: 3 to 4 servings

1 pound turkey breast, ¾ to 1-inch thick
¼ cup soy sauce
¼ cup canola oil
2 tablespoons fresh lemon juice
¼ cup dry sherry
2 tablespoons dried onion flakes
dash of garlic powder
¼ teaspoon ground ginger
freshly ground pepper to taste

- Rinse turkey, pat dry and place in shallow dish.
- Combine remaining ingredients in blender jar; process until smooth. Pour over turkey, turning to coat well.
- Cover and marinate, refrigerated, for several hours.
- Preheat grill.
- Grill over hot coals 6 to 8 minutes on each side or until done to taste. Do not overcook.

LIME TURKEY CUTLETS

Yield: 6 to 8 servings

⅓ cup flour
½ teaspoon freshly ground pepper
16 turkey breast cutlets, about 2 pounds
3 tablespoons butter *or* margarine
½ cup chicken broth–*see page 262*
3 tablespoons fresh lime juice
¼ teaspoon dried dill
1 tablespoon chopped fresh parsley
lime slices

- Combine flour and pepper; dredge turkey cutlets.
- Lightly coat a large skillet with vegetable cooking spray. Add butter to skillet and place over medium heat until butter melts.
- Add turkey and cook 2 to 3 minutes on each side or until browned; set aside. Dry skillet with paper towels.
- Combine chicken broth, lime juice and dill in skillet. Add turkey, cover and simmer over low heat 10 minutes or until turkey is tender. Remove to a warm platter.
- Sprinkle with parsley and garnish with lime slices.

TRADITIONAL TURKEY STUFFING

Yield: Enough for a 10 to 12-pound turkey

½ cup butter
6 small onions, chopped
½ cup chopped fresh parsley
1 cup chopped celery
1 1-pound loaf day-old bread, cubed
salt and pepper to taste
2 tablespoons dried poultry seasoning
2 eggs, lightly beaten

- Melt butter in a large saucepan. Add onions, parsley and celery. Cook until onions and celery are tender. Remove from heat.
- Add bread cubes, seasonings and eggs. Mix well and stuff lightly into turkey.
- Do not stuff turkey until ready to roast.

MICROWAVED STUFFED PEPPERS

Yield: 4 to 6 servings

1 pound poultry Italian sausage, casing removed
1 cup instant rice
2¾ cups spaghetti sauce, divided
⅓ cup finely chopped onion
1 egg
1 tablespoon chopped fresh oregano *or* 1 teaspoon dried
3 large sweet green peppers
1 cup grated part-skim mozzarella cheese

- Mix sausage with rice, 1 cup spaghetti sauce, onion, egg and oregano.
- Halve peppers lengthwise and remove seeds. Place peppers skin side down in a microwave-safe dish with cover and fill pepper halves with sausage mixture.
- Pour remaining spaghetti sauce over peppers. Cover and microwave on High for 20 minutes, turning dish halfway through cooking.
- Uncover, sprinkle with cheese, cover again and let stand 5 minutes.

Jane Andrews, M.S., R.D.
–Wegmans Consumer Affairs

A quiet place for calling home

Seafood

Seafood

Fish

Shellfish

Sauces

BAKED CATFISH

Preheat oven to 400°F Yield: 4 servings

zest from 1 lemon, minced
1 tablespoon cracked black pepper
¾ teaspoon ground fennel seed
½ teaspoon anise seed
½ teaspoon celery seed
1 tablespoon paprika
½ cup bread crumbs
2 tablespoons freshly grated Romano cheese
4 catfish fillets
8 tablespoons butter, melted
1 cup dry white wine
½ cup Dijon mustard

- Topping: combine lemon zest, seasonings, crumbs and cheese.
- Place catfish in a single layer in a 9x13-inch baking dish. Add melted butter and wine. Spread 2 tablespoons mustard over top of each fillet. Pile topping on mustard.
- Bake 25 minutes in preheated oven.

Daniel Lombardo, Chef
–Mendon House Restaurant

Cook's Notes

Catfish has firm flesh, is low in fat and is mild in flavor. It can be purchased fresh or frozen, dressed or cut into steaks and fillets.

SOLE in PUFF PASTRY

Yield: 4 servings

1 sheet frozen puff pastry
2 teaspoons olive oil
2 teaspoons butter
1 cup chopped mushrooms
½ cup minced shallots
2 medium garlic cloves, minced
4 fillets of sole, about 4 ounces each
salt and pepper to taste
2 tablespoons chopped fresh dill *or* 2 teaspoons dried
1 egg yolk lightly beaten with 1 tablespoon water
Béarnaise Sauce-*recipe follows*
chopped fresh parsley

- Remove pastry from freezer to thaw.
- Heat oil and butter in a small sauté pan. Add mushrooms, shallots and garlic; cook over medium heat, stirring frequently, for about 5 minutes or until vegetables are softened and mushrooms have given up their liquid.
- Rinse fillets and pat dry with paper towels. With skin side down, season with salt, pepper and dill.
- Spread mushroom mixture down the middle of each fillet and, starting at wide end, roll up in jellyroll fashion.
- After pastry has thawed 20 to 30 minutes, roll it out on a lightly floured board to about 12x16 inches; cut into 4 rectangles.
- Place a fillet on each rectangle and fold into a neat package, sealing seams securely with a little water. Chill 15 minutes.
- **Preheat oven to 400°F.**
- Brush packets with beaten egg and place on a moistened baking sheet. Bake 20 to 25 minutes.
- Serve with Béarnaise Sauce and sprinkle with chopped fresh parsley.

BÉARNAISE SAUCE

Yield: 1 cup

2 tablespoons white wine
1 tablespoon tarragon vinegar
2 teaspoons chopped shallots
1 tablespoon chopped fresh tarragon
or 1 teaspoon dried
¼ teaspoon freshly ground pepper
¼ cup egg substitute
2 tablespoons fresh lemon juice
¼ teaspoon salt
dash of cayenne pepper
½ cup butter, melted and bubbly

- In a small pan, bring wine, vinegar, shallots, tarragon and pepper to a rapid boil, cooking until all liquid disappears.
- Place egg substitute, lemon juice, salt and cayenne in container of blender or food processor. Flick motor on and off at high speed for a few seconds.
- Remove cover and slowly drizzle in hot butter with motor running at high speed. Add herbs, cover and blend for 4 seconds.
- Keep warm over hot, not boiling, water.

BARBECUED SALMON

Yield: 6 to 8 servings

¾ cup fresh apple cider
6 tablespoons soy sauce
2 tablespoons unsalted butter
1 large garlic clove, minced
2 salmon fillets, 2½ to 3 pounds each, *or* about 5 pounds of salmon steaks, 1 inch thick
sprigs of fresh parsley *or* cilantro
lemon slices

- In a small saucepan, combine cider and soy sauce. Bring to boil over high heat, reduce heat to moderate and simmer 3 minutes.
- Add butter and garlic; continue cooking, stirring occasionally, until liquid thickens enough to coat the back of a spoon, about 20 minutes. Remove marinade from heat and let cool to room temperature.
- Pat salmon fillets or steaks dry and place them skin side down in a single layer in a deep dish. Brush marinade evenly over salmon. Cover and refrigerate at least 30 minutes.
- Preheat and oil grill.
- Place salmon, skin side down, on hot grill. Cook 15 to 20 minutes, turning once during cooking.
- These can also be broiled in the oven 6 inches from heat for about 12 to 15 minutes.
- Serve garnished with parsley and lemon slices.

SHRIMP DIANE

Yield: 4 servings

1 pound shrimp with shells
6 tablespoons basic seafood stock, divided–*see page 261*
8 ounces angel hair pasta
6 ounces unsalted butter, divided
¼ cup finely chopped green onions
¾ teaspoon salt
½ teaspoon minced garlic
¼ teaspoon cayenne pepper *or* to taste
¼ teaspoon freshly ground white pepper
¼ teaspoon freshly ground black pepper
¼ teaspoon dried basil
¼ teaspoon dried thyme
⅛ teaspoon dried oregano
½ pound mushrooms, cut into ¼-inch-thick slices
3 tablespoons finely chopped fresh parsley

- Early in the day, rinse, peel and devein shrimp, reserving shells for seafood stock. Refrigerate.
- Make Basic Seafood Stock.
- In a large pot of boiling water, cook angel hair pasta about 5 minutes, or until al dente. Drain and keep warm.
- In a large skillet, melt 4 ounces of butter over high heat. When almost melted, add green onions, salt, garlic, peppers and herbs. Stir well.
- Add shrimp and sauté just until they turn pink, about 1 minute, shaking pan in a back-and-forth motion to keep butter from separating.
- Stir in mushrooms and ¼ cup seafood stock. Add remaining 4 tablespoons of butter in chunks and continue cooking, still shaking pan.
- Before butter chunks are completely melted, add parsley, then remaining 2 tablespoons of stock. Continue cooking and shaking pan until all ingredients are thoroughly mixed and sauce is consistency of cream.
- Serve immediately with cooked angel hair pasta and lots of French bread.

SHRIMP in a CATAPLANA

Yield: 4 to 6 servings

- 2 tablespoons extra virgin olive oil, divided
- ¼ pound prosciutto in 1 piece, trimmed and cut into ¼-inch dice
- ½ pound chorizo *or* other garlicky, spicy sausage, thinly sliced
- 3 medium yellow onions, thinly sliced
- 1 sweet white onion, thinly sliced
- 3 large garlic cloves, minced
- ½ medium sweet green pepper, thinly sliced
- 2 large bay leaves
- 1½ teaspoons paprika
- ¼ teaspoon red pepper flakes
- 1 28-ounce can chopped tomatoes, drained and juice reserved
- ⅔ cup dry white wine, divided
- 24 small clams *or* mussels, scrubbed well
- 1 pound large raw shrimp, shelled and deveined
- ¼ cup coarsely chopped flat-leaf parsley, divided

- In a very large heavy skillet, heat 1 tablespoon of the olive oil until a haze forms on the surface. Add prosciutto and sausage; stir-fry 2 minutes. Remove with a slotted spoon; drain on a paper towel.
- Add remaining tablespoon of oil to skillet and stir in onions, garlic, green pepper and bay leaves. Sauté, stirring now and then, 5 minutes, or until onions are golden. Blend in paprika and red pepper flakes; cook 2 minutes over moderate heat.
- Stir in tomatoes, ½ the reserved liquid and ⅓ cup white wine. Cover and simmer over low heat about 40 minutes. If mixture gets too dry, add more tomato liquid. When finished, stir in prosciutto and sausage.

✓ *This can be done up to 2 days ahead, covered and refrigerated.*

- A cataplana is a Portuguese cooking pan shaped like a clam shell. Since most kitchens don't have cataplanas, use a large Dutch oven or lidded ovenproof skillet. To assemble the cataplana, spoon ½ the tomato mixture into bottom of pan. Bring to simmer over moderate heat.
- Arrange clams or mussels and shrimp on top; add balance of tomato mixture. Add remaining ⅓ cup white wine and ½ of parsley. Cover tightly and simmer gently about 20 minutes. If clams or mussels are not open, simmer another 5 minutes. Discard any which do not open.
- Serve in large soup plates and sprinkle with remaining parsley.

SHRIMP and VEGGIE OVEN ROAST

Preheat oven to 400°F

Yield: 4 generous servings

16 large raw shrimp, shelled
1 tablespoon olive oil
1 garlic clove, minced
½ cup chopped fresh parsley
3½ teaspoons dried rosemary
or herbes de Provence, divided
salt and freshly ground pepper to taste
4-8 medium new potatoes, cut into chunks
1 pound carrots, cut into chunks
2 onions, cut into chunks
35 garlic cloves, peeled and left whole
⅓ cup olive oil
1 pound kielbasa *or* other smoked sausage, cut into large chunks
1 large zucchini, cut into chunks
1 large sweet red pepper, cut into chunks

- Put shrimp in large flat dish. Marinate in a mixture of 1 tablespoon olive oil, minced garlic, parsley, ½ teaspoon rosemary, salt and pepper. Set aside.
- In a 9x13-inch flat baking dish, place potatoes, carrots, onions, garlic cloves, ⅓ cup of oil, more salt and pepper and 3 teaspoons rosemary. Toss to coat and roast 30 minutes in preheated oven.
- Add kielbasa and roast 15 minutes longer.
- Add zucchini and red pepper; roast another 10 minutes.
- Add shrimp and marinade; roast 8 to 10 minutes.
- Stir often while roasting.

Dick and Ginger Howell
–*The Seasonal Kitchen*

SHRIMP and WILD RICE CASSEROLE

Preheat oven to 300°F   Yield: 4 servings

- **5 tablespoons butter, divided**
- **1 tablespoon flour**
- **¼ teaspoon salt *or* to taste**
- **1 cup chicken broth-*see page 262***
- **½ cup thinly sliced onion**
- **½ cup thinly sliced mushrooms**
- **1 tablespoon Worcestershire sauce**
- **few drops hot pepper sauce**
- **2 cups cooked wild rice**
- **1 pound cooked shrimp**

- Cream Sauce: melt 1 tablespoon butter over medium heat in small saucepan. Add flour and salt; cook, stirring, until bubbly. Slowly whisk in chicken broth; cook until slightly thickened. Set aside.
- In medium skillet, sauté onion and mushrooms in 4 tablespoons butter until soft. Add seasonings, rice, shrimp and cream sauce. Mix well and place in buttered casserole.
- In preheated oven, bake 20 minutes, or until hot.

Cook's Notes

Shrimp: Whether or not to devein shrimp is a matter of personal preference. In general, small and medium shrimp do not need deveining except for cosmetic purposes. However, because the vein of larger shrimp contains noticeable grit, it should be removed.

SHRIMP CURRY

Yield: 4 servings

- 5 tablespoons butter *or* margarine
- 1 large onion, chopped
- 1 apple with skin, cored and chopped
- 2 ribs celery, chopped
- 1 tablespoon curry powder *or* to taste
- 1 tablespoon flour
- salt to taste
- 1½ cups chicken broth-*see page 262*
- 2 teaspoons mango chutney, coarsely chopped
- 1 pound large cooked shrimp, shelled and deveined
- condiments of choice

- Melt butter in a large skillet. Add chopped onion, apple and celery. Sauté vegetables gently until transparent.
- Sprinkle with curry powder, flour and salt; cook 3 to 4 minutes. Add broth and cook until thickened. Force sauce through a food mill or large sieve.
- Just before serving, add chutney and shrimp and reheat. Serve with cooked rice.
- Indonesian curry dinners include a number of condiments. Use any or all of the following suggestions: minced hard-boiled egg, white and yellow separate; grated fresh coconut; chopped peanuts or almonds; chopped green onions; chopped green pepper; sliced banana; sliced avocado; chopped unpared cucumber; raisins soaked in brandy; currants soaked in Madeira; crumbled crisp bacon; fried onion rings and chutney.
- This Indonesian curry sauce can be used with other cooked meats or shellfish.

SHRIMP CREOLE

Yield: 4 servings

¼ pound bacon, diced
⅓ cup chopped onion
1 garlic clove, minced
½ medium sweet green pepper, chopped
1 14-ounce can tomatoes in juice, diced
⅓ cup chili sauce
1 tablespoon red wine vinegar
½ teaspoon dry mustard
⅛ teaspoon red pepper sauce *or* more to taste
1 bay leaf
1½ teaspoons sugar
salt and pepper to taste
1 pound raw shrimp, peeled and deveined

- Fry bacon until crisp; drain and set aside.
- Sauté onion, garlic and green pepper in bacon fat for a few minutes until softened. Add tomatoes with their juice, chili sauce, vinegar and seasonings.
- Cook over low heat about 25 minutes. Add water or tomato juice if too thick.

✓ *Recipe can be prepared ahead and refrigerated at this point.*

- Bring tomato mixture to a simmer, add shrimp and cook, stirring, about 5 minutes. Do not overcook.
- Sprinkle with reserved bacon and serve with cooked rice.

SHRIMP ÉTOUFFÉE

Yield: 8 servings

- 2 pounds medium shrimp
- 3 cups basic seafood stock-*see page 261*
- 2 teaspoons salt
- 1 teaspoon cayenne pepper *or* to taste
- 1 teaspoon freshly ground white pepper
- 1 teaspoon freshly ground black pepper
- 1 teaspoon dried basil
- ½ teaspoon dried thyme
- ½ cup chopped onion
- ½ cup chopped celery
- ½ cup chopped sweet green pepper
- 7 tablespoons vegetable oil
- ¾ cup flour
- 8 ounces unsalted butter, divided
- 1 cup finely chopped green onions

- Early in the day, shell and devein shrimp; refrigerate. Make basic seafood stock.
- Thoroughly combine salt, peppers, basil and thyme for seasoning mix and set aside.
- In a separate bowl, combine the onion, celery and green pepper; set aside.
- Refer to page 262 for information on making a brown roux.
- In a large heavy skillet, heat oil until hot. Lower heat and add flour gradually, stirring constantly with a long-handled whisk or wooden spoon, until roux is dark brown.
- Remove from heat and immediately stir in vegetables and 1 tablespoon of seasoning mix. Continue stirring until cooled, about 5 minutes.
- In a 2-quart saucepan, bring 2 cups of stock to boil over high heat. Gradually add roux and whisk until thoroughly dissolved. Reduce heat to low and cook until flour taste is gone, about 2 minutes, whisking almost constantly. Remove from heat and reserve.
- In a 4-quart saucepan, melt 4 ounces of butter over medium heat. Stir in shrimp and green onions; sauté 1 minute, stirring. Add remaining butter, stock mixture and remaining cup of stock. Cook until butter melts, 4 to 6 minutes, shaking pan back and forth. Add remaining seasoning mix, stir well and remove from heat.
- Serve with cooked white rice.

LEMON SHRIMP SAUTÉ

Yield: 2 servings

- 1 lemon
- 3 tablespoons butter *or* margarine
- 2 tablespoons vegetable oil
- 1 tablespoon minced green onion
- 4-5 garlic cloves, minced *or* pressed
- ¼ teaspoon salt
- ¾ pound large raw shrimp, shelled and deveined
- 2 tablespoons minced parsley
- dash of hot pepper sauce

- Grate ¼ teaspoon of lemon peel and reserve. Squeeze half of the lemon.
- Place wok or large skillet over medium-high heat. When wok is hot, add butter and oil. When butter has melted, add onion, garlic, lemon juice and salt. Stir-fry until onion is limp, about 30 seconds.
- Turn heat to high, add shrimp; stir-fry until pink, 2 minutes.
- Stir in lemon peel, parsley and hot pepper sauce.
- Garnish with lemon wedges to squeeze over each serving.
- Serve with hot buttered noodles, rice or spaghetti.

Jackie Cannizzaro
–Demonstrator and Cooking Teacher

BROILED GARLIC SHRIMP

Yield: 4 servings

- 2 pounds shelled medium shrimp, thawed if frozen
- 2 tablespoons chopped fresh garlic
- ¼ cup chopped fresh parsley
- ¼ cup bread crumbs
- ½ cup olive oil
- salt and freshly ground pepper

- Combine all ingredients gently and lay in 1 layer in a large baking dish. Cover and refrigerate 4 hours.
- Preheat oven to 450°F.
- Bake, uncovered, 10 minutes.
- Turn shrimp and place under broiler briefly to brown.

BAKED SCALLOPS with HERBS

Preheat oven to 425°F

Yield: 2 servings

½ pound sea scallops
2 tablespoons butter
2 tablespoons dry white wine
2 tablespoons snipped fresh parsley
2-3 tablespoons snipped fresh chives
1 small garlic clove, peeled and minced
3 shallots, chopped,
or 1 green onion, chopped
1 teaspoon dried basil
½ teaspoon salt
freshly ground pepper
2 tablespoons bread crumbs

- Wash and drain scallops. Divide between 2 individual ramekins or place in an 8-inch au gratin dish.
- Melt butter and mix with wine. Mince parsley and chives together, reserving 1 tablespoon; stir the rest into the butter and wine. Add the garlic, shallots, basil, salt and pepper and pour over scallops.
- Top with bread crumbs and reserved parsley and chives. Cover and bake in preheated oven for 10 minutes for ramekins or 20 to 25 minutes for au gratin dish until frothy but not overcooked.
- To brown topping, uncover last few minutes of baking or brown under broiler. Serve over cooked rice.

Jackie Cannizzaro
–Demonstrator and Cooking Teacher

Cook's Notes

Scallops are usually sold shucked. They should be firm and free of excess cloudy liquid. Look for those with a sweet smell and a fresh, moist sheen.

PAELLA VALENCIANA

Yield: 8 servings

4 lobster tails, thawed if frozen
24 large raw shrimp
24 hard-shelled clams
3 chorizos *or* ½ pound of other spicy sausage
1 teaspoon dried oregano
2 peppercorns
1 garlic clove, chopped
1½ teaspoons salt, divided
10 tablespoons olive oil, divided
1 teaspoon red wine vinegar
8 serving-sized pieces of chicken
2 ounces ham, diced
½ cup finely chopped onion
1 sweet green pepper, cut into thin strips
1 large tomato, peeled, seeded and chopped
3 cups long-grain rice
¼ teaspoon saffron
6 cups boiling water
1 cup frozen peas, thawed
8 asparagus spears, cooked
1 4-ounce jar whole pimientos, cut into 8 pieces

- Scrub lobster tails and, without removing shells, cut into 1-inch-thick slices. Set aside.
- Shell and devein shrimp and set aside.
- Scrub clams and set aside.
- With a sharp fork, prick sausages in several places and put in a skillet with enough cold water to cover. Bring to boil, reduce heat and simmer, uncovered, 5 minutes. Drain on paper towels and slice into ¼-inch rounds.
- Combine oregano, peppercorns, garlic, ½ teaspoon salt, 2 tablespoons oil and vinegar; mash in a mortar or bowl. Rub chicken pieces with mixture.
- In a deep heavy skillet, heat 4 tablespoons of oil and brown chicken lightly over moderate heat. Remove to a plate.

- Add lobster pieces to skillet; cook over high heat, turning frequently, 2 to 3 minutes, until shell begins to turn pink. Set aside.
- Add sausage to pan and brown quickly on both sides; spread on paper towel to drain.
- Discard fat in skillet and replace with 4 tablespoons of oil. Heat until light haze forms, add ham and brown quickly on all sides over high heat. Add onion, pepper and tomato. Stirring constantly, cook until most of liquid evaporates and mixture holds its shape. Set aside.

✓ *Paella can be prepared to this point and held for several hours before proceeding.*

- **Preheat oven to 400°F.**
- In a paella pan or other large shallow ovenproof pan, combine onion mixture, rice, 1 teaspoon salt and saffron. Pour in boiling water and, stirring constantly, bring to boil over high heat. Remove from heat and correct seasoning.
- Arrange chicken, lobster, sausage, shrimp and clams on top of rice, pushing pieces down into rice slightly. Scatter peas over all.
- Set on bottom shelf of preheated oven and bake, uncovered, 25 to 30 minutes, or until liquid is absorbed by rice. Do not stir.
- When done, remove from oven and drape a clean kitchen towel loosely over top; let paella rest 5 to 8 minutes.
- Garnish with warmed asparagus spears and pimiento. Serve directly from pan.
- Meat and shellfish can be varied or omitted.

CRAB MEAT STEW

Yield: 6 servings

- 2 cups crab meat
- ½ cup dry sherry
- 2 small garlic cloves, minced
- 2 tablespoons unsalted butter
- 1½ tablespoons flour
- 1½ teaspoons chopped fresh rosemary *or* ½ teaspoon dried
- 3 tablespoons chopped mild onion
- 1 tablespoon chopped fresh chives
- 3 tablespoons chopped sweet red pepper
- ¾ cup peeled, seeded and chopped tomato
- salt and pepper to taste
- 1 cup half-and-half

- Marinate crab meat in sherry, refrigerated, for 1 hour.
- In a large skillet, sauté garlic lightly in butter. Do not brown. Add flour and cook about 30 seconds.
- Stir in rosemary, onion, chives, sweet red pepper and tomato. Season to taste. Simmer 5 minutes.
- Stir in crab meat and sherry; heat through. Add half-and-half and cook 5 to 10 minutes longer. Add additional half-and-half *or* milk if stew appears too thick.
- Serve over toast points or fine pasta cooked al dente.

Cook's Notes

Crab: Use freshly cooked crabmeat within 2 days or freeze for up to 1 month. Once opened, canned crabmeat should be used within 2 days.

SCALLOPED OYSTERS BIENVILLE

Yield: 6 servings

4 ounces salted butter
1 cup finely sliced green onions
¼ cup finely minced parsley
1½ teaspoons finely minced garlic
½ cup flour
½ cup heavy cream
1½ cups milk
4 large egg yolks, well beaten
¼ cup dry sherry
1 teaspoon salt
1 teaspoon freshly ground white pepper
½ teaspoon cayenne pepper *or* to taste
⅔ cup finely chopped fresh mushrooms
½ pound cooked shrimp, finely diced
2-3 pints shelled oysters
6 tablespoons freshly grated Romano cheese
4 tablespoons dry bread crumbs
½ teaspoon paprika

- In a large heavy saucepan, melt butter over low heat. Add green onions, parsley and garlic; cook, stirring frequently, until soft.
- Gradually stir in flour and mix with a wooden spoon until smooth. Add cream and milk slowly, stirring constantly, until mixture is quite smooth. Slowly add egg yolks, sherry, salt, pepper and cayenne; blend until mixture begins to thicken.
- Stir in mushrooms and cook 2 minutes, then add shrimp and continue cooking over low heat about 3 minutes, until sauce is thick. Allow sauce to cool; refrigerate until ready to put casserole together.

✓ *This can all be done the day before.*

- **Preheat oven to 400°F.**
- Coat bottom of a glass 9x13-inch baking dish with vegetable spray.
- Drain oysters thoroughly and pat dry with paper towels. Place oysters in baking dish and top with sauce.
- Mix Romano cheese, crumbs and paprika; sprinkle over top of sauce. Bake 15 to 18 minutes.

OYSTERS ITALIANO

Yield: 2 servings

- 24 large, heavy oysters in shells *or* 24 shelled oysters with their juice
- 3 tablespoons virgin olive oil
- ¼ cup unsalted butter
- ½ Bermuda *or* sweet red onion, halved vertically and thinly sliced
- 1 garlic clove, minced
- 1 hot cherry pepper
- 2 ounces fresh mushrooms, thinly sliced
- 1 large ripe tomato, peeled, seeded and cut into thin strips
- pinch of salt
- ¼ teaspoon freshly ground black pepper
- 8 fresh parsley sprigs, finely chopped

- Open oysters, saving any juice.
- Combine olive oil and butter in a skillet; heat. Add onion and garlic; stir and cook slowly for about 5 minutes.
- Halve cherry pepper, discard seeds, wash carefully and cut into thin slices. Add to skillet along with mushrooms and tomato. Cover and cook slowly for about 10 minutes.
- Add oysters and juice, salt and pepper; cook for 3 minutes. Turn oysters, add parsley, cover and cook 3 minutes longer.
- Serve in deep bowls with slices of fresh Italian bread and a green salad.

Cook's Notes

Oysters are a low-cholesterol seafood. They have their best flavor in September through April when they are not spawning.

Sunshine and music, great healers

Puddings

Fruit Desserts

Refrigerated Desserts

Frozen Desserts

Dessert Sauces

Candy & Nuts

Pies

CHOCOLATE BREAD PUDDING

Preheat oven to 375°F Yield: 6 to 8 servings

2 cups French bread cubes
2 cups milk
1 cup sugar
½ cup unsweetened cocoa powder
½ teaspoon ground cinnamon
2 eggs, lightly beaten
½ cup raisins
1 tablespoon butter, melted
2 teaspoons vanilla extract

- Place bread cubes in a large bowl; add milk and let stand about 10 minutes. In a small bowl, stir together sugar, cocoa powder and cinnamon.
- In another bowl, combine eggs, raisins, butter and vanilla; add sugar mixture and mix well. Stir into bread.
- Pour bread mixture into an ungreased 6x10-inch baking dish and bake in preheated oven for 40 to 45 minutes, or until knife inserted near center comes out clean.
- Serve warm with ice cream.

Dick and Ginger Howell
–*The Seasonal Kitchen*

GUILTLESS RICE PUDDING

Preheat oven to 325°F Yield: 6 generous servings

16 ounces egg substitute, equivalent of 8 eggs
3 12-ounce cans evaporated skim milk
1 tablespoon vanilla extract
sugar substitute to equal ½ cup sugar
¾ cup raisins
1½ cups cooked rice

- Mix egg substitute with evaporated milk. Whisk until well blended. Add vanilla and sugar substitute.
- Place raisins in bottom of a heavy casserole dish. Put cooked rice over raisins. Pour liquid mixture over raisins and rice.
- In preheated oven, bake 1½ hours, or until firm. Refrigerate after cooling. Serve cold.

LOW-FAT RAISIN BREAD PUDDING

Preheat oven to 350°F

Yield: 6 servings

4 cups skim milk
¾ cup sugar
1 tablespoon butter *or* margarine
¼ teaspoon salt
3 cups cubed white bread
1 cup egg substitute *or* 4 eggs
1 teaspoon vanilla extract
½ cup raisins *or* chopped dates
dash of freshly grated nutmeg
whipped topping *or* Lemon Sauce–*recipe follows*

- In a large saucepan, scald skim milk; add sugar, butter and salt. Add bread cubes and let mixture soak a few minutes.
- Stir in egg substitute, vanilla and raisins. Stir well and pour into 1½-quart baking dish. Sprinkle with nutmeg.
- Place baking dish in a pan of hot water and bake 1 hour in preheated oven.
- Can be served with whipped topping or Lemon Sauce.

LEMON SAUCE

Yield: About 1½ cups

½ cup sugar
1 tablespoon cornstarch
dash of salt
dash of freshly grated nutmeg
1 cup boiling water
2 tablespoons butter *or* margarine
1½ tablespoons fresh lemon juice

- In a small saucepan, mix sugar, cornstarch, salt and nutmeg; gradually stir in water.
- Cook over low heat, stirring constantly, until clear and thick. Blend in butter and lemon juice.

CRANBERRY CRUNCH

Preheat oven to 350°F	Yield: 6 to 8 servings

1 cup oatmeal
⅓ cup flour
½ cup brown sugar
⅓ cup butter
1 16-ounce can cranberry sauce, jellied *or* whole
1 quart vanilla ice cream

- Grease an 8-inch square cake pan.
- In a medium bowl, mix oatmeal, flour and brown sugar. Cut in butter until crumbly.
- Place half of this mixture in prepared pan and cover with cranberry sauce. Top with remaining mixture.
- Bake 45 minutes in preheated oven. Remove from oven and let rest ½ hour. Serve in squares topped with vanilla ice cream.
- As an option, mix 2 cups chopped and pared apples and ¼ cup chopped nuts into cranberry sauce.

STRAWBERRY-RHUBARB CRISP

Preheat oven to 375°F	Yield: 8 servings

1½ cups flour
½ teaspoon salt
¼ teaspoon ground cinnamon
1½ cups sugar, divided
⅓ cup butter *or* margarine
4 cups sliced rhubarb, fresh *or* frozen
2 cups strawberries, fresh *or* frozen
⅛ teaspoon salt
1 tablespoon fresh lemon juice

- In a large bowl, mix together flour, ½ teaspoon salt, cinnamon and ½ cup sugar. Cut in butter until mixture is crumbly.
- Spread half of this mixture in bottom of a 7x11-inch baking dish. Press firmly.
- Combine rhubarb, strawberries, 1 cup sugar, ⅛ teaspoon salt and lemon juice in a bowl. Spread evenly over bottom layer. Sprinkle remaining crumb mixture over fruit and press firmly.
- Bake 45 to 50 minutes in preheated oven. Serve warm or cold with vanilla ice cream or whipped cream.

RHUBARB AMBROSIA

Preheat oven to 350°F Yield: 4 to 6 servings

1 navel orange
5 cups rhubarb, cut in ½-inch pieces
1¾ cups sugar
1 tablespoon flour
4 cups small bread cubes, divided
½ cup melted butter, divided
½ cup flaked coconut

- Grease an 8-inch square baking pan.
- Grate or zest and chop the orange-colored rind of a navel orange. Cut off white membrane and cut orange into cubes.
- In a large bowl, combine rhubarb, sugar, ¾ teaspoon orange zest, orange pieces and flour. Add 2 cups bread cubes and ¼ cup melted butter. Spread in prepared baking pan.
- Combine 2 cups bread cubes, ¾ teaspoon orange zest, ¼ cup melted butter and coconut for topping. Sprinkle over rhubarb.
- Bake 40 minutes in preheated oven. Serve warm.
- A little cream or ice cream is a nice addition.

MAPLE WALNUT BAKED APPLES

Preheat oven to 375°F Yield: 6 servings

6 large baking apples
½ cup chopped walnuts
½ cup maple syrup
½ cup apple cider *or* apple juice
3 tablespoons butter *or* margarine, melted
ground cinnamon

- Core apples, pare across top and a strip around middle of each.
- Place in a baking dish and fill centers of apples with nuts.
- Mix syrup, cider and butter and pour into each apple; pour remainder into dish. Sprinkle with cinnamon.
- Bake 40 to 45 minutes in preheated oven, basting periodically with juice.
- Apples can be served plain, with vanilla ice cream or with whipped cream.

PHYLLO PEAR SURPRISE

Yield: 6 to 8 servings

6 tablespoons butter *or* margarine
1 tablespoon honey
1 tablespoon fresh lemon juice
1 teaspoon sugar
¼ teaspoon ground cinnamon *or* cardamom
5 pears, pared and thinly sliced
½ cup ground vanilla wafers, about 12 to 14 cookies, divided
8 sheets phyllo dough, thawed
2 tablespoons confectioners' sugar

- In a small saucepan, melt butter and set aside to cool.
- In a medium saucepan, melt honey with lemon juice, sugar and cinnamon. Stir in pear slices and 6 tablespoons vanilla wafer crumbs.
- Refer to page 261 for information regarding handling of phyllo dough.
- Unroll 1 sheet of phyllo and brush with butter. Fold sheet together lengthwise, buttered side in, and then fold again and again until sheet is about 2 inches wide.
- Brush top with butter and place on an ungreased cookie sheet, buttered side down, so that ⅓ of dough extends beyond edges of sheet. Place slightly damp towel over work in progress.
- Continue buttering and folding balance of sheets in same way and arranging them atop each other like 8 overlapping spokes of a wheel.
- **Preheat oven to 400°F.**
- Mound pear mixture in center of dough and sprinkle last 2 tablespoons of wafer crumbs over pears.
- Starting with last strip put on baking sheet, fold each strip over filling and twist it about 3 inches from its end. The twisted strips should almost meet in the middle. Open each end to form a petal.
- Brush top with remaining melted butter and bake about 8 minutes, until top begins to brown.
- **Lower temperature to 325°F** and bake until filling is soft and top is golden, about 30 to 45 minutes more. Let cool until just lukewarm. Dust with confectioners' sugar and cut into wedges. Do not refrigerate.

Jackie Cannizzaro,
–Demonstrator and Cooking Teacher

APPLE DESSERT PANCAKE

Yield: 6 servings

5 tablespoons sugar, divided
1 teaspoon ground cinnamon
2 tablespoons butter
2 McIntosh apples
3 tablespoons flour
¼ teaspoon baking powder
dash of salt
2 eggs separated
3 tablespoons milk
sour cream *or* ice cream, optional

- Combine 2 tablespoons sugar with cinnamon and set aside.
- In a 10-inch skillet, melt butter and swirl all over bottom of pan. Sprinkle cinnamon-sugar mixture evenly over butter.
- Pare and core apples and cut into ¼-inch slices. Arrange slices in skillet in overlapping circles. Cook over low heat for 5 minutes.

✓ *Recipe can be prepared ahead to this point and baked later.*

- **Preheat oven to 400°F.**
- Combine flour, baking powder, salt, egg yolks and milk; set aside. Beat egg whites with remaining 3 tablespoons of sugar until soft peaks form. Fold into flour mixture and pour over apple slices, spreading evenly.
- Bake 10 minutes, or until golden and puffy.
- Remove from oven, loosen edges with a spatula and invert onto a plate. Cut into wedges and serve immediately with sour cream or ice cream.

APRICOTS DELICIOUS

Yield: 4 servings

¼ pound dried apricots
⅓ cup sugar *or* more to taste
3 bananas
1 cup heavy cream, whipped

- Soak apricots in water for 3 hours.
- Place apricots in a small saucepan and add enough cold water to cover. Cook until tender.
- Stir in sugar while apricots are hot. Strain through a food mill. Place in a bowl and chill.
- At serving time, add sliced bananas and whipped cream.

BLUEBERRY COBBLER

Preheat oven to 400°F | Yield: 6 servings

½ cup sugar
1 tablespoon cornstarch
4 cups fresh blueberries
or unsweetened frozen berries
1 teaspoon fresh lemon juice
1 cup flour
1 tablespoon sugar
1½ teaspoons baking powder
½ teaspoon salt
3 tablespoons solid vegetable shortening
½ cup milk

- Blend ½ cup sugar and cornstarch in medium saucepan. Stir in blueberries and lemon juice. Cook, stirring constantly, until mixture thickens and boils. Boil and stir 1 minute.
- Pour into ungreased 2-quart casserole. Keep fruit mixture hot in oven while preparing biscuit topping.
- Blend flour, 1 tablespoon sugar, baking powder and salt in a bowl. Add shortening and milk. Cut through shortening six times with a pastry cutter. Mix until dough forms a ball.
- Drop dough by spoonfuls onto hot fruit.
- In preheated oven, bake 25 to 30 minutes or until topping is golden brown. Serve warm with or without ice cream.

–Cornell Cooperative Extension Service

Cook's Notes

A *cobbler* is a dessert made with fruit filling and a biscuit topping. Cobblers can be made with many different combinations of fruit. Always put batter on hot fruit mixture. Topping cooks more evenly.

LEMON CHIFFON DESSERT

Yield: 12 servings

1 3-ounce package lemon gelatin
1 cup boiling water
½ cup sugar
grated rind and juice of 2 lemons
1 12-ounce can evaporated milk, chilled
12 graham crackers, crushed
½ cup brown sugar
¼ cup butter, melted

- Dissolve gelatin in boiling water; add sugar, rind and juice. Cool until syrupy.
- Beat chilled milk to 3 times its bulk; fold into lemon mixture.
- Mix graham cracker crumbs, brown sugar and butter. Press all but ¼ cup into a 9x13-inch pan. Pour in lemon filling and sprinkle with reserved crumbs. Refrigerate.

CHOCOLATE RICOTTA BOMBE

Yield: 10 to 12 servings

2 3-ounce packages ladyfingers
1 7-ounce bar milk chocolate
3 cups ricotta cheese
1 cup + 2 tablespoons confectioners' sugar, divided
1 cup heavy cream
½ teaspoon vanilla extract
2 tablespoons sliced almonds, toasted

- Line bottom and side of a 2-quart bowl with wax paper.
- Line bottom and side with ladyfinger halves, set aside.
- Break chocolate bar into food processor; process until crumbly. Add ricotta cheese and 1 cup confectioners' sugar; process until blended.
- Pour half of mixture over ladyfingers in bowl. Top with additional ladyfinger halves and remaining chocolate mixture. Gently press on additional ladyfinger halves, split sides down.
- Cover and refrigerate several hours or overnight.
- In small mixer bowl, whip heavy cream, 2 tablespoons confectioners' sugar and vanilla until stiff peaks form.
- To serve, invert bombe onto a large serving plate. Frost with sweetened whipped cream and garnish with almonds.

–Specialty Bakers, Marysville PA

TIPSY TRIFLE

Yield: 8 servings

- ½ cup sugar
- 3 tablespoons cornstarch
- ¼ teaspoon salt
- 3 cups milk
- ½ cup dry sherry
- 3 egg yolks, beaten
- 3 tablespoons butter *or* margarine
- 1 tablespoon vanilla extract
- 1 6 *or* 8-ounce sponge cake *or* angel food cake, *or* 2 packages ladyfingers
- ½ cup raspberry preserves
- 1 12-ounce package frozen strawberries *or* raspberries, thawed
- 1 11-ounce can mandarin oranges, drained
- 2 kiwi fruits, pared and sliced
- 2 tablespoons toasted slivered almonds

- In a 3-quart saucepan, mix sugar, cornstarch and salt. Gradually add milk and sherry. Heat to boiling over medium heat, stirring constantly. Boil and stir for 1 minute
- In a separate bowl, very slowly pour at least half the hot mixture into egg yolks. Return to saucepan; boil and stir for 1 minute. Remove from heat and stir in butter and vanilla.
- Cover with plastic wrap and refrigerate at least 3 hours.
- Split ladyfingers or cut cake into rectangular slices about 1x3 inches.
- Spread 1 side of each piece with preserves and make 1 layer in bottom of a deep glass bowl. Cover with half of berries and ½ of pudding.
- Arrange kiwi slices and mandarin oranges along outside edge so that they show through sides of glass bowl.
- Continue with another layer of ladyfingers or cut cake and remaining berries. Put other ½ of pudding on top; sprinkle with toasted almonds. Decorate top with additional fruit.
- If you prefer a more traditional English trifle, omit kiwi and orange slices and use 2 cups of fresh berries.

APRICOT TART

Yield: 8 to 10 servings

- **2 3-ounce packages ladyfingers**
- **½ cup apricot fruit spread, divided**
- **1 cup heavy cream**
- **⅓ cup unsifted confectioners' sugar**
- **2 teaspoons vanilla extract**
- **½ cup sour cream**
- **1 16-ounce can apricot halves in light syrup, drained well**

- Line bottom of a 9-inch springform pan with ladyfinger halves, split sides up.
- Separate 10 to 12 ladyfingers; cover bottoms with fruit spread. Replace tops and cut in half crosswise. Use to line side of pan, allowing cut ends to rest on ladyfingers in bottom of pan; set aside.
- In small mixer bowl, whip heavy cream, confectioners' sugar and vanilla until stiff peaks form. Fold in sour cream. Spoon and spread into ladyfinger-lined pan.
- Arrange apricots, cut sides down, over cream mixture in pan.
- Place remaining fruit spread in small microwave-proof bowl. Microwave on High for 15 seconds, or just until warm. Spoon over apricots, covering completely.
- Cover and refrigerate several hours or overnight. Remove side of pan just before serving.

Specialty Bakers
–Marysville PA

Cook's Notes

When whipping *cream*, thoroughly chill bowl and beaters in the freezer first. Make sure cream is very cold.

BERRIED ALMOND TORTE

Preheat oven to 350°F

Yield: 6 to 8 servings

½ cup unsalted butter, softened
¾ cup granulated sugar, divided
2 eggs divided
1 teaspoon vanilla extract
2 cups flour
¼ teaspoon salt
½ teaspoon almond extract
1 cup heavy cream
2 tablespoons confectioners' sugar
1 tablespoon brandy, type compatible with berries chosen
1 quart strawberries *or* other fresh berries

- Butter and flour two 9-inch cake pans.
- Cream butter with ½ cup granulated sugar; add 1 egg, vanilla, flour and salt. Divide evenly between cake pans, pressing dough into bottoms of pans.
- Beat 1 egg until foamy. Gradually add ¼ cup sugar and almond extract. Beat until thick and ivory-colored. Spread over pastry layers in pans.
- In preheated oven, bake 25 minutes, or until light golden brown. Cool 5 minutes and remove from pans

✓ *Pastry layers can be wrapped and frozen at this point for later use.*

- Whip cream until stiff. Fold in confectioners' sugar and brandy. Slice half of strawberries or leave small berries whole. Fold sliced berries into cream.
- Place 1 pastry layer on serving dish; spread with half of berries and cream mixture. Place second layer on top and cover with remaining cream. Decorate top with remaining fruit. Chill before serving. Serve within the hour.

RASPBERRY HAZELNUT CLOUD

Preheat oven to 375°F   Yield: 8 servings

4 egg whites
½ teaspoon white vinegar
1¼ cups sugar
1 cup hazelnuts, toasted, husked and ground–*see page 255*
2 cups heavy cream
2 tablespoons confectioners' sugar
2½ cups fresh raspberries

- Lightly grease two 8-inch cake pans.
- Beat egg whites until stiff but not dry. When whites form soft peaks, add vinegar and continue beating until stiff. Fold sugar into whites, then fold in ground nuts.
- Divide batter between prepared pans and bake for 30 minutes in preheated oven.
- Remove meringues from pans immediately and cool.
- Whip cream with confectioners' sugar until stiff peaks form. Fold in raspberries, reserving 8 for decorating.
- Spread ½ of whipped cream and raspberry mixture on top of 1 meringue; place other meringue on top and spread with remainder of cream. Decorate top with reserved raspberries.
- Serve immediately or refrigerate.

PIÑA COLADA ICE CREAM

Yield: 8 to 10 servings

½ gallon vanilla ice cream, slightly softened
16 ounces piña colada mix, slightly thawed
coconut flakes for garnish

- Mix ice cream and piña colada mix and refreeze in wine goblets.
- **Preheat oven to 375°F.**
- Spread coconut flakes on a cookie sheet and toast 5 to 7 minutes. Stir once or twice. Watch carefully to prevent burning.
- When serving, sprinkle ice cream with toasted coconut.
- This can also be made with low-fat frozen yogurt and topped with a sprig of fresh mint.

Dick and Ginger Howell
–The Seasonal Kitchen

FROZEN STRAWBERRY PIE

Preheat oven to 350°F | Yield: 8 servings

1⅔ cups pecans
2½ tablespoons confectioners' sugar
pinch of salt
2½ tablespoons unsalted butter, softened
¼ cup piña colada drink mix
1 quart strawberry frozen yogurt
***or* ice cream, partially softened**

- Lightly butter a 9-inch pie plate.
- In food processor, coarsely chop pecans with confectioners' sugar and salt. Stir in butter with a fork. Press mixture evenly into prepared pie plate.
- Bake in preheated oven until lightly browned, about 5 minutes. Cool completely. Freeze at least 10 minutes before filling.
- Stir piña colada mix into frozen yogurt and spread on pecan crust; freeze until firm.

STRAWBERRY SORBET

Yield: 1 quart

1 quart fresh strawberries
juice of 1 orange
juice of 1 lemon
2 tablespoons light rum
***or* Grand Marnier, optional**
1 cup sugar

- Wash and slice berries. Put in blender with orange juice, lemon juice and rum; purée. Stir in sugar. Refrigerate mixture until cold.
- Stir well and transfer mixture to an ice cream maker; freeze following manufacturer's instructions.
- Move sorbet from freezer to refrigerator about ½ hour before serving to soften slightly.
- Alternate method: Pour purée into ice cube trays and freeze until about 1 inch appears frozen around edges of trays. Remove to a bowl and beat until smooth. Return to trays and freeze until firm.
- This recipe can be made with red raspberries and raspberry liqueur instead of strawberries and rum.

MOCHA ICE CREAM CAKE

Yield: 10 to 12 servings

1 pint chocolate ice cream
2 3-ounce packages ladyfingers
¾ cup almond brickle chips *or* crushed toffee candy
2 tablespoons instant coffee granules
1 pint coffee ice cream
1 cup heavy cream
¼ cup unsifted confectioners' sugar
2 tablespoons Kahlua
½ teaspoon vanilla extract
additional almond brickle chips for garnish

- Let ice cream stand at room temperature about 10 minutes to soften.
- Line bottom and side of a 9-inch springform pan with ladyfinger halves, split sides up.
- Stir chocolate ice cream with a spoon until of spreading consistency. Spoon and spread into ladyfinger-lined pan. Working quickly, sprinkle with almond brickle chips and instant coffee granules.
- Stir coffee ice cream with a spoon until of spreading consistency. Spoon and spread over coffee granules in pan. Top with additional ladyfinger halves, split sides down. Place in freezer.
- In small mixer bowl, combine heavy cream, confectioners' sugar, Kahlua and vanilla. Whip until stiff peaks form.
- Spread Kahlua whipped cream over cake and garnish with additional brickle chips. Cover and freeze several hours or overnight. Remove side of pan just before serving.

Specialty Bakers
Marysville PA

LEMON CREAM SAUCE

Yield: About 3 cups

2 eggs
⅓ cup sugar
⅓ cup fresh lemon juice
1 tablespoon cornstarch
½ cup water
⅓ cup sugar
1 teaspoon vanilla extract
1 cup heavy cream

- In a medium bowl, beat eggs, sugar and lemon juice about 1 minute.
- In a saucepan, combine cornstarch, water and sugar. Cook over low heat until thickened, stirring frequently.
- Gradually add egg mixture to sugar mixture; stir frequently and continue to cook on low heat until thickened. Remove from heat and cool.
- Whip vanilla and cream together until soft peaks form. Fold into lemon mixture.
- Serve with fresh fruit or as a topping for pound cake or angel food cake.

MELBA SAUCE

Yield: About 2 cups

1 cup seedless black raspberry jam
¼ cup sugar
½ cup water
2 tablespoons Kirsch

- Combine jam, sugar and water in a small saucepan, Simmer until thickened a little, about 10 minutes. Add Kirsch and chill. Sauce keeps indefinitely refrigerated.
- Serving suggestion: Put a scoop of vanilla ice cream in a dish. Top with half a poached or canned peach. Spoon some Melba Sauce over all and garnish with toasted slivered almonds.

PECAN PUMPKIN SAUCE

Yield: 3 cups

- 2 tablespoons butter *or* margarine
- 1 cup pecans, chopped
- 1 16-ounce can solid-pack pumpkin
- 1½ cups maple-flavored syrup
- 2 teaspoons ground cinnamon
- ¾ teaspoon ground ginger
- ¼ cup half-and-half
- 1 tablespoon fresh lemon juice

- In a medium saucepan, melt butter; stir in pecans. Cook over medium heat, stirring occasionally, 4 to 5 minutes or until lightly browned.
- Stir in remaining ingredients. Cook over medium heat 4 minutes, stirring occasionally.
- Serve warm or cool over ice cream, pancakes or waffles. Cover and store refrigerated.
- The sauce improves with age.

–Cornell Cooperative Extension Service

BUTTER RUM SAUCE

Yield: About 1⅓ cups

- 1 cup firmly packed dark brown sugar
- ¼ cup light corn syrup
- 4 tablespoons unsalted butter
- pinch of salt
- ½ cup heavy cream
- ½ teaspoon vanilla extract
- ¼ teaspoon fresh lemon juice
- 1½ tablespoons dark rum *or* to taste
- ½ cup shopped pecans

- In a small saucepan, combine brown sugar, corn syrup, butter and salt. Cook over moderate heat until sugar is dissolved.
- Boil undisturbed for 12 minutes or until candy thermometer registers 280°F.
- Remove pan from heat and stir in cream, vanilla, lemon juice, rum and pecans. Serve warm or at room temperature over ice cream.

Dick and Ginger Howell
–The Seasonal Kitchen

HOT FUDGE SAUCE

Yield: 3 cups

- 5 ounces unsweetened chocolate
- ½ cup butter
- 1 12-ounce can evaporated milk
- 3 cups unsifted confectioners' sugar
- 1¼ teaspoons vanilla extract

- Melt chocolate and butter in a large saucepan over low heat. Remove from heat. Mix in evaporated milk alternately with sugar.
- Bring to boil over medium heat, stirring constantly. Cook and stir about 8 minutes, or until thickened and creamy.
- Remove from heat and stir in vanilla. Serve warm.

ALMOND TOFFEE

Yield: About 3 pounds

- 1 pound butter
- 1⅓ cups sugar
- 3 tablespoons light corn syrup
- 6 tablespoons water
- 1 cup almonds, coarsely chopped and toasted
- 2 8-ounce milk chocolate bars
- 1 cup almonds, finely chopped and toasted

- Grease 2 cookie sheets and set aside.
- Melt butter in 3-quart saucepan; add sugar, corn syrup and water. Cook over medium heat until mixture reaches hard crack stage, 300° F. This will take about ½ hour.
- Immediately stir in coarse almonds and spread very thinly onto cookie sheets. Set aside and cool completely.
- Melt chocolate bars in top of double boiler over barely simmering water until smooth. Spread on top of toffee. Sprinkle with finely chopped almonds. Cool completely. Crack into portions.

SPICED PECANS

Preheat oven to 225°F   Yield: 1 pound

1 egg white
1 teaspoon cold water
1 pound pecan halves
½ cup sugar
¼ teaspoon salt
½ teaspoon ground cinnamon
½ teaspoon freshly grated nutmeg

- Beat egg white and water in a large bowl until frothy but not stiff. Fold in nuts and mix until coated.
- Mix sugar, salt and spices; add to mixture in bowl.
- Place on a buttered cookie sheet and bake 1 hour in preheated oven, stirring every 15 minutes.
- When cool, pack in an airtight container.

RUM PECAN PIE

Preheat oven to 375°F   Yield: 8 servings

1 8-inch unbaked pie crust-*see page 263*
3 eggs
⅔ cup sugar
1 cup light corn syrup
¼ cup melted butter *or* margarine
¼ cup light rum
1 teaspoon vanilla extract
1 cup chopped pecans *or* walnuts
20 pecan *or* walnut halves, optional
whipped cream for garnish, optional

- Prepare pie crust and set aside.
- In large mixer bowl, combine eggs, sugar, corn syrup, melted butter, rum and vanilla; beat 3 to 4 minutes.
- Fold in chopped pecans and pour into unbaked pie shell. If desired, place pecan halves on top of mixture in a circular pattern.
- Bake pie 35 to 45 minutes in preheated oven. Remove from oven and cool on wire rack.
- To serve, garnish with whipped cream.

BLUEBERRY PIE with ROSE PETALS

Preheat oven to 450°F — Yield: 6 to 8 servings

- pastry for a 9-inch double-crust pie–*see page 263*
- 4 cups fresh or frozen blueberries
- 1 cup sugar
- 2 level tablespoons tapioca
- 1 tablespoon butter *or* margarine
- sugar
- 1 fresh rose blossom in full bloom, rinsed

- Prepare pastry and line a 9-inch pie plate. Roll out top crust and set aside.
- Wash and sort berries; mix with sugar and tapioca. Pour into pie shell and dot with butter. Place a single layer of rose petals over berries. Rose petals bring out the flavor of the berries. Cover with top crust and sprinkle lightly with sugar.
- Set on cookie sheet to catch drips; bake 20 to 30 minutes in preheated oven. Crust should be lightly browned.

BLUEBERRY CREAM PIE

Preheat oven to 400°F — Yield: 6 servings

- 1 unbaked 9-inch pie crust–*see page 263*
- 1 cup sour cream, regular, low-fat *or* nonfat
- 5 tablespoons flour, divided
- ¾ cup sugar
- 1 teaspoon vanilla extract
- ¼ teaspoon salt
- 1 beaten egg *or* ¼ cup egg substitute
- 2½ cups fresh *or* frozen blueberries
- 1½ tablespoons butter *or* margarine
- 3 tablespoons chopped walnuts

- Prepare pie crust and set aside.
- Combine sour cream, 2 tablespoons flour, sugar, vanilla, salt and egg. Beat 5 minutes at medium speed, or until smooth. Fold in blueberries.
- Pour filling into pie crust and bake in preheated oven 25 to 30 minutes, or until nearly set. Remove from oven.
- Combine remaining ingredients and sprinkle over pie. Bake 10 minutes more. Chill before serving.

LAKE COUNTRY GRAPE PIE

Preheat oven to 425°F — Yield: 8 servings

- pastry for a 10-inch double-crust pie–*see page 263*
- 3 pounds fresh Concord grapes
- 1 cup sugar *or* to taste
- 2 tablespoons cornstarch
- 3 tablespoons tapioca
- ¼ teaspoon ground cinnamon
- ½ cup red wine
- 2 tablespoons butter, melted

- Prepare pastry and line a 10-inch pie plate. Roll out top crust and set aside.
- Slip skins from pulp of grapes; set aside. Heat pulp to a boil. Rub heated pulp through strainer to remove seeds. Stir reserved skins into strained pulp; cool.
- Mix sugar, cornstarch, tapioca and cinnamon. Stir dry ingredients, wine and melted butter into grapes.
- Spoon filling into pastry-lined plate. Cover with top crust, flute edge and vent well. Place on a baking sheet and bake on bottom rack of preheated oven until crust is set and edge is lightly browned, approximately 15 minutes.
- **Reduce oven temperature to 400°F.** Continue to bake pie on bottom rack approximately 1 hour, or until bubbling and golden brown. Protect edge with a strip of foil, if necessary, to prevent burning.

Cook's Notes

Look for plump, fresh *grapes* without bruises, mold or soft spots and with good color for the variety. Grapes often have a frosty white cast or bloom. The bloom is typical and does not affect quality

DEEP DISH PLUM PIE

Preheat oven to 400°F — Yield: 8 servings

4 **cups pitted and diced Italian prune plums**
1 **cup sugar**
¼ **cup flour**
¼ **teaspoon salt**
1 **tablespoon butter *or* margarine**
pastry for a single-crust pie-*see page 263*
beaten egg, optional

- Arrange plums in an 8-inch square baking pan.
- Combine sugar, flour and salt; sprinkle over plums. Dot with butter.
- Roll pastry into a square. Place over plums, seal edges and prick top. Brush crust with egg if desired. Bake 35 to 40 minutes in preheated oven.

PAPER BAG APPLE PIE

Preheat oven to 425°F — Yield: 6 to 8 servings

1 **9-inch unbaked pie crust-*see page 263***
2½ **pounds tart apples**
1 **cup sugar, divided**
2 **tablespoons + ½ cup flour, divided**
½ **teaspoon freshly grated nutmeg**
2 **tablespoons fresh lemon juice**
dash of ground cinnamon
½ **cup cold butter *or* margarine**

- Prepare pie crust.
- Pare, core and slice apples about ¼ inch thick. Place in large bowl.
- In a small bowl, combine ½ cup sugar, 2 tablespoons flour and nutmeg. Sprinkle over apples and toss well. Spoon mixture into pie shell; drizzle with lemon juice.
- Combine ½ cup sugar, ½ cup flour and cinnamon for topping. Cut in butter until it resembles coarse crumbs. Sprinkle over apples.
- Slide pie into heavy brown paper bag large enough to cover loosely. Fold over end of bag and close with paper clips. Place on baking sheet.
- Bake 1 hour in preheated oven. Remove from bag and cool on wire rack.
- Serve with Cheddar cheese or ice cream.

STRAWBERRY CREAM CHEESE PIE

Yield: 8 to 10 servings

- 1 9-inch baked pie crust–*see page 263*
- 3 cups strawberries, washed and hulled
- ½ cup sugar
- dash of salt
- ½ cup cold water, divided
- 1½ tablespoons cornstarch
- 1 tablespoon fresh lemon juice
- 3 ounces cream cheese, softened
- 3 tablespoons milk

- Prepare pie crust and set aside.
- Slice 1 cup strawberries; place in saucepan with sugar, salt and ¼ cup water. Bring to boil and cook 3 minutes. Mix cornstarch and ¼ cup cold water; stir into berries and cook, stirring, until thick. Add lemon juice.
- In a small bowl, beat cream cheese and milk until smooth. Spread in bottom of pie shell. Cover cheese with half of strawberry sauce. Arrange remaining whole strawberries on top, stem ends down. Spoon remaining glaze over berries.
- Chill 2 hours before serving.

Cook's Notes

Choose fully-ripened *strawberries* because berries do not ripen after picking. Do not wash or hull berries until you are ready to use them.

The library, a spot for reading or doing homework

Cakes

Cheesecakes

Drop Cookies

Shaped & Rolled Cookies

Bars & Squares

Frostings

BLACK CHOCOLATE CAKE

Preheat oven to 350°F | Yield: 6 to 8 servings

1 cup sugar
4 tablespoons butter *or* margarine, softened
1 egg
1 teaspoon vanilla extract
1 cup flour
¼ teaspoon salt
1 teaspoon baking soda
½ cup unsweetened cocoa powder
1 cup hot water mixed with 1 teaspoon instant coffee
6 ounces semisweet chocolate chips
1 cup sour cream
pinch of salt

- Grease and flour a 1-quart aluminum ring mold.
- Cream sugar and butter; mix in egg and vanilla.
- Sift flour with salt, baking soda and cocoa. With mixer set at low speed, add sifted dry ingredients to creamed ingredients alternately with hot water. Batter will be thin.
- Pour into prepared pan. Bake in preheated oven 30 to 35 minutes, or until cake tests done. Cool 20 to 30 minutes in pan, then turn out onto cooling rack.
- When cake has cooled, melt chocolate chips over barely simmering water, stir in sour cream and salt and mix well. Frost cake.

RAISIN PUDDING CAKE

Preheat oven to 350°F | Yield: 2 loaves

1 pound raisins
4 cups water, divided
1 cup solid vegetable shortening
2 cups sugar
2 tablespoons baking soda
1 tablespoon ground cinnamon
dash of ground cloves and freshly grated nutmeg
4 cups flour
¼ teaspoon salt
1 teaspoon lemon extract

- Grease and flour two 5x9-inch loaf pans.
- In a large saucepan, boil raisins in 3 cups water for 15 minutes.
- Add remaining ingredients, including 1 cup water, and pour into prepared pans. Bake 45 to 60 minutes in preheated oven.

MAZARIN TORTE

Yield: 10 to 12 servings

1½ cups flour
1 teaspoon baking powder
1 cup sugar, divided
1 cup softened butter *or* margarine, divided
3 eggs
½ cup raspberry jam, divided
1 cup blanched almonds, ground *or* finely chopped
½ teaspoon almond extract
½ cup confectioners' sugar
2 teaspoons fresh lemon juice

- Grease a 9-inch springform pan.
- In mixer bowl or food processor, blend flour, baking powder and ⅓ cup sugar. Mix in ½ cup butter and 1 egg until all flour is moistened. Press dough evenly on bottom and sides of pan.
- Spread ¼ cup jam over dough; cover with plastic wrap and chill.
- **Preheat oven to 350°F.**
- In mixer bowl, cream ½ cup butter and ⅔ cup sugar. Stir in almonds and extract. Add 2 eggs, 1 at a time, beating well after each addition. Spoon filling over jam and bake about 40 minutes.
- Cool in pan, then remove to plate. Spread with remaining jam.
- Combine confectioners' sugar and lemon juice, mixing until smooth. Drizzle over top of cake.

ALMOND CAKE

Preheat oven to 350°F

Yield: 10 to 12 servings

2 cups flour
1 teaspoon baking soda
1 teaspoon baking powder
¼ teaspoon salt
1 cup sugar
½ cup butter, softened
2 eggs, beaten
1 teaspoon vanilla extract
1 cup sour cream
1¾ cups toasted sliced almonds, divided
½ cup half-and-half
¼ cup brandy
8 ounces almond paste–*see page 261*
4 tablespoons milk
4 tablespoons confectioners' sugar

- Grease and flour a 9 or 10-inch tube pan.
- Sift flour, baking soda, baking powder and salt into a large bowl and set aside.
- In electric mixer bowl, cream sugar and butter. Add beaten eggs and vanilla and blend well. Add dry ingredients to butter mixture alternately with sour cream until batter is stiff. Stir in 1 cup almonds and set aside.
- Combine half-and-half, brandy and ½ cup almonds; set aside.
- Knead almond paste with fingers until soft and pliable. Add brandy mixture a little at a time until well blended.
- Spread half of cake batter in prepared pan. Spread half of almond paste mixture over cake batter. Spread remaining batter over paste layer. To remaining almond paste mixture, add milk and confectioners' sugar. Pour over cake.
- Bake 30 minutes in preheated oven. Remove from oven and garnish top with remaining almonds. Bake 30 minutes longer, or until cake tests done when inserted toothpick comes out clean. Remove from pan and cool completely.

TWO-CUP CAKE

Preheat oven to 350°F Yield: 20 servings

- 2 cups flour
- 2 cups sugar
- 2 teaspoons baking soda
- 2 eggs
- 1 20-ounce can crushed pineapple with juice
- 2 cups chopped walnuts, divided
- 4 ounces butter, softened
- 8 ounces cream cheese, softened
- 1½ cups confectioners' sugar
- 1 teaspoon vanilla extract

- Stir together flour, sugar, baking soda, eggs, pineapple and 1 cup nuts. Pour into 9x13-inch ungreased baking pan. Bake 30 to 40 minutes in preheated oven.
- While cake is baking, make frosting. Cream butter, cream cheese and confectioners' sugar; stir in 1 cup walnuts and vanilla.
- When cake is done, spread frosting on hot cake and then refrigerate. Serve when cool.

BLUEBERRY GINGERBREAD

Preheat oven to 350°F Yield: 15 servings

- 1 cup sugar
- ½ teaspoon ground cloves
- ½ teaspoon ground cinnamon
- ½ teaspoon ground ginger
- 1 teaspoon salt
- 1¼ heaping teaspoons baking soda
- ½ cup molasses
- 2 eggs
- ½ cup vegetable oil
- 1 cup hot tea
- 2½ cups flour
- 2 cups blueberries, fresh *or* frozen

- Mix all ingredients, folding in blueberries last. If using frozen berries, do not thaw.
- Place in a nonstick 9x13-inch pan. Bake 45 minutes in a preheated oven.
- Serve plain or with whipped cream.

MOLASSES SPONGE CAKE

Preheat oven to 350°F — Yield: 8 to 10 servings

- 4 tablespoons butter *or* margarine
- ½ cup molasses
- 1 cup boiling water
- 1 cup sugar
- 1½ cups flour
- 1 scant teaspoon baking soda
- 1 scant teaspoon baking powder
- 1 teaspoon ground cinnamon
- ½ teaspoon ground allspice
- ½ teaspoon salt
- 1 egg, lightly beaten

- Grease and flour an 8-inch square baking pan or angel food cake pan.
- In a saucepan, mix butter, molasses and water; boil until butter is melted.
- In mixer bowl, combine all dry ingredients and then add hot ingredients. Add egg and beat 1 minute on medium speed.
- Pour into prepared pan and bake in preheated oven 30 to 40 minutes or until cake tests done.
- Top with whipped cream if desired.

Cook's Notes

Light and dark *molasses* are interchangeable in recipes, the latter having a slightly more robust flavor. Store molasses tightly sealed in a cool, dark place at room temperature for up to 2 years.

STRAWBERRY JAM CAKE

Preheat oven to 350°F

Yield: 12 servings

1 cup sugar
⅔ cup butter *or* margarine, softened
3 eggs
1 teaspoon baking soda
½ cup sour milk *or* sour cream
1 teaspoon ground cinnamon
¼ teaspoon salt
2 cups flour, sifted
1 cup strawberry jam
Seven-Minute Frosting–*recipe follows*

- Grease and flour two 9-inch round cake pans.
- Cream sugar and butter. Add eggs and beat well.
- Add baking soda to sour milk or cream.
- Stir cinnamon and salt into sifted flour.
- Alternately add flour mixture and cream to butter mixture. Stir in jam.
- Pour batter into prepared pans and bake in preheated oven for 30 minutes or until cake tests done.
- Remove from oven; cool 10 minutes in pans. Remove layers from pans and cool on racks. Frost with Seven-Minute Frosting.

SEVEN-MINUTE FROSTING

Yield: Enough for 2-layer cake

2 egg whites
½ cup firmly packed brown sugar
¾ cup white sugar
dash of salt
½ cup water
¼ teaspoon cream of tartar
1 teaspoon vanilla extract

- In bottom of double boiler, bring 2 cups water to boil.
- In top of double boiler, combine egg whites, sugars, salt, water and cream of tartar. Beat 1 minute. Place over boiling water.
- Using highest speed of electric mixer, beat constantly 5 to 7 minutes or until frosting stands in stiff peaks. Remove from heat and add vanilla.

CHOCOLATE TRUFFLE SUPREME

Preheat oven to 425°F

Yield: 10 to 12 servings

1½ cups butter
1 cup + 1 tablespoon sugar, divided
¾ cup unsweetened cocoa powder
1 tablespoon flour
2 teaspoons vanilla extract
4 eggs, separated
1 cup heavy cream, chilled
chocolate curls–*see page 261*

- Grease bottom of 8-inch springform pan.
- Melt butter in medium saucepan over low heat. Add 1 cup sugar and ¾ cup cocoa, stirring until well blended. Cool slightly.
- Stir in flour and vanilla and mix well. With electric mixer, add egg yolks, one at a time.
- In medium bowl, beat egg whites with remaining 1 tablespoon sugar until soft peaks form. Gradually fold into chocolate mixture.
- Spoon batter into prepared pan and bake in preheated oven 16 to 18 minutes, or until edges are firm. Center will be soft but cake sets as it cools.
- Remove to wire rack until completely cooled; remove sides of pan. Refrigerate at least 6 hours.
- Beat cream at high speed until thickened. Spread over top of cake and garnish with chocolate curls. Cut cake while cold, but let stand at room temperature 10 to 15 minutes before serving.

RUM CAKE

Preheat oven to 325°F | Yield: 12 servings

1 cup coarsely chopped pecans
1 cup vegetable oil
3 cups sugar, divided
4 eggs *or* 1 cup egg substitute
2½ cups flour
¼ teaspoon salt
2¼ teaspoons baking powder
½ cup milk
1 cup dark rum, divided
½ cup butter *or* margarine
¼ cup water

- Grease and flour a 9 or 10-inch tube pan or a bundt pan. Sprinkle pecans over bottom of pan.
- With an electric mixer, beat oil with 2 cups sugar until light and creamy. Add eggs, 1 at a time, beating well after each addition.
- Sift together dry ingredients and add alternately with milk and ½ cup rum.
- Pour into prepared pan and bake in preheated oven 1 hour or until cake tests done.
- Just before cake is finished baking, make a syrup of butter, 1 cup sugar and water. Boil 5 minutes, stirring constantly. Remove from heat and carefully stir in ½ cup rum.
- Remove cake from oven and, while still hot, prick top all over with a bamboo skewer or something similar. Spoon hot glaze all over top and let it soak into cake. When cake has cooled, invert onto a serving plate. Allow cake to sit a few hours before serving.

Cook's Notes

N*uts* are easier to chop when they are warm. Either heat in microwave at 100% power for 2 to 3 minutes or in a conventional oven at 325°F for 5 minutes.

GERMAN TORTE

Preheat oven to 350°F

Yield: 12 servings

8 **eggs, separated**
½ **cup sugar**
½ **cup flour**
2 **teaspoons baking powder**
1 **pound walnuts, finely ground**
¼ **cup sugar**
6 **tablespoons instant cocoa mix**
4 **whole eggs**
8 **ounces butter**
1 **tablespoon vanilla extract**
½ **pint heavy cream**

- Grease two 9-inch round cake pans.
- Cream egg yolks and ½ cup sugar until fluffy.
- Sift flour and baking powder 3 times. Add to creamed mixture.
- Beat egg whites until stiff and fold into batter. Place in prepared pans and bake 30 minutes in preheated oven. Cool.
- In a saucepan, mix all remaining ingredients except cream and cook over low heat until butter is melted and filling is smooth, stirring constantly. Cool.
- Remove cakes from pans and split each horizontally into 3 layers. Stack layers, spreading filling between layers.
- Whip cream until stiff and frost top and sides of cake. Refrigerate at least 2 hours before serving.

Cook's Notes

To *split cake layers*, loop a piece of unflavored dental floss tightly around cake horizontally. Cross the ends, then slowly but firmly pull on each end. The floss will cut cleanly through the cake.

DATE NUT TORTE

Preheat oven to 350°F | Yield: 20 servings

1¼ cups sifted flour
¾ teaspoon baking soda
½ teaspoon salt
8 ounces pitted dates, finely chopped
¾ cup firmly packed brown sugar
½ cup water
½ cup butter *or* margarine
6 ounces semisweet chocolate chips
2 eggs
½ cup milk
½ cup orange juice
1 cup chopped walnuts
Chocolate Cream Whip–*recipe follows*

- Thoroughly grease and flour a 10x15-inch jelly roll pan.
- Sift flour, baking soda and salt together onto wax paper.
- Combine dates, brown sugar, water and butter in large saucepan. Cook over low heat, stirring constantly, until dates soften. Remove from heat and immediately add chocolate chips, stirring until chocolate melts.
- Beat in eggs and then flour mixture alternately with milk and orange juice. Fold in nuts.
- Pour batter into prepared pan and bake in preheated oven 25 minutes or until top springs back when lightly touched with finger. Let cool in pan 15 minutes, then loosen with spatula and turn out onto wire rack to cool.
- While cake is cooling, make Chocolate Cream Whip.
- When torte has cooled thoroughly, cut crosswise into 3 pieces, each 5 inches wide. Place bottom layer on serving tray and spread with ⅓ Chocolate Cream Whip. Add second layer and half remaining Whip. Top with remaining layer; frost top. Refrigerate. To serve, cut into 1-inch slices, then in half again.

Cook's Notes

Keep *dates* in a tightly closed container in the refrigerator up to several months or in the freezer up to a year. Dates can be diced more easily if placed in the freezer for an hour or so.

CHOCOLATE CREAM WHIP

Yield: About 3 cups

½ cup semisweet chocolate chips
2 tablespoons honey
1 tablespoon water
½ teaspoon vanilla extract
1 cup heavy cream
⅛ teaspoon salt

- In small saucepan, combine chocolate, honey and water. Stir over low heat until chocolate melts. Remove from heat and stir in vanilla. Cool until mixture thickens slightly.
- In a bowl, combine heavy cream and salt; whip until soft peaks form. Gently fold in chocolate mixture.

OATMEAL CHOCOLATE CHIP CAKE

Preheat oven to 350°F

Yield: 12 servings

1¾ cups boiling water
1 cup quick-cooking oatmeal
½ cup butter
1 cup granulated sugar
1 cup brown sugar
1¾ cups flour
1 tablespoon unsweetened cocoa powder
1 teaspoon baking soda
½ teaspoon salt
12 ounces chocolate chips

- Grease and flour a 9x13-inch baking pan.
- Mix boiling water and oatmeal and let stand 7 to 10 minutes.
- Add butter to oatmeal and let melt. Add both sugars and mix well.
- Sift flour, cocoa, baking soda and salt together; add to oatmeal mixture and mix well. Stir in 8 ounces chocolate chips.
- Pour into prepared pan and sprinkle remaining chips on top. In preheated oven, bake 35 to 40 minutes, or until cake tests done. No frosting is needed.

PRALINE CHEESECAKE

Preheat oven to 350°F

Yield: 10 to 12 servings

1 cup graham cracker crumbs
3 tablespoons sugar
3 tablespoons butter *or* margarine, melted
3 8-ounce packages cream cheese, softened
1¼ cups packed brown sugar
2 tablespoons flour
3 eggs
1½ teaspoons vanilla extract
½ cup finely chopped pecans
maple syrup
pecan halves, optional

- Combine crumbs, sugar and butter and press into bottom of a 9-inch springform pan. Bake 10 minutes in preheated oven.
- Combine cream cheese, brown sugar and flour, beating with electric mixer at medium speed until blended. Add eggs, one at a time, mixing well after each addition. Blend in vanilla and chopped nuts.
- Pour mixture over crumbs and bake 50 minutes in preheated oven. Cake is done when knife inserted in center comes out clean. Cool and loosen side of pan. Chill at least 6 hours.
- Brush with maple syrup and garnish with pecan halves.

Cook's Notes

Graham crackers: 14 square crackers = 1 cup fine crumbs. To make crumbs, place crackers in a zip-top plastic bag, leaving a small opening. Roll with a rolling pin.

FROSTED CHEESECAKE

Preheat oven to 350°F — Yield: 8 servings

- 3 8-ounce packages cream cheese, softened
- 1¼ cups + 2 tablespoons sugar, divided
- 5 eggs
- ½ teaspoon salt
- 2¼ teaspoons vanilla extract, divided
- 1 cup sour cream
- chocolate curls–*see page 261*

- With an electric mixer, beat cream cheese. Add 1¼ cups sugar, eggs, salt and ¾ teaspoon vanilla, beating until thick and lemon colored. Pour into an ungreased 9-inch springform pan and bake 45 to 50 minutes in preheated oven.
- Remove from oven and cool 20 minutes; cake will drop in center.
- Mix sour cream, 2 tablespoons sugar and 1½ teaspoons vanilla; pour over top of cake. Bake an additional 10 minutes.
- Cool thoroughly and decorate with chocolate curls.

LOW-FAT CHEESECAKE PIE

Preheat oven to 325°F — Yield: 8 servings

- ½ cup chocolate graham cracker crumbs
- 2 8-ounce packages nonfat cream cheese, softened
- ½ cup sugar
- 1 tablespoon flour
- ½ cup nonfat sour cream
- 3 egg whites
- 1 teaspoon vanilla extract
- 2 cups sliced strawberries, optional

- Coat a 9-inch pie plate with vegetable spray. Add crumbs and shake plate to coat entire surface; set aside.
- Combine cream cheese, sugar and flour in large mixing bowl. Beat on medium speed until thoroughly mixed and creamy. Beat in sour cream, egg whites and vanilla.
- Pour mixture into prepared crust and place in center of preheated oven. Bake 40 minutes; remove from oven and cool on rack. Refrigerate at least 3 hours.
- Before serving, spoon sliced strawberries over top of cake.

POTATO CHIP COOKIES

Preheat oven to 350°F

Yield: 4 dozen

2 cups brown sugar
1 cup solid vegetable shortening
2 eggs
2 cups flour
1 teaspoon baking soda
1 teaspoon vanilla extract
1 cup crushed potato chips
1 cup chopped nuts

- Grease a cookie sheet and set aside.
- Cream sugar and shortening; beat in eggs. Stir in remaining ingredients and drop by teaspoonfuls onto cookie sheet.
- Bake 10 to 12 minutes in preheated oven. Cool on wire racks.

OATMEAL COOKIES

Preheat oven to 350°F

Yield: 6 dozen

1 cup butter *or* margarine, softened
1 cup granulated sugar
1 cup brown sugar
2 eggs
1 teaspoon vanilla extract
1 cup flour
1 teaspoon baking powder
½ teaspoon salt
1 teaspoon ground cinnamon
¼ teaspoon freshly grated nutmeg
3 cups oatmeal

- Grease a cookie sheet and set aside.
- Cream butter, sugars, eggs and vanilla.
- Sift together dry ingredients except for oatmeal and add to creamed mixture. Fold in oatmeal and mix well.
- Drop by teaspoonfuls onto cookie sheet. Bake 10 minutes in preheated oven, or 12 minutes for a crisper cookie.

APRICOT NECTAR COOKIES

Preheat oven to 300°F | Yield: 3½ dozen

2¾ cups flour
1 teaspoon baking soda
¾ cup sugar
¼ cup dark brown sugar
1 cup butter, softened
1 large egg
¼ cup apricot nectar
½ cup apricot preserves
¾ cup dried apricots, chopped

- Sift together flour and baking soda; set aside.
- Blend sugars with mixer at medium speed. Add butter and mix to form a grainy paste. Add egg, nectar and preserves; beat at medium speed until smooth.
- Add flour mixture and apricots; blend just until combined. Do not overmix.
- Drop by rounded tablespoonfuls onto ungreased cookie sheet, 1½ inches apart. Bake in preheated oven until cookies just begin to brown on edges, about 22 minutes. Cool 5 minutes then remove with spatula to cool, flat surface.

SOUR CREAM COOKIES

Preheat oven to 350°F | Yield: 6 dozen

1 cup butter *or* margarine, softened
2 cups sugar
2 eggs, lightly beaten
1½ cups sour cream
1 teaspoon vanilla extract
1 teaspoon baking soda
1 teaspoon baking powder
½ teaspoon freshly grated nutmeg
5 cups flour, unsifted
6 ounces semisweet chocolate chips, optional
1 cup chopped walnuts, optional

- Cream butter and sugar; add eggs, sour cream and vanilla.
- Sift together baking soda, baking powder, nutmeg and flour; add 1 cup at a time to creamed mixture. Mix well. Fold in chocolate chips and walnuts.
- Drop by teaspoonfuls onto greased cookie sheet. Bake 10 minutes in preheated oven.

GOURMET CHOCOLATE CHIP COOKIES

Preheat oven to 375°F
Yield: 5 dozen

1 cup butter *or* margarine, softened
1 cup granulated sugar
1 cup brown sugar
2 eggs
1 teaspoon vanilla extract
2 cups flour
2½ cups oatmeal, reduced to powder in blender
½ teaspoon salt
1 teaspoon baking powder
1 teaspoon baking soda
12 ounces semisweet chocolate chips
4 ounce milk chocolate bar, finely chopped
¾ cup chopped pecans
¾ cup chopped walnuts

- Cream butter and sugars together in large bowl. Add eggs and vanilla.
- Mix together flour, oatmeal, salt, baking powder and baking soda. Add dry ingredients to creamed mixture. Add chocolate chips, milk chocolate and nuts.
- Drop by heaping tablespoonfuls 2 inches apart on ungreased cookie sheet.
- In preheated oven, bake 6 to 8 minutes until just lightly browned. Cool on wire racks.

TOASTED ALMOND MERINGUES

Preheat oven to 350°F Yield: 5 dozen

3 cups sliced almonds
4 egg whites
1½ cups sugar

- Place almonds on baking sheet and toast at 350°F for 8 to 10 minutes. Turn baking sheet halfway through toasting. Watch carefully to prevent burning. Remove from oven and cool completely.
- **Reduce oven heat to 300°F.**
- Beat egg whites, gradually adding sugar, until stiff peaks form. Fold in toasted almonds.
- Line baking sheet with foil. Drop meringue by rounded teaspoonfuls onto foil. Bake 30 minutes.

CREAM CHEESE COOKIES

Preheat oven to 350°F Yield: 3 dozen

½ cup solid vegetable shortening
3 ounces cream cheese, softened
½ cup sugar
½ teaspoon vanilla extract
1 egg yolk
1 cup flour
¼ teaspoon salt
½ teaspoon baking powder
¼ cup chopped nuts
1 cup semisweet chocolate chips, optional
½ cup raisins, optional

- Cream shortening with cream cheese, sugar, vanilla and egg yolk.
- Sift together dry ingredients and mix thoroughly into creamed mixture. Add nuts and optional chocolate chips and raisins.
- Drop by teaspoonfuls onto a baking sheet and flatten with a moist knife.
- Bake 10 to 12 minutes in preheated oven. Watch carefully because tops should not brown.

CHOCOLATE SURPRISE COOKIES

Preheat oven to 350°F

Yield: 2 dozen

- ½ cup butter *or* margarine, softened
- 1 cup sugar
- 1 egg
- 1¾ cups flour
- 1 teaspoon baking soda
- ½ teaspoon salt
- ½ cup unsweetened cocoa
- ¼ cup milk *or* more if needed
- 1 teaspoon vanilla extract
- ½ cup chopped pecans
- 12 large marshmallows, halved
- Chocolate Frosting-*recipe follows*

- Grease a cookie sheet and set aside.
- Cream butter, sugar and egg.
- Sift together flour, baking soda, salt and cocoa. Add to creamed mixture alternately with milk. Add vanilla and pecans, folding in well.
- Drop by heaping teaspoonfuls onto cookie sheet and bake 8 minutes in preheated oven.
- Remove from oven and place ½ a marshmallow on top of each cookie. Return to oven for 2 minutes. Remove from oven and cool.
- Frost each cookie so that marshmallow does not peek through. That makes the surprise! Do not freeze these cookies.

CHOCOLATE FROSTING

- 2 cups confectioners' sugar
- 5 tablespoons unsweetened cocoa
- pinch of salt
- 4 tablespoons butter, melted
- 4 tablespoons cream *or* whole milk
- 1 teaspoon vanilla extract

- Sift confectioners' sugar, cocoa and salt together. Add remaining ingredients and mix well with electric beater.

MAPLE PECAN DROPS

Preheat oven to 350°F Yield: 3 dozen

- 8 ounces butter, softened
- ¾ cup sugar
- 1½ teaspoons maple extract
- 2 cups flour
- pinch of salt
- 36 pecan halves

- Lightly grease cookie sheet and set aside.
- In food processor, cream butter, sugar and maple extract. Add flour and salt and mix just until combined, scraping sides of bowl if necessary.
- Roll into balls and place 3 inches apart on cookie sheet. Gently press pecan half on each cookie. In preheated oven, bake 10 to 12 minutes until golden brown. Cookies will keep a week in airtight container.

Dick and Ginger Howell
–*The Seasonal Kitchen*

NEW-FASHIONED BUTTER COOKIES

Yield: 4 dozen

- 1 cup butter, softened
- 1 cup sugar
- 2 eggs
- 1 tablespoon milk
- 1 teaspoon vanilla extract
- ½ teaspoon freshly grated nutmeg
- 3 cups flour
- ½ teaspoon salt
- 1½ teaspoons baking powder

- Prepare cookie dough a day before baking. In electric mixer, cream butter and sugar until light and fluffy. Add eggs, milk, vanilla and nutmeg.
- Sift flour with salt and baking powder and stir into creamed mixture. Chill overnight.
- **Preheat oven to 375°F.**
- Roll dough on floured board to ⅛-inch thickness and cut with any cookie cutters. Place on greased cookie sheet and bake 8 to 10 minutes.
- Cookies can be decorated with colored sugars, nuts or a drop of jelly in center of each.

BAKLAVA COOKIES

Yield: 24 to 30 cookies

- 2 cups sugar
- 1½ cups water
- 1 tablespoon honey
- 1 teaspoon fresh lemon juice
- 2½ cups chopped walnuts
- 2 teaspoons ground cinnamon
- 12-15 phyllo dough sheets, thawed
- ½ cup butter, melted

- In a small saucepan, heat sugar and water to 220°F; boil 5 minutes. Remove from heat and add honey and lemon juice. Set aside.
- Mix nuts and cinnamon in bowl and add 2 to 3 tablespoons of syrup, enough to make mixture stick together.
- Grease a baking sheet and set aside.
- **Preheat oven to 375°F.**
- Refer to page 261 for suggestions regarding handling of phyllo dough.
- Working with 1 phyllo sheet at a time, brush sheet with butter and cut in half lengthwise.
- Place heaping tablespoon of nut mixture in middle of one end of half sheet. Fold sheet lengthwise on both sides over nuts. Begin to roll until entire sheet is rolled. You should have a log about 2 to 3 inches wide. Place on baking sheet and repeat with remainder of ingredients. Brush rolls with butter.
- Bake 8 to 10 minutes or until brown. Pour syrup over hot cookies and let stand about 5 minutes. Remove and place in paper muffin cups to cool. Cookies will keep 1 week in sealed container or can be frozen.

PINE NUT COOKIES

Yield: 2 dozen

8 **ounces almond paste, purchased**
_or_ homemade-*see page 261*
2 **tablespoons Amaretto _or_ other liqueur, such as Kirsch**
1 **egg white, lightly beaten**
½ **cup pine nuts**

- Butter a baking sheet and set aside.
- Blend almond paste with liqueur. Shape into equal patties about 1½ inches wide. Place on baking sheet 1 inch apart.
- Brush each cookie with egg white. Pat pine nuts on top of each and press lightly into paste. Let stand 2 hours.
- **Preheat oven to 400°F.**
- Bake 5 to 8 minutes. Do not overbake. They should be firm and pale brown.
- Cool on a rack and place in airtight container. Cookies can be frozen.

PECAN BUTTERBALLS

Preheat oven to 350°F — Yield: 30 to 36

1 **cup butter, softened**
¼ **cup brown sugar**
1 **cup finely chopped pecans**
1 **teaspoon vanilla extract**
2 **cups sifted flour**
¼ **cup confectioners' sugar**

- Cream butter and brown sugar in food processor. Add nuts, vanilla and flour; process until soft ball forms. Remove to floured board.
- Roll a heaping teaspoon of dough into a ball and place on ungreased cookie sheet. Repeat until all dough is used.
- Bake 7 to 9 minutes in upper third of preheated oven. Place cooling rack on a towel; remove cookies to rack.
- Sift confectioners' sugar over hot cookies. When cool, discard excess sugar. Cookies can be frozen.

LEMON SNOWFLAKES

Preheat oven to 375°F

Yield: 4 dozen

1¼ cups softened butter, divided
2½ cups confectioners' sugar, divided
¾ cup cornstarch
1½ cups flour
¾ cup chopped walnuts
2 tablespoons fresh lemon juice

- Grease a cookie sheet and set aside.
- Cream 1 cup butter and ½ cup sugar until pale yellow. Combine cornstarch and flour and beat into creamed mixture.
- Shape into 48 small balls and flatten with the floured bottom of a glass. Sprinkle nuts on cookies and pat in firmly.
- Place 2 inches apart on prepared cookie sheet and bake 15 minutes in preheated oven, rotating pan after 7 minutes. Remove and let cool on plate.
- Melt remaining ¼ cup butter and combine with 2 cups confectioners' sugar and lemon juice. Frost cookies. If frosting is too runny, let it sit; if too thick, add lemon juice. Top with cinnamon candy or nonpareils while frosting is still soft, if desired.

Cook's Notes

When baking *cookies,* let baking sheet cool between batches. Cookies keep their shape better.

RUM BOURBON BALLS

Yield: 100 or more

- 24 ounces vanilla wafers, crushed
- 2 cups unsweetened cocoa
- ½ cup light corn syrup
- 1 cup dark rum
- 1 cup bourbon
- 5 cups confectioners' sugar, sifted, plus more for dusting
- 3 cups finely chopped pecans *or* walnuts
- 3 cups coconut flakes

- Mix all ingredients thoroughly. Form into 1-inch balls and roll in additional confectioners' sugar.
- Let sit overnight, then store in airtight container. The longer you let them age, the better they taste.

HAZELNUT BISCOTTI

Preheat oven to 350°F

Yield: 25 to 35 cookies

- 4 ounces butter, softened
- 1 cup sugar
- 2 teaspoons fresh lemon zest
- 2 tablespoons fresh orange zest
- 2 teaspoons fresh lime zest
- 2 eggs
- 1 teaspoon vanilla extract
- 1 teaspoon baking powder
- ¼ teaspoon salt
- 2 cups flour
- ¾ cup hazelnuts, blanched, toasted and rough chopped
- ¼ cup shelled pistachios, rough chopped

- Cream butter, sugar and zests until fluffy. Add eggs one at a time, then vanilla.
- Sift dry ingredients and add to butter mixture. Mix at low speed to form a smooth dough. Fold in nuts.
- Divide dough and form into 2 logs, each 3 inches thick. In preheated oven, bake 30 minutes on unfloured cookie sheet; cool 15 minutes.
- Slice ½ inch thick, lay flat on cookie sheet and toast lightly in oven, turning once.

RUGALACH

Yield: 32 cookies

1 cup butter, softened
8 ounces cream cheese, softened
2 cups flour
1 teaspoon baking powder
½ cup sugar
3 teaspoons ground cinnamon
1 jar apricot marmalade
1 cup chopped walnuts

- In food processor, mix butter, cream cheese, flour and baking powder. When dough forms a ball, divide into 4 parts. Flatten each and wrap in plastic wrap. Refrigerate ½ hour.
- **Preheat oven to 375°F.**
- Grease a cookie sheet and set aside.
- In a small bowl, mix sugar and cinnamon.
- On floured board, roll 1 portion of dough into circle. Spread with 2 tablespoons marmalade; sprinkle with sugar mixture and ¼ cup nuts.
- Cut dough into 8 wedges. Starting at wide outside edge, roll toward center, pressing tip to seal. Roll rugalach in sugar mixture and place on cookie sheet. Repeat with other 3 portions of dough.
- Bake 10 to 12 minutes in upper part of oven. Cool on rack and store in airtight container. Cookies can be frozen.

RAISIN-FILLED COOKIES

Preheat oven to 400°F

Yield: 3 dozen

1½ cups sugar, divided
⅔ cup solid vegetable shortening
2 eggs
⅓ cup milk
3 cups + 1 heaping tablespoon flour, divided
3 teaspoons baking powder
½ teaspoon salt
1 teaspoon vanilla extract
½ cup water
1 cup raisins

- Grease a cookie sheet and set aside.
- Cream 1 cup sugar and shortening; beat in eggs and then milk. Stir in 3 cups flour, baking powder, salt and vanilla.
- On a floured board, roll dough ⅛ inch thick and cut with a round cookie cutter. Place half of circles on cookie sheet.
- Mix ½ cup sugar with heaping tablespoon flour in small saucepan. Add water and raisins and cook until thick, stirring constantly.
- Place heaping teaspoon of raisin filling on each circle, top with another circle and press edges with tines of a fork to seal. Bake 10 to 15 minutes in preheated oven.
- Cookies can be filled with fruit jam instead of raisins.

ALMOND CANDY COOKIES

Preheat oven to 375°F

Yield: 16 cookies

1 cup butter
1 cup sugar
⅓ cup honey
⅓ cup heavy cream
4 cups slivered almonds
1 cup semisweet chocolate chips

- Grease 16 small aluminum foil tart pans and set aside.
- In saucepan, combine butter, sugar, honey and cream. Heat to boiling, stirring frequently. Cook 1½ minutes; remove from heat and add almonds.
- Divide evenly among greased pans. Press flat using fingers dipped in cold water.
- In preheated oven, bake 10 to 14 minutes or until golden brown. Cool completely and then refrigerate 10 minutes. Carefully pop cookies out of pans by pressing bottoms. Stack between sheets of wax paper and refrigerate.
- Melt chocolate and spread on half of each cookie. Keep refrigerated until serving.

GINGER COOKIES

Preheat oven to 350°F

Yield: 3 dozen

¾ cup butter, melted
1 cup sugar + more for rolling
4 tablespoons dark molasses
1 large egg
2 cups flour
¾ teaspoon salt
2 teaspoons baking soda
1 teaspoon ground ginger
1 teaspoon ground cloves
1 teaspoon ground cinnamon

- In large bowl, cream butter with sugar. Beat in molasses and egg. Add remaining ingredients and combine thoroughly.
- Shape dough into walnut-sized balls, roll in sugar and flatten with fingers on ungreased baking sheet.
- In preheated oven, bake 9 to 12 minutes or until cookies are golden brown and cracked on top. Cool on wire racks and store in airtight container.

HAZELNUT BARS

Preheat oven to 350°F

Yield: 12 to 18 bars

Crust:

1½ cups flour
¼ cup + 2 tablespoons firmly packed light brown sugar
½ teaspoon salt
½ cup unsalted butter, cut into bits

- In a bowl, whisk together flour, brown sugar and salt; add butter and blend mixture until it resembles very loose and crumbly meal. Press mixture onto bottom of a 9x13-inch baking pan. Bake 12 minutes in middle of preheated oven. Set on a rack to cool.

Topping:

1½ cups firmly packed light brown sugar
3 tablespoons flour
½ teaspoon baking powder
3 large eggs, lightly beaten
1½ teaspoons vanilla extract
1½ cups coarsely chopped hazelnuts, toasted

- In a bowl, whisk together brown sugar, flour, baking powder, eggs and vanilla; stir in hazelnuts.
- Pour topping evenly over crust and bake in middle of oven 25 to 30 minutes, or until golden. Place pan on rack to cool; cut into squares or bars.

Cook's Notes

To remove the brown skins from *hazelnuts* place in cold water; drain but do not dry. Bake in 400°F oven for 10 minutes. Place hot nuts in a towel and rub vigorously to remove skins.

RASPBERRY SQUARES

Preheat oven to 325°F

Yield: 2 dozen

1 cup flour
¼ teaspoon salt
1 teaspoon baking powder
½ cup solid vegetable shortening
2 eggs
1 tablespoon milk
1 cup raspberry jam
2 tablespoons butter *or* margarine, softened
1 cup sugar
2 cups shredded coconut
1 teaspoon vanilla extract

- In a large bowl, mix flour, salt and baking powder. Cut in shortening with pastry blender. Add 1 egg and milk; stir until well blended.
- Spread this mixture in 7x11-inch baking pan, bringing dough up a bit on sides of pan to hold jam. Spread jam over dough.
- Cream butter and sugar; add 1 egg and beat well. Stir in coconut and vanilla. Drop from spoon onto top of jam. Bake 30 to 35 minutes in preheated oven. Top should be lightly browned.
- Cool slightly and cut into squares.

DECADENT PEANUT BUTTER BARS

Yield: 5 dozen

1 pound confectioners' sugar
1 cup graham cracker crumbs
1 cup peanut butter
1 cup butter *or* margarine, melted
12 ounces semisweet chocolate chips

- In a bowl combine sugar and crumbs. Add peanut butter and melted butter; mix well with a spoon or with your hands. Spread in a 9x13-inch ungreased pan.
- Melt chocolate chips and spread over mixture. Refrigerate 30 minutes, or until chocolate just begins to look dull around edges. Remove and score chocolate into 60 pieces. Return to refrigerator. Cut all the way through before serving.
- Bars can be eaten in less than an hour after refrigerating. They can be stored frozen up to 3 months.

Ellie Klein, Owner
–Dartmouth House Bed and Breakfast

Cook's Notes

When making *bar cookies* line the pan with foil. When done, turn out onto rack to cool. Peel the foil off before cutting into bars.

NUTTY BUTTER BARS

Preheat oven to 375°F — Yield: 5 dozen

- 8 ounces butter, softened
- 1 cup sugar
- ½ teaspoon vanilla extract
- 1 egg, separated
- 2 cups flour
- pinch of salt
- 2 cups chopped nuts

- Cream butter and sugar in a large bowl; beat in vanilla and egg yolk. Add flour and salt and blend thoroughly.
- Press into an 11x17-inch jelly roll pan. Beat egg white lightly and spread over top of dough. Sprinkle with chopped nuts, pressing nuts lightly into dough.
- Bake 16 to 18 minutes in preheated oven. Cut into small squares or diamond shapes while warm.

DOUBLE CHOCOLATE WALNUT BROWNIES

Preheat oven to 350°F — Yield: 2 dozen

- 1 cup butter *or* margarine
- 4 ounces unsweetened chocolate
- 2 cups sugar
- 3 eggs
- 1 teaspoon vanilla extract
- 1 cup flour
- 1½ cups chopped walnuts, divided
- 6 ounces semisweet chocolate chips

- Grease a 9x13-inch baking pan and set aside.
- In medium saucepan, melt butter and chocolate over moderate heat. Remove from heat.
- With a wooden spoon, beat in sugar gradually until combined. Add eggs, one at a time, beating well after each addition. Stir in vanilla. Add flour and stir until well blended. Stir in 1 cup walnuts. Spread onto bottom and sides of prepared pan.
- Combine remaining walnuts with chocolate chips and sprinkle over top of batter; press them down lightly. Bake 35 minutes in preheated oven.

THREE-STORY BARS

Preheat oven to 375°F

Yield: 2 dozen

¾ cup melted butter, divided
7 tablespoons sugar, divided
5 tablespoons unsweetened cocoa
1 teaspoon vanilla extract
1 egg
2 cups graham cracker crumbs, 28 square crackers
½ cup coconut flakes
½ cup chopped nuts
6 tablespoons milk, divided
2 tablespoons instant vanilla pudding dry mix
2 cups confectioners' sugar
6 ounces semisweet chocolate chips

- Combine ½ cup melted butter with 5 tablespoons sugar, cocoa, vanilla and egg. Add graham cracker crumbs, coconut and chopped nuts; mix well.
- Press into an 8-inch square pan and bake 8 to 10 minutes in preheated oven.
- Mix ¼ cup melted butter with 3 tablespoons milk, pudding mix and confectioners' sugar. Spread over first layer; refrigerate at least 1 hour.
- Melt together 3 tablespoons milk, 2 tablespoons sugar and chocolate chips until smooth. Spread over cookie mixture. Store refrigerated. To serve, cut into bars.

APPLE BARS

Preheat oven to 350°F

Yield: 2 dozen bars

1 cup vegetable oil
2 eggs
1½ cups white *or* brown sugar
3 cups flour
½ teaspoon salt
½ teaspoon baking powder
1 teaspoon baking soda
1 teaspoon ground cinnamon
1 teaspoon vanilla extract
3 cups chopped pared apples
½ cup chopped nuts, optional
½ cup chocolate chips, optional

- Lightly grease a 9x13-inch pan.
- Mix together oil, eggs and sugar. Sift together dry ingredients and add to creamed mixture. Add vanilla, chopped apples, nuts and chips.
- Place in prepared pan, patting batter down with a spoon. Bake 50 minutes. When cool, cut into bars.

The laundry, another place to feel "at home"

Cook's Pantry

ALMOND PASTE

Yield: 1 pound

8 ounces blanched almonds
2 egg whites, lightly beaten
1 cup sugar

- Coat almonds with egg white. Remove from whites and place in bowl of a processor fitted with metal blade. Process nuts until very finely chopped.
- Blend remaining egg white with sugar. Add to chopped almonds. Process until smooth.

BASIC SEAFOOD STOCK

shells from 1 pound raw shrimp, rinsed
2 quarts cold water
1 medium onion, unpeeled, quartered
1 rib celery, chopped
1 garlic clove, unpeeled, quartered

- Bring all ingredients to a boil; simmer 4 hours. Replenish water to keep 1 quart of liquid in pot.
- Strain, cool and refrigerate until ready to use. Stock can be frozen and used as needed.

CHOCOLATE CURLS

- To make chocolate curls to decorate desserts, warm a square of chocolate in the palm of your hand and then use a vegetable parer which has been heated in very hot water. Pare shavings from the flat side of the chocolate. Keep repeating the warming process if the chocolate begins to shred.

HANDLING PHYLLO DOUGH

- Phyllo sheets are paper-thin and dry out quickly. When working with phyllo, thaw according to package instructions. Open up the roll of pastry and lay it on a sheet of plastic wrap on a flat surface. Cover with another sheet of plastic wrap and then a slightly dampened towel. Always keep the pastry sheets covered until ready for use.

BROWN ROUX

- Roux adds flavor, thickness and color to Cajun and Creole cooking. Usually roux is made from a mixture of equal parts of flour and vegetable oil, cooked in a large heavy pot until the mixture is brown–the color of milk chocolate–and has a nut-like aroma. It serves as a base for bisques, gumbos, gravies and stews.
- Roux must be stirred constantly and the temperature kept under control to keep the mixture from scorching. If it is darkening too fast, remove it from the heat for a few minutes. If it scorches, start over.
- The safest method is to use very low heat and cook, stirring constantly, for 45 to 60 minutes. Always start with a large, clean pot or skillet, preferably cast iron, and stir with a long-handled whisk or wooden spoon.
- Roux can be made ahead and stored in a covered jar in the refrigerator for several weeks. To use, bring back to room temperature, stir to recombine and remove amount needed. Reheat slowly, stirring constantly. Any liquid to be added should be at least lukewarm.

BASIC CHICKEN BROTH

Yield: 2 quarts

1 whole boiling chicken,
***or* 4 pounds backs and wings**
1 peeled onion stuck with 2 cloves
1 carrot, coarsely chopped
1 rib celery, coarsely chopped
1 teaspoon dried thyme
1 sprig parsley
1 bay leaf
salt and freshly ground pepper to taste
4 quarts water

- Place all ingredients in large pot. Bring to boil, cover and simmer over low heat for 2½ to 3 hours.
- Strain broth, chill and skim fat from surface. If using whole chicken, meat can be stripped from bones and used for salads or entrées.
- Broth can be frozen in small containers to use as needed.

PASTRY • PIE CRUST

Yield: Enough for a 2-crust pie

- 2½ cups sifted all-purpose flour
- 1 teaspoon salt
- 1 cup chilled solid vegetable shortening
- ⅓ cup ice water
- ¼ cup unsifted flour

- Sift flour and salt together or pulse on and off several times in the bowl of a food processor fitted with a metal blade.
- Cut in the shortening with a pastry cutter or with quick pulses in the processor. Don't overmix.
- Add the ice water and gather into a ball. Dust with additional flour. Wrap and refrigerate for ½ hour before using.
- For a fully baked crust, line the pie pan with pastry and prick all over with a fork. Line the crust with buttered foil, butter down, and fill with dried beans or pastry weights. Bake at 375°F for 8 minutes. Remove foil and weights and bake an additional 10 to 13 minutes.

POACHED CHICKEN

- If you need cooked chicken for a salad or other recipe, poach chicken on the stove or in the microwave. For 2 cups of cooked chicken, you will need two 6-ounce skinned and boned chicken breasts.
- To poach chicken on the stove, place chicken pieces in a large skillet with 1⅓ cups of water or broth. Bring to a boil, reduce heat, cover and simmer 12 to 14 minutes, or until chicken is tender and cooked through. Let cool in the broth for up to ½ hour before refrigerating.

HARD-COOKED EGGS

- Place eggs in a saucepan in one layer. Add enough cold water to cover by 1 inch. Bring to boil, reduce heat to low, cover and simmer for 15 minutes.
- Run cold water over cooked eggs until cool enough to handle. Drain and tap shells lightly on counter and roll between palms of hands. Carefully peel shells.

CLARIFIED BUTTER

- Melt butter over low heat in a small saucepan. Pour off the oily layer on top–the clarified or drawn butter–and discard the milky solids in the bottom of the pan.
- Clarified butter is good for cooking because it does not burn easily. It can be kept in the refrigerator for several weeks. Another popular use for clarified butter is for dipping lobster or artichokes.

POWDERED SUGAR FROSTING

Yield: 1½ to 2 cups

⅓ cup butter, softened
1 pound confectioners' sugar
5-6 tablespoons half-and-half
2 teaspoons vanilla extract
pinch of salt

- Place butter in mixing bowl. Alternately beat in sugar and half-and-half. Mix in vanilla and salt. Beat until of spreading consistency, adding more sugar or cream as needed.

CRÈME FRAÎCHE

- Mix ¼ cup sour cream or buttermilk with ¼ cup heavy cream in a large shallow bowl. Cover tightly with plastic wrap and leave at room temperature for 24 to 48 hours. Cream will thicken and can be stored in the refrigerator for up to 2 weeks.

BASIC WHITE SAUCE

- For 1 cup of a thin white sauce, melt 1 tablespoon of butter in a saucepan. Stir in 1 tablespoon of flour and cook, stirring, over moderate heat for 2 minutes. Heat 1 cup of milk and add to butter and flour all at once, stirring. Season to taste.
- For medium sauce, use 2 tablespoons of flour; for thick sauce, use 3 tablespoons of flour.

FLAVORED BUTTERS

- For a tasty addition to meat, poultry, fish and vegetable dishes, keep flavored butters in your refrigerator or freezer. Chop any one of the following in a food processor and then add 4 ounces of butter. Process until smooth and blended.
  - ¼ cup Dijon mustard and ¼ cup chopped basil leaves
  - 3 tablespoons any fresh chopped herb
  - 3 tablespoons mixed chopped shallots and fresh chives
  - 1½ tablespoons drained horseradish and 1½ tablespoons minced fresh chives
  - 1 roasted sweet red pepper and 1 teaspoon lemon juice
  - 2 ounces any of the blue cheeses
  - 1 oil-packed sun-dried tomato and 1 garlic clove
- On a sheet of plastic wrap, form butter into a log, roll in wrap and chill.

HARD SAUCE

- Cream ½ cup softened butter in bowl of electric mixer. Gradually add 1 cup sugar and beat until light and fluffy. Flavor to taste with rum, sherry or brandy. Form into a roll, wrap and chill. Cut off slices to serve on warm pie. Hard sauce is so named because it is served while hard.

BEURRE MANIÉ

- To thicken a sauce, knead 2 tablespoons butter with 2 tablespoons flour. When blended, form into small balls and add them gradually to the simmering liquid. Stir until butter is dissolved and sauce is thickened.

CHICKEN or TURKEY GRAVY

- Strain pan juices and pour off fat from roasted fowl. In saucepan, heat ¼ cup fat. Stir in ¼ cup flour until blended. Add enough chicken broth to pan juices to make 2 cups. Stir broth into flour and fat slowly; simmer and stir 5 minutes. Season to taste.

TABLE OF EQUIVALENTS

1 large egg white = about 2 tablespoons
¼ cup egg substitute = 1 egg
1 stick butter or margarine = ½ cup
¼ pound Cheddar cheese = 1 cup shredded
3 medium apples = 1 pound
1 teaspoon dried herbs = 1 tablespoon fresh
3 ounces reconstituted dried mushrooms = 1 pound fresh
½ pound pasta = 3 to 4 main course servings
1 large onion = about 1 cup chopped
3 medium potatoes = 1 pound
3 medium tomatoes = 1 pound
1 cup raw white or wild rice = 3 cups cooked
1 cup instant rice = 2 cups cooked
6 ounces chocolate pieces = 1 cup
1 slice fresh bread = ½ to ⅔ cup crumbs
1 medium lemon yields about 3 tablespoons juice
1 medium lemon yields about 1 tablespoon grated zest
1 medium lime yields about 2 tablespoons juice
1 medium lime yields about 2 teaspoons grated zest
1 medium orange yields about ½ cup juice
1 medium orange yields about 2 tablespoons grated zest
1 slice uncooked bacon = 1 tablespoon crisp-cooked, crumbled
1 pound fresh green beans = 4 cups whole
1 pound dried beans = 6 to 7 cups cooked
1 slice fresh bread = ¾ cup soft crumbs
1 slice dry bread = ¼ cup fine dry crumbs
2 medium carrots = 1 cup sliced
1 cup heavy cream = 2 cups whipped
14 graham cracker squares = 1 cup fine crumbs

Acknowledgments

This book would not exist without the help of many other people. We wish to recognize them and thank them for sharing their recipes and for generously giving time, effort and talent toward the completion of the book. We sincerely hope that we have not inadvertently omitted any names.

NEW YORK (by County)

Allegany
Dorothy Ellis Berg

Broome
Dolly Furman
Virginia Irons
Mary Ann Russik
Jeanette Zebrowski

Cattaraugus
William K. Abrams

Chautauqua
Nancy Gaden

Chemung
Mary Bailey Bowers
Susan DeFilippo
Donna Hastings
Hill Top Inn
Michele Wielk Mazzela
Tom Moretti
Ann O'Brien
Mary B. Randolph
Mrs. Donald Rosenberg

Erie
Joanne Hill

Fulton
Mary A. Maceyka

Genesee
Rose Bergin-Zook
Julia Dzierzanowski
Janet King
Evelyn Seaman

Herkimer
Stephanie Litwen

Jefferson
Marion Amoroso Benedetto
Marcia Canale-Bracken
Brenda Cavallario
Laura T. Cavallario
Sue Chellis
Mary Elaine Costantino
Lisa M. Pecori
Sherry Steblen
Charlotte Yehle

Livingston
Gladys M. Browne
Pati Clark
Barbara Cole
Jeanne Coyne
Martha Cullinan
Marcella Davin
Terry Haynes
Rosemary Horan
Kelly Houghton
Marianne Houghton
Kath Hulburt
Rita Hulburt
Sharon Hulburt
Mary Lou Joynt
Kim Krauss
Stephen Krauss
Vicki M. Lewis
Linda Marion
Mary Marschke
Dolores Meath
Betty Neubeck
Marlene Perry
Henrietta Robinson
Tallman Family
Evelyn Taylor
Sylvane Ann Treible
Rhonda Westmiller

Kings
Shirley Sonkin

Monroe
Maureen Agosto
Mrs. June L. Amies
Lucille Ammenheuser
Jane Andrews
Patricia Andrews
Paula Ayers
Betty Barrett
Luisa Barsema
Barb Barteld
Elaine Benedict
Monica Benedict
Sandy Berrettone
Ann Binazeski
Marjorie Biondi
Clara D. Bishop
Laurie Bittner
Barbara Blake
Deidre Blakely
Jeff Bleier
Big Bob's
Priscilla Bolduc
Lita Boudakian
Barbara Brayer
Vivian Brennan
Joann M. Brickler
Elaine Brigman
Emmy Briner
Sanndi Brochu
Gina Broderick
Barbara A. Brown
Leslie Brown
Newman R. Brown
Nicholas S. Brown
Denise Bruns
Carol Bryan
Wendy Budgar
Helen Burness
Eleanor O. Buss
Terryl S. Butwid
Marlene Camardo
Norma Campbell
Jackie Cannizzaro
Sylvia Cappellino
Mrs. Joseph Carpenter
Elaine Carpin
Jean Carroll
Jane Casey
Barbra Cerio
Judi Chamberlain
Jean Chandler
Jackie Chesler
Nate Cianciola
Donna Cink
Evelyn Clare
Josephine Clemente
Bob Cleveland
Carolyn R. Clouser
Dolores Bubb Coates
June Codding
Joan Cohen
Mary T. Coleman
Bobbi Colgan
Jackie Colicchio
Julie Colombo
MaryJo Coniglio
Gwen Conners
Lois Conradt
Kitty Conroy
Terry Conroy
Katie Coon
Lori Cooper
Theresa Cooper
Joann Cortese
Carol Costello
Ellie Craig
Marsha Cross
Patty Cubbin
Brenda Cvejic
Eva Wright Dailey
Jack Decker
Lisa DeGirolamo
Martha Thigpen Denison
Barbara DeWaters
Mary M. DeWolf
Patricia J. Diehl
Marion Dietz
Michael DiGuiseppe
Barbara Dinse
Mrs. Frederick Dobles
Jack Dolan
Dorothy Donovan
Mary Lou Dowling

Irene Downes
Kathleen C. Downey
Betty Doyle
Judy Drake
Rita Drew
Karol DuBois
Carl Dumbauld
JoAnn Dunlevy
Kathleen Zello Eckler
Donna Edelstein
Stephenie Eisenschmid
Claudia Elliot
Carolyn Engel
Starr Englert
Anne P. Erbland
Suzanne M. Ernst
Jean M. Erskine
Dorothy W. Farrell
Sally Fay
June Palmer Feldman
Jenny Ferguson
Greg Fitch
Kathleen S. Fithen
Pamela Flynn
Beth Forester
Betty Fouquet
Sandy Frasch
Elfriede Frey
Marion Frine
Carol Fullerton
Ellen M. Gaffney
Lois Gallea
Debbi Galloway
Handy Gelbard
Marcia German
Karen Gilbert
Sally Gillan
Marge Gleason
Catherine Glenning
Katie Culhane Goldsmith
Eunice Goldstone
Cindy Goodenberger
Pam Gosnell
Jim Gould
Bernice Graham
Barbara Granite
Pat Grassi
Anita Pincelli Green
Margaret Guinan
Carole Haas
Sue Haefner
Linda Halldow
Betty Halpin
Lorraine Hannon
Lynn Harris
Kathy Hartmann
June Harvey
Gail Hayes
Mary Ann Hayes
Cindy Heagerty
Kathy Heerkens
Sharon Heiligman
Jeannetta Hermans
Penny Hetzer
Noreen M. Hogan
Anne Hossenlopp
Dick Howell
Ginger Howell
Deena Banks Hucko
Toddy Hunter
Ginny Hurley
Laurie Ireland
Barb Jackson
Gwenda Jacobs
Evie Jacobson
Peggy Jeffries
Kathyrn Jensen
Amy Jewett
Judy Johnson
Laurie Johnson
Karola Jones
Mary Kalamaroff
Bernice Kaluza
Cookie Kaplan
William E. Kerley
Margaret M. Kidd
Ellie Klein
Mary Louise Koch
Beth Koopman
Joyce Kosters
Margie Kowalski
Carol Krause
Lynne T. Kroner
Barbara Krug
Sylvane Kuter
Geri Kwiatkouski
Ladies District #1
Knights of St. John
Janet Lady
Cay Laglia
Darlene M. Lake
Bill Lamb
Rhoda Lamb
Debra Lancto
Bill Lang
Betty Larter
Carol Later
Susan Lawson
Kay Layton
Mary Lefler
Frances Lennie
Ray Lenz
Elsie Lesyk
Vicki Lewin
Nancy Leyendecker
Kathy Lindsley
Julie Littell
Kristine Littrell
Michele A. Lobene
Jeanne Loberg
Dan Lombardo
Jill D. LoMonaco
Liz Long
Sharon R. Lonthair
Mike Loveland
Sandy Lovell
Millie Lowe
Jackie Lucas
Pat MacDonald
Mary Kay Mahar
Rena Maiuri
Judy Malone
Joyce Manley
Julie Marcoux
Barbara G. Marsaw
Francie Marx
Sandy Maslona
Barbara Mason
Cheri Massella
Margaret Mathe
Carla A. Mattioli
Chris Matyjakowski
Mary Wallace McAdam
Gloria McCleary
Jan McGlynn
Sherry McKellar
Catherine McKenna
Joanne McNutt
Kathleen M. Meade
Elaine Meath
Betty Mechler
Barbara Mehnert
JoAnn Melia
Sue Millard
Helen Miller
Julie Carr Miller
Kathy Miller
Pat Mitchell
Sandy Monahan
Donna Mooney
Norma Mooney
Jean Morley
Faith G. Morrell
Karen Morris
Gail Mulkeen
Pat Murray
Anne Nary
Joan Nash
Lynn Natapow
Nella Neeck
Maureen Nielsen
Donna Norris
Patricia Norris
Glenda Nothnagle
Margaret Nothnagle
Barbara Noval
Marietta Nye
Oatka Garden Club
Julie Odenbach
Alice O'Dwyer
Gene Olcott
Ann Olson
Ernie Olson
Paula Oppedisano
Betty Oswald
Bill Oswald
Kimberly Palma
Adele Pappas
Julie Paternico
Peggy Patterson
Michelle Pavone
Janice Pellegrini

Eileen G. Perryman
Kelly Petracchi
Dianna Petrella
Sally Phelps
Mike Pickard
Germaine C. Pierson
Maryann L. Platania
Pat Polidor
Emily M. Polizzi
Barbara Porter
Helen E. Preston
Prevention Partners
Connie J. Profeta
A. Prokop
Elaine Pugliese
Jan Rae
Sandy Ranalli
Carol Rauscher
Mary Redlin
Nadine Reich
Kellie Reynolds
Gloria Riccardi
Dot Ridley
Linda Hellebush Riordan
Jeanne Rivers
Nancy Robbins
Ducky Robinson
Eddie Roland
Marcia D. Rosenberg
Nina Rupp
Sue F. Russell
Dinny Ryan
Gloria Sargent
Betty Sauer
Carol Schacht
Margaret Schenkel
Pat Schmugler
Gretchen Shafer
Betty W. Shamblen
Mary Sharpe
Dinny Shaw
Alicia J. Sheridan
Margaret Shero
Grace R. Sibbald
Dale Simmons
Leslie Sladdin
Mary Anne Slaudenmayer
Alma Smith
Charlene Smith
Darcy Smith
Jean Sobraske
Diane Sommers
Jacquie Sonkin
Alisha Southern
Tracy Springer
Ellen Stahl
Susan Stahl
L. S. Stahlman
Mary Ann Staudenmeyer
Elsa Steo
June L. Stewart
Sarah Stimson
Marta Stockdale
Mrs. Mary Ann Stone
Nicole Stout
Mary M. Strong
Debbie Strott
Sharon A. Sullivan
Ruth Sundell
Suzie Syracuse
Betty Szembrot
Dan Tack
Martha Tack
Eileen K. Tanner
Linda Taylor
Mary Teall
Toby Ten Eyck
Caitlin Thomsen
Martha Thomson
Barbara Timlim
Nancy Tinnes
Barbara Totedo
Linda Traphagan
Timothy Trembley
Betsy Tschorke
Shirley Tschorke
Carolyn Turner
Sally Twaits
Jinny Ussel
Bonnie Vahey
Mark A. Vahey
Julie Van Benthuysen
Patti Van Nostram
Leonard Vancheri
Roseanne Vane
Marie Vara
Pat Vazzana
Peggy Drew Vianco
Tony Vitale
Sophie Vollmer
Ellen Wagner
Liz Wakefield
Patty Walsh
Bunny Walton
Nora Ward
Ruth Ward
Anne G. Watts
Greg Wegman
Jean Wegman
Lorrie Weis
Carol Weiss
Pat Werner
Catherine Wetjen
Peg Whiteford
Lee Wiedrich's Mother
Darlene Wilcox
Karen A. Wiler
Paula Willard
Carol Williams
Laurie Williams
Diane Wilmot
Marion G. Wilmot
Alice B. Wilson
Pat Witt
Carol Wright
Irene Wynne
Carolyn Yaekel
Judy Zelony
Hanna Zukoski
Ruth Zukoski

New York

Rose Levy Beranbaum
Anna Teresa Callen
Ladies Home Journal

Onieda

Jeanne Guarascio

Onondaga

American Dairy Assoc.
Suzanne B. Beeching
Sharon James

Ontario

Sue Anderson
Dorothy I. Archer
Nancy Becker
Bill Bold
Linda Campbell
Pat Cargnoni
Marilyn Carr
Cathy Caster
Pamela Chiverton
Rosalie Clarke
Debbie Clune
Laura K. Colmerauer
Carol Conklin
Cornell Cooperative Ext.
Mark Cupolo
Thelma Ernst
Linda Fox
Fran Gordon
Cynthia Hanford
Jan Haynes
Norma Herendeen
Scott Herendeen
Patricia Howk
Edwina Lange
Carol Lee
Mrs. Dean Lewis
Dorothy Markham
Jeanne Marten
Greg Monteleone
New York Apple Assoc.
New York Cherry Growers Assoc.
Susan O'Mara
Robyn Prince
Candy Riccione
Gloria Riccione
Shirley Sackett
N. Scammell
Betty Stahlbrodt
Mrs. Tandle's 2nd Grade
Liz Towner
Marilyn Tschorke
Mary Wallace
Shielee Weidner
Patricia Wilder
Joan M. Willis
Bill Young
Bert Zimmerman

Orange
Marge Kriney
Orleans
Amy Donahue
Rensselaer
R. S. Ambuhl
Rockland
Marla Silverman
Seneca
Cindy Campbell
Terry Miner
Marguerite O. Smith
Bessie Woodward
Steuben
Jody Applebee
Anne Eckert
Elizabeth Hammond
Mary Jo Hanna
Neal O'Donnell
Stella Pulver
The Ures
Carol Young
Tompkins
Mary Beth Willis
Wayne
Krystal Beauchemin
Donna Bellenger
Frank Carlesimo
Jodi Carlesimo
Vee Carlesimo
Pat Codding
Virginia Compitello
Patti Costich
Charlene Desens
Joyce Downey
Paula Ewing
Sue Foley
Irene Fry
Phyllis Gibson
Colleen M. Gray
Fern Guggino
Anita Gwara
Carol Watson Haak
Mary Hansen
John Hill
Carol Holzschuh
Bev Jacobs
Ruth Kotvis
Lynn H. Kouwe
Kay Kruk
Dorotha Loder
Lori Miller
Chris Page
Barbara Peck
Laurie Peters
Gerrie Pruner
Robin Shurgot
Bonnie Sonneville
Linda Taft
Shirley Timmerman
Jean White
Arlene S. Youngman
Kathy Zingler
Wyoming
Edna R. Meyer
M. Michele Rechberger
Dave Sheffield
Pat Van Buren
Yates
Sharon Herendeen
Lois Oswald

ALABAMA
Mrs. Richard Reitz
Gen Turner

ARIZONA
Jessie Saunders

CALIFORNIA
Louise Farley
Martin Yan

CONNECTICUT
Linda Gray
Lisa Oswald

DISTRICT OF COLUMBIA
Andrea Sonkin

FLORIDA
Linda Gassenheimer
Susan Hespin
Doris M. Kerr
Jean Klein
Phyllis Madden
Patty Pierce

GEORGIA
Harvey Brickley
Mary Brickley

INDIANA
Janet Gardner

MASSACHUSETTS
Mary LaVerge
Ted Place

MARYLAND
Peggy Ryan

MICHIGAN
Joie DeWolf

MINNESOTA
Mary E. Fischer

NORTH CAROLINA
Jean Keating
Carol Lonthair
Lina Treleaven
Barbara Tack Turkheimer

NEW JERSEY
Sherry Nehs

NEW MEXICO
Dorothy Doolittle

OHIO
Janet Felt

OREGON
Don Malagamba

PENNSYLVANIA
Ethel G. Hofman
Specialty Bakers
Patricia W. Young

TENNESSEE
Mary Stumb

TEXAS
Juliet Breeze
Donna J. Brugler
Mrs. Curt Grubb
Mary Beth Paul
Susan Wilhite

VERMONT
Hill Farm of Vermont

WASHINGTON
Sharon Kramis

CANADA
Betty Moffit
Bonnie Stern

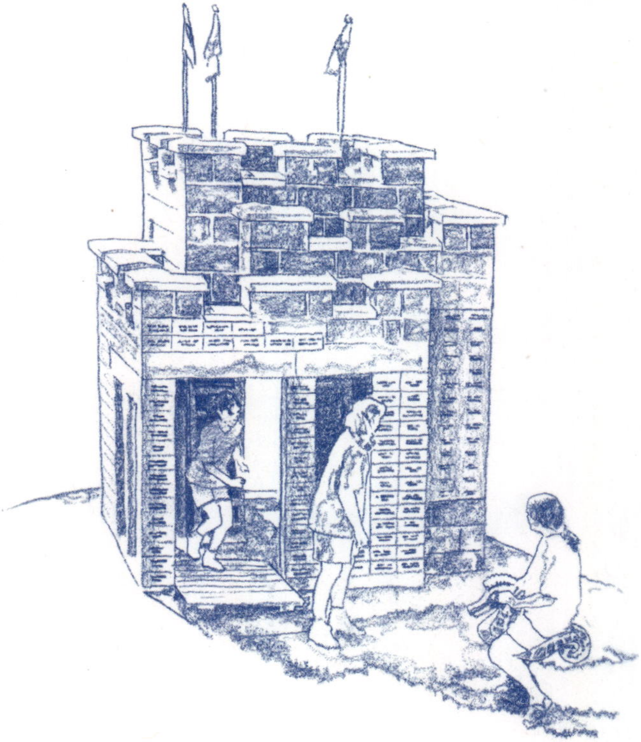

Patients and siblings enjoy the play yard

Index

Index

Specialities of the House Publications
Ronald McDonald House of Rochester
333 Westmoreland Drive, Rochester, NY 14620

Order Today!

Please send copies of *Specialties of the House* ______ @ $18.95 ea. $ ________
Add Shipping & Handling Charges ______ @ $ 3.50 ea. $ ________
New York Sales Tax if delivered within the state ______ @ $ 1.80 ea. $ ________
TOTAL $ ________

Make Checks Payable to: SOTH PUBLICATIONS
OR, bill my Charge Card (VISA or MASTERCARD only) Card#________________
Name as appears on card________________ Expires ________

SHIP TO: (*Please print legibly*) Phone (______) ________
Name ________________
Address ________________
City________________ State______ Zip ________

Specialities of the House Publications
Ronald McDonald House of Rochester
333 Westmoreland Drive, Rochester, NY 14620

Order Today!

Please send copies of *Specialties of the House* ______ @ $18.95 ea. $ ________
Add Shipping & Handling Charges ______ @ $ 3.50 ea. $ ________
New York Sales Tax if delivered within the state ______ @ $ 1.80 ea. $ ________
TOTAL $ ________

Make Checks Payable to: SOTH PUBLICATIONS
OR, bill my Charge Card (VISA or MASTERCARD only) Card#________________
Name as appears on card________________ Expires ________

SHIP TO: (*Please print legibly*) Phone (______) ________
Name ________________
Address ________________
City________________ State______ Zip ________

Specialities of the House Publications
Ronald McDonald House of Rochester
333 Westmoreland Drive, Rochester, NY 14620

Order Today!

Please send copies of *Specialties of the House* ______ @ $18.95 ea. $ ________
Add Shipping & Handling Charges ______ @ $ 3.50 ea. $ ________
New York Sales Tax if delivered within the state ______ @ $ 1.80 ea. $ ________
TOTAL $ ________

Make Checks Payable to: SOTH PUBLICATIONS
OR, bill my Charge Card (VISA or MASTERCARD only) Card#________________
Name as appears on card________________ Expires ________

SHIP TO: (*Please print legibly*) Phone (______) ________
Name ________________
Address ________________
City________________ State______ Zip ________

TP
APEX

9780964795501